AF600533

Contemporary Italian Women Philosophers

SUNY series in Contemporary Italian Philosophy

Silvia Benso and Brian Schroeder, editors

Contemporary Italian Women Philosophers

Stretching the Art of Thinking

Edited and
with an Introduction by

Silvia Benso and Elvira Roncalli

Published by State University of New York Press, Albany

Printed in the United States of America

For information, contact State University of New York Press, Albany, NY
www.sunypress.edu

Library of Congress Cataloging-in-Publication Data

Names: Benso, Silvia, editor. | Roncalli, Elvira, editor.
Title: Contemporary Italian women philosophers : stretching the art of thinking / Silvia Benso and Elvira Roncalli, editors.
Description: Albany : State University of New York Press, [2021] | Series: SUNY series in Contemporary Italian Philosophy | Includes bibliographical references and index.
Identifiers: ISBN 9781438484914 (hardcover : alk. paper) | ISBN 9781438484938 (ebook)
Further information is available at the Library of Congress.

10 9 8 7 6 5 4 3 2 1

Contents

Part Three: Responsibility, Emotions, Time

Part Four: Everyday Life, Action, Transcendence

Coda

Acknowledgments

Over many months, in various places of the world, and in different manners, numerous individuals have given us the motivation, encouragement, and support that have helped lead to the publication of this volume. Spouses, children, other family members, friends, colleagues, students, and occasional interlocutors have gifted us many times with the generosity of an inspirational word, a kind gesture, a joyful smile, a reassuring comment, or even a critical but insightful remark. There are too many of these individuals for us to list all their names here, but we trust that they know who they are. And they should also know that our gratitude to them is sincere and deep.

We are especially thankful to James Peltz, Michael Rinella, Diane Ganeles, and the staff at SUNY Press not only for their editorial competence, good-humored attitude, and enthusiastic backing of this volume but also for their constant support of the SUNY Series in Contemporary Italian Philosophy in which this book appears.

We wish to thank the anonymous reviewers who took time to read the initial version of the manuscript thoroughly and carefully and who offered important insights to help us make the volume a better work.

We wish to thank each other for the meaningful collaboration on this volume, for the numerous conversations we had about its themes and content, and for all the words we shared, wherein life and philosophy have met to cement a beautiful, personal and professional friendship.

And last but not least, we extend our sincerest and deepest appreciation and thanks to the contributors of this volume for their prompt responsiveness, ongoing collaboration, and unending patience. Without them, their work, and their thinking, there would be no volume, and philosophy in general (and Italian philosophy in particular) would not be as rich.

Silvia Benso and Elvira Roncalli

Introduction

Contemporary Italian Women Thinkers: Attending to Thinking, Extending the Art

Silvia Benso and Elvira Roncalli

This volume brings together a diverse collection of philosophical essays written by contemporary Italian women—scholars, activists, in some cases both—who have made of the practice of thinking an integral part of their lives. Whether they teach and do research in academic settings or practice philosophy while engaging politics and the public world, these women exhibit a familiarity with thought and a savoir faire that demand attention.

The collection is unique in that it provides an opening onto a variety of perspectives in contemporary Italian thought rarely, if ever, displayed in the front window. If, at least until recently, translation into English of Italian philosophers has been slow, somewhat haphazard, and ultimately a niche, translation of philosophical works by Italian *women* thinkers has been even sparser, more random, and quite selective, ultimately precluding ease of access and the possibility of broad recognition. In Italy, the women thinkers featured in this collection are all highly respected, widely published, and justly renowned. In the global reality of our times, it is not unlikely that the English-speaking reader may have come across some of their names before. Some of these authors may indeed be already known through their translated work.[1] Many have taught or lectured outside Italy, and all have, no doubt, relations of various nature with colleagues in other parts of the world. Whereas it may come as no surprise that, in this volume, there are more voices than those one may be already familiar with, the reader may nevertheless be surprised by the variety of writing styles, the breadth of the issues examined, or simply the thinking that is here exhibited. The outcomes of this all are for each reader to uncover, appraise, and relish.

Two features immediately stand out about the volume, if only by consideration of the book's title; namely, that it gathers essays by *women* thinkers and that these thinkers live and work in *Italy*. Indeed, gender and the geopolitical/cultural context provide the broader frame for this volume. In the current times of identity politics and dangerous nationalistic exclusionary policies, one cannot avoid thinking about gender and national identity, and think about them seriously one must. Nevertheless, we would like to caution against making hasty assumptions or coming to rushed conclusions about the overall content of the collection; instead, we would like to invite the reader to problematize the questions that the volume elicits and solicits.

To what extent does the geopolitical and cultural context wherein the essays in the collection originate provide a lens by which to read and understand the contents of this volume?

Does being a woman affect, and to what extent, the kind of philosophical truth delivered to the world?

These questions arise spontaneously and inevitably—invited by the title and reinforced by even a quick glance at authors' names and table of content—and gesture toward two possible paths for reading the book. Rather than eclipsing these queries through facile and ready-made answers one may already have available, what if one were to dwell on the issues, suspend one's views on the matter, and hold the questions near, keep them open, and return to them while reading the collection? The essays will not provide *a way* to answer these important queries. Yet they will offer us *ways* to problematize them further.

As said, the philosophers in this collection live and work in Italy. Italy is the place they call home, where they have established meaningful and long-standing relationships, where they engage and participate in many ways in the cultural, political, and academic life by teaching, writing, and engaging in public speaking. They share a common history, even though this history has many sides; they partake of a similar cultural milieu even when their personal and intellectual stories are different; and they live among buildings and palaces evocative of the past—a past that is diversified and mostly gone, but in some way still standing, casting its shadows into the present. They speak the same Italian language, in their different cadences reflecting the regions of their birth, and they are familiar with a landscape that morphs into plains, lakes, and mountains, that has drawn many from afar because of its reputation for beauty, and that has been referred to as the "blue peninsula"—a strip of land that stretches into the Mediterranean sea and toward the countries, cultures, and peoples bordering its waters.

Appealing to the shared geopolitical and cultural background, one may try to situate these women's thought—their approaches, themes, and methods—in relation to the philosophical works of other contemporary Italian thinkers one may be already familiar with and whose names are well known in the English-speaking world (such as Agamben, Esposito, Negri, or Vattimo, to name a few). A comparison would lead, no doubt, to identifying some interesting elements of parallelism, commonality, and contrast. Yet such an approach would also implicitly divert the light from the essays at hand. Seeking to identify some "resemblance" would be analogous to comparing, for instance, the Alps to the Rocky Mountains or the other way around. Of course, it can be done, but if that is how one looks at these geological formations, one sees neither the Alps nor the Rocky Mountains. One sees only what one thinks one already knows of them. Resemblance is a subtle way to trace back what one encounters to an already known place, to something familiar or to some starting point. It tells us something, provided that an origin or a source can be identified; but it also distracts us from what lies right in front of us. Once again, our invitation is to not take the path that sends us looking for what we already know, which results in measuring discrepancies and similarities, and instead keep the light focused on the essays (and their authors) themselves. One would then notice that each piece stands on its own and offers original threads that come to form unique and original compositions. It is as if, in each of them, new sites unravel just as, in moving through a landscape, new vistas open up. If one expects to come to a panoramic point from which to see all around, one may be disappointed. The essays stand together, yet each stands alone; there is no all-encompassing view to be gained in this volume.

Deliberately, these essays have not been written in response to a particular question, nor assembled with a theme in mind, not even with the sole aim of furnishing a window on the contemporary Italian philosophical scenario. The essays definitely give us a distinctive taste of the philosophical work that is done in Italy, but not in the sense that one gains a grand, overarching view. These essays do not lend themselves to a grasp of this kind. What they do, each in its own specificity and heterogeneity, is to take the reader along on a thinking exercise that is deeply involved and involving as well. Each essay shows how to think about the issue at hand, an issue that is representative of the long-term scholarly interests of its author and with which she continues to wrestle. Hence, what each essay offers and demands is far from being a superficial and detached reading exercise; on the contrary, the thinking each exemplifies leaves the reader with a personal, participatory, and, at times, even intimate feeling toward its author.

Employing the Italian geopolitical, cultural context as a reading register does not lead to any one specific feature that alone could qualify this collection. Even if we were to consider the Italian language, which is the shared language in which these essays were originally written,[2] it would be hard to say what this linguistic commonality might mean concretely. Any spoken language is alive only insofar as it is interwoven with a lived environment. A pure language, that is, a language disconnected from its life-world, would require a process of distillation, a cleansing procedure that sanitizes it of its "impurities" such as accents, cadences, and the likes. Provided this were possible, if at all desirable, what one would obtain would be a "dead" language, a language no one speaks. It is instead clear that all the thinkers whose essays are collected here exhibit a love for the written word, an elegance of linguistic expression, a passion for practices, and an attention to the nuances of life in its many facets that remind us that philosophy does not speak by way of concepts alone. Rather, living philosophy speaks the language of embodied life.

"But I am a woman," Luisa Muraro writes unflinchingly in her essay, and such an epiphany, which emerges from her embodied condition, turns her way of thinking around. Her exclamation resonates with the figure of Plato's enchained prisoner who, after escaping from the dark cave, is turned around again and again, experiencing dizziness and disorientation; but finally, adjusting to the light of the sun, the now liberated captive comes to see clearly and sharply. For Muraro, being a woman is the unthought that requires being thought, and commands the creation of a language that makes sexual difference visible and real. To her, seeing clearly and sharply means being able to see the words and deeds of women, mostly unseen and forgotten by the tradition, and to bring them into the world. She writes that "if there is something true, right, good it can only enter the world by passing through the inner self of a free rational human being."[3] Truth is subjective, she claims: it comes into the world in and through our very being. The authors of these essays are, indeed, all women. Even the last piece, the Coda—a conversation between Nidesh Lawtoo and Adriana Cavarero—places the work and thought of a woman, Cavarero herself, at the center of the dialogue.

The history of Italian women is fascinating and complex, and certainly too rich to be addressed in this introduction. It is nevertheless worth mentioning that the postwar Italian women's liberation movements were strong and successful,[4] especially in the 1960s and the 1970s, in ushering in important legal and political recognitions in terms of civil law, equality, and social and economic rights.[5] These legal and political successes remained however somewhat formal and did not fully translate, for Italian women, into cultural and structural transformations radically affecting the concrete, material realities of everyday life, thereby attesting to patriarchy's pervasive and obstinate stronghold on Italian society. Nonetheless and moving from diverse positions situated internally or externally to the establishment, women in Italy have persistently partaken in many intellectual and political activities—from writing to debating, from thinking to engaging in public dialogues, from mobilizing to creating spaces for alternative structures of learning and education.[6] Women's copious and relevant editorial work in some select presses, newspapers, and magazines alike illuminates yet again their indefatigable activism and their undeniable presence in the production of knowledge at large, in Italy, during the last decades. The Italian academic philosophical universe has stood out as an enclave particularly slow to change, with a small presence of women, especially at the highest academic ranks, and a widespread, if not unrelenting, indifference toward Women's/Gender Studies programs, which remain rare and few. The present volume attests to the vitality, creativity, and originality of Italian women thinkers, both within and outside the academic world—reminding us that there are more sites of knowledge than just the traditional ones.

Italian women's history aside, being *a woman* may be upheld, just like the Italian geopolitical and cultural context, as a possible lens through which to read this collection. It is undeniable that, as we have remarked, this volume shines light on the philosophical work of thinking women in Italy. Yet this does not, by itself, provide the sole or even privileged interpretative key to the entire collection. One detects a serious and unmistakable vein of critique across the texts, but this critique does not find its roots in the fact of being a woman per se or, at least, not for all the authors in the volume. In other words, this volume does not present a collection of feminist essays or, better, not in its entirety. The first three chapters comprising part one—by Luisa Muraro, Maria Luisa Boccia, and Lea Melandri, respectively—certainly place the question of being a woman forefront and at the center of the discussion, notably with regard to the role of "the maternal." Muraro explicitly examines the topic of being a woman, as mentioned before. Boccia speaks of the "irreplaceable womb" that cannot be ignored in the new era of artificial reproductive technologies, and where at stake is still the question of female freedom. The maternal, in the form of a symbolic, is also where, for Melandri, the struggle between women's liberation—rooted in women's struggle for a freedom outside and beyond established male paradigms—and emancipation—which rests on equality achieved through formal changes in the law[7]—carries on. Is the maternal the site of a new frontier? Is it the old redressed in new clothes? Melandri's chapter spurs us to reflect on these critical questions.

The maternal, women's freedom, and woman subjectivity are not the primary focus of the chapters in the subsequent parts of the volume. Nonetheless, questions relating to freedom, subjectivity, and (political and ethical) responsibility remain central throughout the volume, and they are approached and examined artfully and freely without any neat tie to a specific philosophical approach or school of thought. The phenomenological method, the hermeneutic strategy, the poststructuralist approach, the deconstructionist angle, and the feminist and critical attitude are all present in some form, at times joined together in inspiring configuration; none of them is however active in such a predominant way as to define the collection in its entirety. In fact, it would be more accurate to say that these chapters defy all categorization of this type, thus displaying a freedom and ingenuity of thinking that are truly remarkable.

A host of past and contemporary philosophers of diverse temporal, geographical, and conceptual backgrounds (Freud, Heidegger, Plato, Ricoeur, Weil, Schleiermacher, Simmel, Arendt, Derrida, Merleau-Ponty, Patočka, Foucault, to name just a few in no specific order) are deftly summoned as interlocutors, and we, the readers, feel summoned as well, picking up on the urgency of what is at stake at every turn of the page. The texts are rich, solidly grounded, manifold, refreshing, surprising. Even when the authors masterfully practice the art of detailed reading of other thinkers, they never simply provide us with a commentary; rather, they approach the texts with a specific concern in mind and so as to take us elsewhere, where we perhaps do not expect. It is as if, through them, one discovers new corners or hidden hooks one had no idea they were there, like playing hide-and-seek, but where the author is not searching for who is hiding; rather, she goes after interstices that dilate and augment the thinking space. "See here?" "And here?" the authors prod the reader, who may be starting to feel slightly unsettled at the continuously new openings, not unlike Plato's prisoner or Muraro's subject at the realization that things are different from what they were initially imagined to be.

In a way, these chapters invite the reader to take hold of the destabilizing effects of thinking. Nothing stands firm when one thinks; everything starts moving. Are we prepared to move with these essays? It is, after all, like a dance. If one worries about not knowing all the steps, one will not get up and dance. But movement, and moving along is what is at stake and all that really matters. Even the pace of the essays is anything but monotonous. It feels slow and tranquil in some, frenzy and hasty in others. These essays are an invitation to engage the art of thinking as if in a dance. For the reader, the point is to move along; to look and see, feel and savor the varying qualities of each piece as it unfolds the art of thinking.

The essays insist, in one way or another, on a close-knit relation between thinking and practice, on the need for a philosophy of and for the world, and on the necessity to engage with everyday life. Underlining these women's thinking is the implicit recognition that the available set of tools inherited from the philosophical tradition is insufficient for thinking through the issues of the day. To employ Simona Forti's term, there is a tinge of "dissidence" and, perhaps, even impertinence in their thinking, in that these thinkers question the delimitations of the art of philosophizing. They "sit apart" from given ways of thought, they reconsider established approaches, they problematize issues in novel and original manners. And they do so while plunging fully into their quests. Theirs is an odd exercise of distancing in immersion—distancing from given parameters while immersing themselves in thinking through these quests anew. It is an exercise that dis-tends, ex-tends, and at-tends to thinking and stretches its reach. A bow has to be carefully and artfully pulled for the arrow to hit the distant mark. Could it be that the given ways of philosophy are a too-tight and constraining bow for a thinking subject whose subjectivity could not even surge as a question for much of the past philosophical tradition? This question emerges powerfully and suggestively from this collection.

Perhaps we come here, with this question, to a common place, to a site of togetherness of all the essays that is better expressed in an image: that of a major Italian piazza, which is where all main roads converge or from which they all depart. It seems that to get wherever each is going, the authors of these essays have to pass through the main piazza. Maybe they have come to the piazza after meandering elsewhere. It is here, though, that they find their bearings: what road to take, or not to take, in order to get more directly to where they intend to go. The piazza, defined by notable and ancient buildings that delimit its perimeter and cannot be ignored and by the large opening that is offered in their midst, is a place that gathers, a place of togetherness where the old and the new, the individual and the public, the personal and the political, the familiar and the unexpected, the given and the hoped for meet. The buildings' old grandness is both intimidating and outdated; perhaps it is decayed, but the space they open up by close proximity and differing styles, a testament to their age, is inviting and alluring, a promise of new relations and negotiations. One could say that these essays fashion and refashion the piazza, if not in its buildings, at least in the ways they articulate the subject that moves through that space.

This subject—a recurrent theme in many of the essays—is far from being an isolated and abstract entity, indifferent and cold, uniform and universal.

There is an urgency running through the essays about various challenges of our time the subject cannot ignore—from immunitary politics to the surge of fascist movements, from modern technologies to new forms of control, from environmental and humanitarian crises to the call for new forms of responsibility, action, and vision. The subjectivity discussed here is rather porous, shaped and reshaped by the winds of time and by the encounters with the other(s) to which it is exposed. The carvings are unmistakable, and the piazza takes on different looks in light of them. In another sense, what these authors do is something that may not seem likely or possible, namely, enlarging the piazza and extending its space.

Will the old buildings have to come down? Maybe, but not necessarily. Perhaps what such old buildings need is to become passages to other kinds of spaces, ensure that their walls are not completely sealed off and can be furnished with gateways or arches that transform the wall into a "*via*," a passageway, a path that connects to another site, a different kind of space, but still one we can partake in and share. Or, yet again, the work of these essays is about opening new piazzas and multiplying the spaces that create the opportunity to meet and interact—spaces that, in turn, may and can transform whoever takes part in the encounter.

Let us briefly consider the kinds of subjectivity these essays set forth. Here, the subject is embodied and vulnerable, relational and changing. It is not the self-sufficient, self-created, and autonomous subject that has dominated much of the modern philosophical tradition; nor is it the impersonal or nomadic self of postmodernity, although there are some echoes of that. It is hard to pin down a model of subjectivity that reflects the various forms subjectivity takes from one essay to the other. It is clear, though, that the subject, as a philosophical concept, is a site of continuous sculpting. Simona Forti suggests a Socratic type of subjectivity that defies all forms of affirmative identities: in the inner dialogue of the two-in-one nothing goes unquestioned, showing a relationality and a plurality at the very core of each of us that demands practices. Relationality is constitutive of our humanity, says Adriana Cavarero, and that means that we are ex-posed, we lean out. Considering how each of us comes into the world, completely dependent on and at the mercy of another being, makes the notion of a self-sufficient and self-created subject crumble. Relationality and vulnerability go hand in hand, one is not self-enclosed, but open. Elena Pulcini speaks of a relational subject too, an emotional subject that is in relation with itself, but not in such a way as to close others off. Rather, the emotional subject lets itself be displaced by the other(s) and in so doing becomes another, in an ongoing process of self-transcending. In evoking the migrant, in a time of increasing nationalistic policies intent on keeping others out, Caterina

Resta reminds us, very concretely, that total displacement is directly tied to a conception of identity as pure and intact. But citizenship cannot be the result of artificial enclosures (can it?), and the migrant or the undocumented person is not any less human for being on the outside of some borders, or some laws, despite having been turned into an anonymous and unspecified entity precisely by those walls and laws. Rather than an impassable barrier that separates, the border needs to be thought of as threshold that relates and connects. Are we capable of this kind of metamorphosis, where we are transformed by the encounter with those that are foreign and come from the outside? Are we up to a vision of relations and connectedness, rather than of division and separation?

These are the kind of questions the essays collected in this volume provoke. They draw us in and keep our hold. After we are done with the reading, the questions are not done with us. The thinking at work here is about attending to and extending, connecting and relating. In the words of Maria Cristina Bartolomei, it is about seeing the connection between action and symbol, it is about seeing the "in-between"; something was there, but no longer is, and nevertheless, or precisely because of that, such a lack points, tends to something beyond, something that is not. This tending is rooted in a "radical interrogation of everyday life," writes Enrica Lisciani Petrini. The everyday, what has been marginalized by a dominant philosophy of transcendence, is the *locus* of this thinking. The view from the everyday is opaque, neither pure nor clear as it is assumed to be when regarded from above. It is only from this close-knit quarters that one can see and probe the tensions, where by "tension" one should understand the ways in which the different forms play out in relation to one another and stretch the ways one thinks about what is being thought.

Let us return to the topic of subjectivity to discover some of the specific tensions that are therein implicated and exemplified. Cavarero affirms a subjectivity that is both relational and vulnerable, one that is exposed and dislodged from its vertical axis by leaning toward the other. At the same time, Cavarero reiterates the subject's uniqueness and distinctiveness that are revealed in responding to the other's call, without becoming one with the other. How is this uniqueness revealed and maintained in a subject that morphs and changes under the dislocation caused by the encounter with the other, as Pulcini discusses, in an incessant process of "self-renewing"? Both Cavarero and Pulcini speak of a relational subject, and not of a self-referential or a self-enclosed one; yet the relationality at work in these two thinkers does not lend to the same subjectivity. And what about the new form of collective subject that Laura Bazzicalupo discusses in her chapter, produced by biopower not through disciplinary methods but rather in and through neoliberal forms? These subjectivities are aggregates described as bottom-up experiments, she writes; they fluctuate and resist being locked in an identity status. This presents, yet again, a different kind of subjectivity, if we can still call it "a subject," and this may be just one of the underlining tensions this collection uncovers.

Other tensions disclosed in these essays stem from our entanglement with the world, in and through our material embodiment. Questions of freedom, liberation, and responsibility arise out of our embodied experience, whose thickness and density reveal political, ethical, and historical grains. There may be an objective and impersonal way of understanding freedom, disentangled from all that inheres to lived experience; that path is not pursued in these essays, though. Instead, tensions emerging from embodied life are laid bare and probed: between mother and woman, between mother and womb, between liberation and emancipation, between identity and uniqueness, between desubjectivation and becoming a subject, between migrant and citizen, just to name a few.

It is fitting to say that these essays question, in one way or another, the rigidity and the enclosures of traditional philosophy as a way of thinking that usually operates via a given set of concepts and categories. They present and exemplify a way of thinking that is agile, open, and subtle. It is not an openness that makes everything the same; rather, it is an openness that does not disdain anything as *un*philosophical and does not refrain from exploring it thoughtfully and inquisitively. Life in all its concrete and varied dimensions is where thinking demurs. From there, thinking moves in and out of such concreteness without ever abandoning it entirely. Without offering final and definitive answers, this way of thinking invites us to pause, to dwell and reflect on many facets and on how they interlace in the issue at hand. If a vision is provided, it is neither static nor final.

Each essay has its own specific way of "wooing" us without making us fall captive. We are drawn, but not coerced; we are in its net, but not caught. In her essay on responsibility, Laura Boella argues that the question is about "being here," being present and taking the initiative, recalling a life that is exposed and not self-centered, but also a life that is in "active tension." In the broad variety of timely and urgent questions gathered in this volume, as well as in the manifold approaches herein displayed, these essays make manifest a way of thinking that delves into tensions. They exemplify an exercise that is enchanted neither with transcendence and purity, nor with a conception of philosophy founded on a hierarchization of life. These essays remind us that there is no separating philosophy from life; rather, philosophy is about delving into life's depths. We tend to look at tensions as problems that need some form of resolution or reconciliation.

But, as these chapters display, in attending to tensions, thinking dis-tends and ex-tends the philosophical art.

~

The volume has been organized around four conceptual clusters—each highlighting distinct yet interconnected themes—followed by a Coda. Part One, "Women, Mothers, Bodies," centers on topics relating to the configuration of women's identity and subjectivity, challenging traditionally patriarchal procedures of philosophizing in light of women's experience. This is, admittedly, the most overtly feminist of all the sections, and, at times, it does not shy away from personal considerations providing a refreshing breath of air in an often asphyctic, overly exegetic and argumentative way of doing philosophy. The part opens with an essay by Luisa Muraro, "The Inner Passage." The core of this chapter—and, for Muraro, the challenge for our times—lies in the question: What happens to thought when faced with something unthought? Starting from the statement recalled earlier, "But I am a woman," and drawing on Descartes' method of making his own thinking "the inner passage" that ushers in the modern world, Muraro argues for women's politics as an intersubjective practice that begins from within, liberates women's desire, names the real in ways other from those that are already known, and imagines ways of living otherwise and elsewhere.

The unthought that Muraro so fervently invokes returns in the next chapter under the guise of the maternal with which women's identity has often and too readily been assimilated. Through a critical consideration of the controversial concept of the "irreplaceable womb," in "Who Is a Mother?" Maria Luisa Boccia considers the effects that the new reproductive technologies have on the meaning of motherhood. The destabilizing role they ultimately play, Boccia argues, complicates the concept of the maternal and opens the way for the possibility of reconfiguring the meaning of being a woman, deconstructing female identity, and getting rid of motherhood as "destiny" through the dissociation of the figures of the woman, the mother, the biological mother, and the person who loves and cares for a child.

The figure of the mother makes a crucial appearance also in Lea Melandri's "Aporias of the Maternal in the Women's Movement." The question at the basis of Melandri's reflection focuses on the notion of the maternal and its ability to operate as a meaningful factor for positive changes and transformations. The question Melandri provocatively consigns us is whether a mere value shift—from negative to positive—in the understanding of the maternal may be sufficient to transform the cause of women's traditional exclusion from public life into an opportunity for women's affirmation, liberation, and empowerment.

Part Two extends the reflections relating to themes of women's identity to a consideration of topics of subjectivity, power, and the political as philosophical concepts broadly understood. In "Toward an Ethos of Freedom: Notes on Subjectivity and Power," Simona Forti raises the question of how to (re)think a notion of subjectivity that, while not being oblivious to relations of power, can be free by enacting forms of resistance against external pressures and constraints. The underlying conviction of Forti's analysis of the figure of Socrates as it appears in texts by Arendt, Foucault, and Patočka is that, to prevent power from becoming domination, political action must be the visible manifestation of an ethics of freedom as the articulation of an anti-fascist practice of life.

The political concern in relation to practices of power, government, and processes of subjectivation is also at the center of Laura Bazzicalupo's "Biopolitics and Economy: Between Self-Government Practices and New Forms of Control." Neoliberal rationality is a form of biopolitics, Bazzicalupo argues, as it governs through the production of processes of subjectivation whose ethos is economic, that is, based on an organizational logic (an economy) that substitutes the modern juridical-political logic based on formal, exclusionary, and dualist law with an unlimited, yet highly selective inclusiveness. This functional system produces the imaginary of self-government and lives' productive power, yet it also exposes such lives to the *ex post* control of evaluation and rating, thereby implying, Bazzicalupo warns, deeply problematic consequences for democratic forms of representation.

The preceding considerations of themes of subjectivity and processes of subjectivation are enriched by the explicit appearance of the other—in the form of the migrant—in Caterina Resta's "Immunitary Politics." In Europe, Resta notes, various forms of "immunitary" politics and sovereignisms have recently emerged, that is, new nationalistic policies based on the fear of contamination by foreign elements—the migrants—seen as a threat to cultural identity and economic wealth. Confronted with this situation and following Derrida's notion of "topolitics," Resta calls for an examination of the very character of sovereignty understood in the form of the connection between sovereignty, ipseity, identity, membership, and territory. Only by deconstructing this nexus and pointing to the need to remain vulnerable, no matter the challenges and risks, will it be possible to imagine new forms of citizenship and planetary cohabitation, Resta courageously concludes.

Whereas Part Two has a somewhat distinctly sociopolitical flavor, Part Three revisits some of the same themes and concerns yet this time from a perspective of individual involvement inclined in an ethical and practical direction. What constitutive elements need to be at work in the individual to orient subjectivity possibly to generate the new forms of world cohabitation invoked by Resta at the end of Part Two? In "Responsibility as Being Here in Our Own Time," Laura Boella notes how, in contemporary thought, the generative source of ethics has become responsibility, which thinkers such as Jan Patočka and Karel Kosík address through the conceptual figure of one's "presence at one's own time" or the courage "to be here." This figure of responsibility appears also in the work of the perhaps little known Swiss thinker Jeanne Hersch. Boella notices the "heretical" value of these still largely unexplored reflections, and argues that the essential moment of responsibility understood as "being here" consists of placing oneself at the center of the contradictions between individual behavior and macroeconomic/technological processes, institutions, needed beliefs, and disappointed hopes.

The need for a change, a revision, or at least an update of the traditional philosophical vocabulary and, more specifically, the thematization of a notion of subjectivity that is capable of meeting the challenges of its time continue in Elena's Pulcini's "Emotional Subjects: For the Care of the Future." Confronted with the many global challenges that threaten the future of the living world, philosophy's only chance to avoid literally becoming world-less is to renew itself, Pulcini argues. This urgently needed renewal invests primarily the subject, which needs to be redefined, according to Pulcini, as an interrelational subjectivity based on *passions* regarded as the relational structures par excellence. Understanding the passions is the prelude to the education and cultivation of those positive emotions Pulcini defines as "empathic passions," that is, those passions that are urgently needed to preserve the possibility of the world future.

The need for alternative conceptual categories and for a reorientation toward affective modes of existence capable of gesturing toward the unthought—a notion that returns, albeit in a different form, from previous chapters in Part One—are some of the themes central to Part Four. In "Everyday Life: For a Vision without Transcendences," Enrica Lisciani-Petrini focuses on reclaiming the notion of everyday life and the productive force intrinsic in this idea. Starting already in the mid-nineteenth century, the category of the "everyday" has imposed itself to philosophical and also artistic thinking, Lisciani-Petrini remarks, thereby shifting the focus from the heights of the rigid protocols of "pure reason" to the lowliness of everyday life considered in its unavoidable material and impersonal interconnections. The shift is accompanied by a changed methodology, which is now aimed at exposing the inescapable complexity of reality in its everyday passing and is situated at the intersection of various linguistic registers—art, politics, anthropology, philosophy, fashion, marketing, and advertisements. This approach is not distant, Lisciani-Petrini concludes, from the "impure reason" that, for many, characterizes that trend of Italian thinking recently become known as "Italian thought."

The invitation to resist ways of thinking that reduce philosophy to purely abstract, cognitive, or conceptual modalities and the desire to assign to thinking more active and affective functions that nevertheless are not closed to transcendence are central to Maria Cristina Bartolomei's "The Symbol in Action." Drawing on Paul Ricoeur and Friedrich Ernst Schleiermacher, Bartolomei looks at the symbol not from a cognitive perspective but from the dimension of action. This leads to acknowledge that the way in which symbols work is by acting, by fulfilling a communicative and affective function that allows the receiver of the symbolic action to lean toward the unthought. According to Bartolomei, the symbol maintains a circular and dialectical relation between various dimensions (words and things, precision and stratification of meanings, the symbol's singularity and the symphonic dimension of its horizon, timelessness and historical and cultural rootedness) and ultimately, as theorized by Ricoeur, it acts in the sense of being an occasion for and spur toward the exercise, practice, and activity of thinking.

The volume concludes with a Coda—an interview with Adriana Cavarero conducted by Nidesh Lawtoo. Not an extemporaneous addition but rather a vibrant testimony and exemplification of the relational subjectivity and collaborative practices of thinking evoked in many of the previous chapters, in "Mimetic Inclinations: A Dialogue with Adriana Cavarero," the Italian thinker responds to Lawtoo's own interest in the role played by the ancient concept of *mimēsis* in the articulation of Cavarero's political thought. In the dialogical space that opens up, Cavarero provides a terse and vivid overview of some major themes that characterize her philosophy. On the background of authors that span from Hannah Arendt to Plato, Karen Blixen, Elias Canetti, Émile Zola, and Emmanuel Levinas among others, she intersects themes that are at the heart of her work, but that also resonate with many topics of this volume. Through her method of "stealing," Cavarero recovers from the depths of a forgetful tradition voices that resound in a new polyphony—the subject, the other, the woman, the mother, the everyday, the political, the body, responsibility. Cavarero's Arendtian conclusion, which can be aptly applied to this volume as a whole, is that, in polyphony, individualities do not dissolve because "uniqueness and plurality are just two categories that implicate one another reciprocally."[8]

At the end of the journey this volume takes through the reflections and positions advanced by these remarkable Italian women thinkers, each distinct in her individuality and yet in relation with the others, one certainly has a sense of the novelty of concepts, the expansion of themes, the subtlety of analysis, the rigor of thought, and the commitment to practice that these authors bring to contemporary philosophy, Italian and beyond. It is our hope as editors that the dance to which they invite us and the piazzas in which they welcome us may not only be enjoyed and treasured but also urge us toward ways of thinking that are daring, creative, and resilient.

Notes

1. One can find information on works by these women thinkers available in English translation in the contributors' notes at the end of the volume.

2. The editors would like to point out that this is also the case for the conversation between Nidesh Lawtoo and Adriana Cavarero, the "Coda"; this conversation too took place in Italian.

3. Luisa Muraro, "The Inner Passage," Part One, p. 24.

4. Women's right to vote was established in Italy in 1945, and Italian women were able to vote for the first time that year in local administrative elections where they were held. Women voted for the first time at the national level in 1946 in the referendum that established Italy as a Republic; twenty-one women, the so-called *madri costituenti* [constituent mothers], were elected to be part of the constituent assembly, made of a total of 556 members, and five women participated in the committee of seventy-five individuals that wrote the Italian constitution.

5. For example, the right to equal pay in factories in 1961, retirement benefits for housewives and equal access to all professions, including courts of law, in 1963, the legitimation of divorce in 1970, the creation of daycare facilities to help working mothers in 1971, a new family law in 1975, a law on equal treatment in matters of work in 1977, and the legalization of abortion in 1978.

6. These activities were carried out through mixed groups of men and women, communities of women alone, collectives of self-reflection and consciousness raising, and gave rise to numerous initiatives such as the various *Casa delle Donne* [Women's House] in many Italian towns, the *Libreria delle Donne* [Women's Bookstore] and the *Libera Università delle Donne* [Women's Free University] in Milan, the Diotima group in Verona, and many others.

7. The feminist struggle in Italy has seen the debate over emancipation versus liberation taking center stage over the years. The question at the heart of this debate is complex and would require more space than this introduction allows. Suffice it to say that while emancipation rests on the struggle for equality in and through recognition of rights and legislation reform, the struggle for liberation considers women's freedom independently from male (or universal) notions of equality and

legal reforms. The three essays in Part One by Muraro, Boccia, and Melandri refer to this debate: Muraro and Boccia do so implicitly and Melandri in a more explicit way. See Melandri, "Aporias of the Maternal in the Women's Movement," p. 48.

8. Adriana Cavarero/Nidesh Lawtoo, "Mimetic Inclinations: A Dialogue with Adriana Cavarero," p. 197.

Part One

Women, Mothers, Bodies

One

The Inner Passage

Luisa Muraro

If I go ahead with my fragmentary visions, the whole world will have to be transformed in order for me to fit in it.

—Clarice Lispector, *The Passion According to GH*

Those who wish to devote themselves to the study of philosophy should know that they must give up defining philosophy ahead of time. Philosophy will provide its own definition. Indeed, there exists such a thing as the philosophical vocation, and it is personal. In my case, it started with my feminist awakening, when I realized: "But I am a woman." At that point, I began to reflect critically on the meaning of my realization and its truth effects, which impacted my own thought as it became aware that sexual difference may have a free meaning.

In my philosophical practice, I find it impossible to separate the aspect that involves research from my commitment to the women's movement. I am reminded of what Simone Weil writes in 1943, in her *Carnet de Londres*, namely that philosophy is "exclusively an affair of action and practice"; and this, she says, is why it is so difficult to write about it, "difficult in the same way as a treatise on tennis or running, but much more so."[1] I share this idea, while allowing that the philosophical pursuit may also be conceived and practiced in other ways, even by feminist thinkers. The only condition is that pluralism be excluded. I do not reject the plural form, "feminisms"; but I do not use it in my own work because it tends to turn plurality (which I accept) into pluralism (which I do not accept). I prefer the use of the singular form, "feminism," and when confronted with conflicts, I maintain that feminism is a battleground where one fights without hate.

One day, my philosophy teacher asked me: "Why do you side with the feminists? You are *homo*." *Homo*: a free, thinking human being—one's admission to philosophy required nothing more. . . . Yet this was both too much and too little. "But I am a woman!" I proclaimed, and I began to try to understand the meaning of such "but." What I found was an argument concerning the relation that reasoning thought establishes with our being living, sensitive bodies. There is a symbolic debt that thought has toward matter and life. Yet to me as a woman, things did not seem right, and maybe my professor understood this even before I spoke.

Some feminists would hesitate to say "I am a woman" because they think that the meaning of the word "woman" has been irremediably corrupted by the patriarchal culture. To these feminists, I would say that the meaning of words is an important part of the feminist challenge, and their position is like surrendering to the enemy even before the battle begins.

I have heard that, according to one feminist scholar, "woman" as it was presented in the 1960s and 1970s is a concept that no theoretically equipped feminist can find acceptable. I find this statement perplexing for two reasons. First of all, there is here a sense of ownership over the meaning of words that I do not approve. I have learned from the linguist Ferdinand de Saussure that the meaning of words belongs first and foremost to the speakers. As far as the concept of "woman" is concerned, feminist scholars are called to engage in thinking within a field that opened up precisely thanks to the feminist revolt of the period. Therefore, while it is right to criticize and analyze, it may be somewhat reckless to depart from this field for reasons that are accessible only to those who are theoretically equipped.

Thus philosophy presented itself to me as a political orientation (that is, to stand on the side of women) and as a commitment to find words to express something that I am deeply certain is true, namely that sexual difference is not an addition to who I am, it does not stand *between* me and who knows whom or what, *nor* is it caused by who knows whom or what. The difference that I consciously assume when I say "I am a woman" is not an I; rather, it is there *within* me independently from me. It keeps my I from coinciding with my "I," thereby giving rise to a never-ending negotiation between being body and being word. This negotiation makes me be what we all are, namely, symbolic animals. In other words, feminism is a challenge regarding the free meaning of sexual difference.

This challenge extends from the present back into the past, producing new narratives. Even when it concerns the past, the "battle of the narrative" (as it has been called) is fought in the present and the benefits are reaped in the present. One can win a challenge even after it has been lost as long as one raises the stakes. This may seem absurd but it is not insofar as facts act on us through the meaning that they take on.

~

Since 2001, I have felt a growing sense of anticipation and urgency within the world, and an awareness that changes are taking place. The signs are both increasingly numerous and self-contradictory. We cannot see the future straight ahead of us because we are at a turning point. Our predictions, like our natural vision, are rectilinear. This is the direction of progress, which is increasingly a false progress and brings us to be suspicious of those who want progress at all cost. Traveling in a vehicle that is only open at the front is dangerous. Yet we can feel the curve—we perceive a centrifugal force that tells us we are turning. Are we entering a new, unknown gravitational field?

In Europe, the passage to modernity has been a long and complex process marked by some salient features. Some of these traits run throughout its history and have brought modernity to its end.

Modern Europe came to an abrupt and disastrous end with World War I, which was a massacre the likes of which had never been seen before. People called it the Great War. The name was later changed because World War I was followed by a second World War that was worse than the first, not to mention the events that took place in the interval between the two. Subsequently, the task of paving the way for a better future for Western civilization fell to the United States. I too was there during this latter stage. As a child, I had never seen a movie or even been to the cinema, but I used to collect the cards of the great Hollywood actors, I chewed gum, and I listened to my older sister tell us about the life of American women, who were so free that they did not even have to wear a petticoat.

There are two main paths in the passage to modernity. The first of these, which is predominant within English-speaking philosophy, concerns the birth of modern law, narrated in the figurative form of an originary social contract.

This path was critically retraced by the feminist Carole Pateman in a book written more than thirty years ago, *The Sexual Contract* (1988), which has taken on increasing importance over the years. This is how she briefly sums up the passage to modernity that extends, with pejorative effects, into postmodernity: "That is to say, in the movement from the old world of status to the new world of contract, the freedom of the individual consists in *emancipation* from the old bonds and constraints, whether those of absolutism, the *patria potestas*, the state—or sexual difference."[2] Contemporary individualism is the outcome of this generalized "unboundedness" with which the very concept of freedom tends to be confused, and in which it tends to be lost. This is not without its contradictions where it comes to concern women, who are assimilated to men even against their own interests and in contrast with their own experience.

The second path, which is prevalent in continental philosophy, is related to the conception of knowledge. The salient, and pejorative, trait here regards, to my mind, the unsettled debt I referred to earlier, that is, the debt owed by thinkers to matter and life. This trait is not as obvious as the one described in *The Sexual Contract*; rather, it resembles a "bracketing," an "overlooking," a "leaving out," as when we leave something "out of consideration." Let us examine this more closely.

I take as the inaugural text of modernity René Descartes' *Discours sur la méthode*, which appeared in 1637. The *Discours* begins with a story related in the first person.

Centuries later, the personal accounts exchanged among themselves by the members of Alcoholics Anonymous or the women of feminist self-consciousness or consciousness-raising groups will also be in the first person. This is a significant coincidence because it better highlights the fracture and the polemic. The ones to which I am referring, in fact, are small groups of individuals who come together voluntarily in the name of something they have in common—in the first case, addiction to alcohol; in the second, gender—and help each other talk about themselves and listen without the censorship of the "leaving it out."

In his choice of autobiographical language, Descartes is said to have drawn inspiration from Michel de Montaigne, the author of *Les Essais*. In several aspects, in fact, the two men are close yet distant. What separates them is precisely the matter we are discussing here.

One of Montaigne's merits was his consideration and condemnation of witch hunting. He was a man endowed with a courageous intellectual honesty. He devoted to witch hunting one of his last *Essais*, written in a characteristically allusive language suggested by the title itself: *Les boiteux* (*Of Cripples*). At the beginning of the essay, he writes that men "more willingly study to find out reasons than to ascertain truth: they slip over presuppositions, but are curious in examination of consequences; they leave the things, and fly to the causes (. . .)." Whereas they should say, "Is such a thing done?," our reason, continues Montaigne, is "able to create a hundred other worlds (. . .); it needs neither matter nor foundation: let it but run on." And he concludes that "both the body and the soul interrupt and weaken the right they have of the use of the world (*le droit qu'ils ont de l'usage du monde*)," where things are felt and endured.[3]

Descartes passes over this "right" to a kind of knowledge that is based on the sensible and passionate partaking or "use" of the world and focuses instead on its rational construction. His *Discours*, as revealed by the subtitle, has the purpose of "rightly conducting one's reason and of seeking truth in the sciences."

How did it turn out? It turned out well, if one judges from the extraordinary development of techno-scientific knowledge. That it turned out well was also the prevalent evaluation until the beginning of the twentieth century. But then, Europe and the areas within the radius of European influence (which was worldwide) were struck by a succession of wars and upheavals, aggravated enormously by the destructive potential that had developed alongside science itself. And it is far from being over, as we know. We have lost, as Montaigne would say, the "right" to the form of knowledge resulting from the practical and sensitive partaking (*frequentazione*) of the world. Montaigne's choice of the word *usage* to name such a partaking refers to a French term that in his day had a connotation closer to what today we refer to as "practice."

The *Discours sur la Methode* begins with a narration in which the philosopher looks back at his own education, of which he speaks well. Yet the purpose of his account is to stress the ensuing profound dissatisfaction he experienced at finding himself with no criteria for distinguishing true from false. He tells how he then began to travel to study "the great book of the world" but, failing to find what he sought, eventually decided to concentrate his studies within himself, relying on his own human capacity for reason. It was only then, in fact, that he found his way. It happened at some insignificant place in Germany, toward the end of 1619, in comfortable lodgings during the winter break from the easy military service that, as a young nobleman, he had opted for himself. Concentrating on putting order among his thoughts, he found within himself, namely in his natural ability to reason, the starting point he needed.

The narration with which Descartes introduces his *Discours sur la Methode* is essential to understanding the spirit of Western modernity.

What happened, he tells us, was that in his consciousness—the consciousness of a man who, though gifted with intelligence, lacked the authority of a teacher like Aristotle or the *magistri* of the Sorbonne, and who lived in circumstances that, while undoubtedly privileged, were nonetheless ordinary—a spark was ignited that shed light on something that had so far remained unseen (and those who did see it, as there were some who could, had failed to express it in comprehensible and acceptable terms).

What was this "something"? Paraphrased in my own words, Descartes' narration shows us that for something that is true to exist, there must be someone who consciously and freely seeks it out and recognizes it. In other words, it shows us that truth, if and when it reveals itself, is subjective truth.

Following and as a result of this discovery, everything appeared and began to move in a different direction, toward establishing an indissoluble relation between personal freedom and true knowledge. I refer here not to rights, which were to come later, but to constitutive, originary relations.

In Descartes' day, the word "subject" and its derivatives did not have the same meaning we give it today. The word still took the originally medieval Latin meaning of *subjectum*. It was Descartes himself, in fact, who made the decisive move to give a new meaning to the word, a meaning that has made the greatest imprint on the civilization of European origin.

Some scholars have attempted to justify Descartes' use of such a markedly subjective language, which appears to be in contrast with the philosophical themes he developed, such as rationalism and the ideal of scientific objectivity. In my view, however, this subjective language needs no justification. The turn Descartes brought about in history consists precisely in the realization that, if there is something true, right, and good, such a something can only enter the world by passing through the inner self of a free, rational human being. There remains the need to explain, however, how this new way of thinking developed into an objective and objectifying science, independent from both context and embodied subject.

Descartes' *Discours* does, in fact, announce these developments, which are made possible by that "leaving out" I described earlier.

Let me go back again to the association I made with the autobiographical language used in feminism. The feminist turn that took place in the 1960s and 1970s also began with subjective consciousness. Based on this, both Descartes and the feminist turn to subjectivity produced a discourse that until that moment was literally unheard-of, and released a transforming power that then spread throughout their respective historical contexts.

Although they resemble each other, Descartes' discourse and the feminist practice diverge macroscopically. The practice of feminism is intersubjective; on the contrary, Descartes narrates a meditation that occurred in solitude. His solitude was conscious and deliberate, and he justified it by claiming that the knowledge that is based on the opinions of many different people never comes as close to the truth as the reasoning of a man of good sense who thinks alone.

Descartes was well aware that his discourse depended on the critiques and contributions of others (so much so that he explicitly sought them out). What he meant to get across, however, is that the truth emerges not as the sum of a multiplicity of varyingly authoritative and well-established positions, but as the result of the mental act of the thinking subject that recognizes it as such. As is well known, the philosopher wanted to do away with the principle of authority. Yet he was aiming higher than this, namely at establishing the thinking subject as the foundation for a universal science subjected only to the authority of reason.

The discourse on the difference between the seventeenth-century philosopher and the feminists, between the solitary meditation of the former and the practice of the latter, is *not* a comparison of two different views on how best to approach the truth, as if it were simply a question of whether it is better to be alone or to be more than one. Solitude or multiplicity is not the point. The point is, rather, a shift in the terms in which questions are posed, including the question of truth. Is this just a shift in perspective? It is more than that! These two moves can be likened to those played in a game of chess—they are two moves that change the whole symbolic "landscape." When the feminist movement erupted fifty years ago, someone said that a new subject had been born. It would have been more correct to say that the term "subject" remains but its meaning will change again. And one could have simply added that thought was finally beginning to pay off more substantially and effectively its debt toward living, sensitive bodies. Carla Lonzi, to whom we owe the seminal texts of the Italian feminism of sexual difference, wrote at the time: "The unforeseen destiny of the world lies in beginning the journey all over again, this time with woman as subject."[4]

In his *Discours*, the philosopher is aware that, in his itinerary, there is an element of fabrication that enables him to reach his conclusion. His idea, he writes, that a man's reasoning can attain a faithful expression of the truth would be true "if we had had the entire use of our reason from our birth and had always been conducted only by it."[5] Yet this was not the case, as he himself acknowledges through his use of the clause of rejected condition.

And in fact, things do not work that way. We human beings come into the world without even being able to talk, let alone reason. Yet we are symbolic animals, in the sense that we are brought into the world by speaking human beings, have the ability to learn how to do the same, and little by little, with the help of others, if all goes well we also learn to reason. The path is long and precarious. Without going into detail, Descartes allocates the responsibility to family upbringing and school education, with their imperfect rationality. And he clearly believes that it is not logically necessary to consider the circumstances in which we are born and develop into thinking beings.

Montaigne, as we have seen, takes a different view. According to Montaigne, reason can come to know reality as long as it acknowledges the contribution made by a basic human partaking of the world, with all its material and immaterial content ("soul and body," he says). The linguist Roman Jakobson would agree with this. According to the theory expounded by the latter in *Two Aspects of Language and Two Types of Aphasic Disturbances*, verbal language develops along two directions, one metaphorical and one metonymic. These two are inseparable, but they occur in historically variable proportions characterizing cultures as well as individuals and social groups. Within the context of the activities of human beings, who are both symbolic and social animals, the two directions correspond, respectively, to imagining the world and to partaking of it. And as such, the two directions both contribute to the human representation of reality. Reflecting on this theory and applying it to my own experience, I have come to realize that we all contribute to building language and culture, but with diverse and unequal tasks; therefore we can speak of a division of the symbolic work that depends on the position (be it incidental or enforced) of the speaker.[6]

And I realized how enormously has the fabrication of the Cartesian man benefited from this division of the symbolic work.

Undoubtedly, the age in which Descartes lived and the social position he enjoyed allowed him to rely on the hardworking presence of a large body of people who catered to his everyday needs as a thinking being without his having himself to attend to such needs. This allowed him to concentrate on his intellectual work and neglect the rest, to the extent that he became convinced that the rest is insignificant from the point of view of the knowledge of reality. This is a mistake Montaigne did not fall into, despite the fact that he shared the same social condition.

This body of people, as present and hardworking as they were unseen and unheard, was made up of women, servants, and manual laborers. In the typical patriarchal society, women and servants are regarded as naturally inferior and subordinate to the head of the family. They are *not*, as Aristotle taught in his *Politics*, to be placed on the same level because women, *along with* physical labor, have always done an essential part of the symbolic work, such as taking care of home economics, teaching how to speak, managing affective relationships in everyday life, and so on. Ultimately, women have always, either by choice or as a result of decisions made by others, been in charge of the symbolic work that is required by our being embodied.

All of this, in Descartes' theory, turns into the metaphysical correspondence, guaranteed by God himself, between body and mind. As far as the concrete "details" are concerned, that is, regarding the part that women play in this work of correspondence, there is no need to turn this issue into a philosophical question, because the answer already lies in the roles assigned to women by the established order.

From ancient times to modern days, a great many (if not all) patriarchal societies have tended to *overlook* women (that is, leave them out) not on a practical level, which would be impossible, but ideally, that is, in the act of their self-representation. Thus, for example, women are present in real life but are hardly mentioned at all in history books. To simply claim that historiography is "androcentric," centered on the male gender, would not be enough because the maneuvers put in place to eliminate women symbolically are diverse and numerous and profoundly shape the different cultures, although not in a manifest way.

The anthropologist Françoise Héritier retraced a perspicacious archaic example of the symbolic elimination of women.[7] In one of the earliest known written codes of our civilization, there is a rule that forbids having sex with two sisters or with their mother. Researching into the taboo of incest, the anthropologist realized that the purpose of this strange rule was simply to establish that a woman cannot have sex with her sister's or her mother's man. To put it in such terms, however, would have meant placing women in the symbolic landscape as subjects responsible for their own behavior; in other words, free.

The symbolic act of "leaving out" the female subject still continues in today's world through recourse to the possibilities offered or promised by techno-science. A certain Italian judge seeking to endorse the practice of surrogate motherhood (which is currently not permitted under Italian law) put forward the argument that because laboratories in various parts of the world are experimenting to create an artificial womb, women who agree to be surrogate mothers are merely doing what, in the near future, will be done by machines.[8] Thus, a woman who agrees to bring a new human being into the world finds herself reduced to being the surrogate of a future machine. It could almost be the sequel to Margaret Atwood's *The Handmaid's Tale*.

~

At this point, a conclusion is imperative: we must raise the stakes if we are to win the challenge that modern Europe, in its time, lost. This was the challenge of proving that one could liberate the powers of desire and, under the guidance of reason, direct them toward the common good. As we can observe, however, things have turned out differently, and what has prevailed is the will to power and the rule of financial economy. This does not mean the end of history; there will be events to come whose accounts will fill the libraries of the future, if there is a future. What this means is the end of politics. Some people believe that politics is intrinsic to social life; this is a delusion and a misconception, because the political game is increasingly restricted by economic calculations and the balance of power.

As I have said earlier, we can still win challenges that have previously been lost if we raise the stakes. To do this, we need to secure symbolic independence and be able to *hear* the *unheard-of*. This has nothing to do with the mystical, but a great deal to do with the practical.

I have been brought to think of symbolic independence on the basis of a simple question: What happens to thought when it is faced with something unthought? In other words, when one finds oneself in a situation where there are no ready-made answers, no criteria of truth for finding them, nor even words to express the problem? How can we think independently from what has already been thought? The unthought is a no-man's-land, the devil's territory. Only the innocent can enter without harm. For the rational mind, it is traumatic to venture into this territory, and it often provokes defensive or aggressive reactions. For example, how does Shakespeare's Macbeth react when he suddenly realizes that the feudal bond of loyalty to the king represents an obstacle to his ambition? The witches' prophecy represents an alarming portent of the end of an era and could have marked the beginning of a new political order. Yet Macbeth's response is violence, with all the effects of symbolic disorder manifested in the madness of Lady Macbeth.[9]

In the 1970s, in her famous book *On Violence*, which was written during the student-led revolts that spread across half the globe, Hannah Arendt criticized the use of violence in politics, declaring that it is not the only way to stop the automatic and predictable course of events. There are other ways, such as engaging in the kind of political action that is worthy of its name:[10] that which is capable of fracturing the order of the dominant discourse so that a breach can be made, what I like to call "the hole in the bushes," in memory of my childhood.

I believe that politics today is women's politics. It is said that in 1966, during the protests by American students against the Vietnam War, something completely unprecedented occurred. In a mixed meeting, many men were discussing the "Woman Question." A group of young women walked out of the meeting and gathered among women only. This represented an interruption of the trajectory of integration in the male world and a turn toward women's freedom. I am just one of the countless others who have followed those young women's example.

The anecdote may have an air of legend to it. Yet the second wave of feminism is indeed a historical fact, and the practice of women's separation marked its beginning. The "revolt within the revolt" is how I describe this feminist turn that embraced the rebellion of the younger generations against the society of their fathers as an opportunity to deepen the rift in the age-old stratum of patriarchal domination.

We do sometimes try to overthrow the dominant order with violence. Yet when faced with the "unthought" that emerges in the desire for change, more often than not we fall back on the "already thought" by giving our *consensus*.

I recall how, when I was a student, now and again my attention would be drawn to the fact that almost no women were mentioned in the history books. This seemed so strange to me, because my everyday world had always been full of women, beginning with my mother and my sisters. And yet I let it go. Now I wonder: how could I?

Those who have reflected on the question, and especially those who have listened to and believed in the testimonies from personal experience, have found themselves focusing on the enormous ambiguity of the word "consensus."

Consensus is not ipso facto an open agreement, nor, conversely, is it the expression of a submissive personality. There is a third interpretation. This very same word with the very same meaning can refer to the mode of living of those who cannot imagine themselves living in any other way than the way they live in: everything they know and can say about themselves and the world prevents them from imagining themselves *elsewhere* and *otherwise*. This brings them to believe that it can be tolerated. And so tolerate it they do, even when they are unhappy.

This third, more profound answer to the question of consensus sheds light on the entire history of women within patriarchy. I found it in Rachel Moran's *Paid For: My Journey through Prostitution*, a book that is surely one of the masterpieces of feminist thought. The book explains how a human being, in this case the author herself, can come to allow such an unacceptable situation as female prostitution, which she practiced in Dublin from the age of fifteen to twenty-two.[11]

After she came out of prostitution, Rachel Moran's mission became that of finding the words to tell the subjective truth of a human condition that is tolerated, despised, and legalized by our society amid a mess of contradictions, which she manages to unravel in a way that no one has ever done before (subjective truth is no less true than objective truth, nor is its pursuit less arduous—on both counts it is quite the contrary, in fact).

Rachel Moran talks about the issue of not believing that one has rights, which represents the zero degree of political awareness. *Non credere di avere dei diritti* [*Don't believe you have any rights*] is the Italian title of a book to which I and a number of others have contributed. It tells the story of the Women's Bookstore, *la Libreria delle Donne*, in Milan, following our political journey from the feminist revolt to the cultivation of a relation of trust among women. The book has also been published in the United States, though with a different title because (we were told) in the United States the original title would have been misunderstood.[12]

Translating the book into other European languages did not pose this problem. Perhaps in the United States more than in Europe there is the idea that freedom is synonymous with the certainty of having rights. But does this also apply to women's freedom? I think not. Neither in the experiences shared by Rachel Moran nor in the accounts relating to 1966 and the feminist awakening does the certainty of having rights appear as primary. What stands out as supreme is the discovery, both personal and shared, of being *otherwise* and *elsewhere* than the place received from others in the world.

This was also the case with the recent Hollywood harassment scandal that gave rise to the feminist movement #MeToo. Through silent and repeated abuses, man signaled that public life (studies, work, politics, etc.) was his domain and that women who wished to enter and be a part of it were expected to pay him a price. Not everyone behaved in this way, yet everyone, tacitly, could behave in such a manner; complicity among men was the confirmation thereof. This was how things stood at the time of women's emancipation, amid forced silence, male complicity, and fruitless legal denouncements. It was a feudal-mafia type regime. Now at last this is over; now we can begin to talk about women's freedom within public life, and the effects of this are unpredictable: we are on the eve of a new season in women's politics.[13]

When I talk about politics, I interpret it in a feminist key, but I do not rule out other ways of conceiving it. The way I see it, the challenge of women's politics, of feminism, is to attain a free sense of sexual difference. Through this path, which is neither unique nor exclusive, I believe that it is possible to resume an evolutionary development of life on Earth that moves from the natural event of sexuation toward the formation of a civilization in which all living beings can coexist, thus bringing about the need for mediation and, therefore, language. This is not a remote event; it is happening here and now, between you and me.

I do not even exclude the possibility of the feminist movement's reaching its conclusion in the form of its own self-surpassing. Alongside the many possible answers that feminism offers in the search for freedom, in fact, there are also solutions that are not feminist. My dream as a writer is to find the words that can shed light on the greatness of women—including that greatness that is invisible, that which is unconscious of itself, and that which has not found its place in this world.

Note: The title of this chapter, The Inner Passage, *names exactly an intuition that is only partially brought to light by the text. Therefore, I consider this text a provisional and imperfect version of an unwritten text. I have kept the original title, and I publish the English translation of that provisional and imperfect text in the hope that reading through it may bring the intelligent reader to a further passage than the one I myself have been able to accomplish.*

(Translated by Geraldine Clarkson;
revised by Silvia Benso and Elvira Roncalli)

Notes

1. Simone Weil, *Oeuvres Complètes* (Paris: Gallimard, 2006), vol. IV, 392.

2. Carole Pateman, *The Sexual Contract* (Stanford, CA: Stanford University Press, 1988), 228.

3. *Essays of Michel de Montaigne*, Ch. XI, "Of Cripples" (Paris 1827).

4. Carla Lonzi, *Sputiamo su Hegel* (Milan: Scritti di Rivolta Femminile, 1974).

5. René Descartes, *Discours de la Methode*, 1637.

6. Roman Jakobson, "Two Aspects of Language and Two Types of Aphasic Disturbances," in *Selected Writings II, Word and Language* (The Hague-Paris: Mouton, 1971), 239–59; Luisa Muraro, *Maglia o uncinetto. Racconto linguistico-politico sulla inimicizia tra metafora e metonimia* (Milan: Feltrinelli, 1981); abridged English translation: "To Knit or to Crochet: A Political-Linguistic Tale on the Enmity between Metaphor and Metonymy," trans. Mark William Epstein, in *Another Mother: Diotima and the Symbolic Order of Italian Feminism*, ed. Cesare Casarino and Andrea Righi (Minneapolis: University of Minnesota Press, 2018), 67–119.

7. Francoise Heritier, *Les Deux sœurs et leur mère: Anthropologie de l'inceste* (Paris: Odile Jacob, 1994).

8. Daniela Danna, *Maternità. Surrogata?* (Trieste: Asterios, 2017), 133–34.

9. Luisa Muraro, "The Symbolic Independence from Power," in *The Italian Difference: Between Nihilism and Biopolitics*, ed. Lorenzo Chiesa and Alberto Toscano (Melbourne: re.press, 2009), 81–94.

10. Muraro, "The Symbolic Independence from Power," 93.

11. Rachel Moran, *Paid For: My Journey through Prostitution* (Dublin: Gill Books, 2013).

12. Libreria delle donne di Milano, *Non credere di avere dei diritti. La generazione della libertà femminile nell'idea e nelle vicende di un gruppo di donne* (Turin: Rosenberg & Sellier, 1987); the English translation appears as The Milan Women's Bookstore, *Sexual Difference: A Theory of Social-Symbolic Practice* (Bloomington: Indiana University Press, 1990).

13. Lia Cigarini, "La battaglia della narrazione," from the September 2018 issue of *Sottosopra*, a non-periodical magazine published by the Women's Bookstore in Milan.

Two

Who Is a Mother?

Maria Luisa Boccia

The abortion debate has recently come back, taking many countries by storm, from Europe all the way to Latin America. Truth be told, the denial of female autonomy in matters of reproductive choices has never been absent. And it has manifested itself in various forms, from prohibitions to restrictions to practical obstacles. The common trait that unites all these various forms is the blame put on the woman: she is made to be guilty of either a legal or an ethical "crime." Modalities and languages may change, but the common end goal is to uphold maternity as female destiny and assert *men's control* over the woman's reproductive power. In the past, the prohibition of abortion had the symbolic function of stigmatizing a practice that was tolerated when not even demanded by men. In the current context, marked by female freedom and by a widening of the spectrum of reproductive choices, the war on abortion signals the decline of patriarchal authority and the last attempt at reinstating the traditional order of sexual relations.

Abortion in the Politics of Sexual Difference

The right to access the female body and control it without limits is the true core of the patriarchal order. Men have upheld it not only through social norms (in relations of kinship, but not limited to them), but also through the construction—which has been interiorized by women—of the mother's body as vessel. The reduction of the body to a physical object has been essential to negate female reproductive power: doing and undoing the body; giving or not giving birth to a new human being. In these actions, the second possibility is as important as the first one. And, of course, it is also the most feared.

For men, the contingency of birth is connected to the inscrutability of maternal desire and to the thrust to contrast it by imposing limits and prohibitions on women's autonomy. This happens, first of all, by shifting the individual right to personal integrity back to conception. The "right-to-life" should, in other words, give men a protection against their precarious relation with procreation and against the "maternal danger" as it is made explicit in the act of abortion.[1] Therefore, abortion can be tolerated only insofar as women suffer from it, only insofar as they are its first victims. To this day, abortion is still considered to be an unjustifiable, even senseless act if it is understood as a woman's responsible and willing choice. And in fact, the real root of the conflict about abortion gets to be disguised behind a contraposition of values (right-to-life versus freedom of choice) and a conflict over rights (the woman's, the fetus', the potential father's).

Within the language of individual rights, subjects are in a position of equality, independent from one another. The woman can claim the right of control over her own body. But this exposes her to the equal yet opposite claims to rights by others. And she has to respond to these claims. Therefore, her body becomes a "public space"[2] that is exposed to interventions and norms in order to protect the other subjects' rights. The argument that states the formal equality of subjects is reinforced within the contemporary context of reproductive medicine. In fact, reproductive technologies, equating organs and biological substances, promise to realize men's and women's equal opportunities, de jure and de facto, to procreate; and they pledge to render irrelevant the sexual difference inscribed in the body. On the one hand, paternity is naturalized because of the increasing relevance of the genetic bond; on the other, the relation that, at the corporeal level and otherwise, unites woman and fetus during pregnancy is transformed into an exchange between two distinct and separate subjects that bear potentially antagonistic rights.

In particular, biological paternity (and men's belief of being "equally" involved in procreation) has become a powerful instrument of the resistance and even the reestablishment of the paternal right to its originary goal, namely the submission of the "natural" female reproductive power to the social and symbolic order of patrilineal descent.

The parental equality that is becoming widespread is, however, the opposite of the path laid out by feminism, which began precisely with abortion. The feminist reflection on abortion in fact started from the need to *give meaning* to the *female* human experience of (pro)creation and wondered about the reasons why women become pregnant, whether they want it or not. And it began with the fundamental question of woman's sexuality: "For whose pleasure did I become pregnant?" In the experience of abortion, women in fact discovered the failure of their dependency on male sexuality because it is male sexuality, and not the woman's own sexuality, that experiences the coincidence between pleasure and coitus.

By exploring this feeling of dependence, inscribed in femininity, it became possible to name what women discover about themselves in the experience of abortion and what meaning emanates from what the body experiences and is forced to live through. It became possible to acknowledge that *being a woman* does not mean being a mother. The initial core of the "theory" of sexual difference took shape here. The reflection on sexuality was probably more explosive and deeper than the reflection on reproductive power. It is a sexuality in which desire, pleasure, and bodily experience have little to do with the reproductive function and the act that makes procreation possible, that is, coitus.[3]

Abortion was therefore the origin rather than the content of the politics of sexual difference. This politics is very different from the vindication of a right, whether the right to abortion or to procreation.

Bodies as Objects vs Embodied Subjects

Thinking about sexual difference has meant, for women, positing themselves as thinking subjects and questioning themselves on their being sexed and embodied. This has led to thinking differently not only, as it is commonly believed, about the meaning of masculinity and femininity but also, and more profoundly, about the relevance of embodiment for thought itself. The affirmation of a different subject and of thought itself as sexed (and gendered) has represented an incredible complication for knowledge and for the disciplinary status of knowing; and this is a fact that can be no longer eluded.

Patriarchy has understood the body either as a factual reality whose truth may be known or, vice versa, as a mystery into which one drowns because its enigma is destined to remain unsolved. Femininity has been the paradigmatic object of this relation between the knowing subject and the body that is to be known. It is not hard to understand why, for women's thinking, the cultural and political project of knowing the body as other-than-oneself creates a fictitious freedom, and so it has been necessary to undo this framework. What ensues is the modification of the very idea of thought as "free" because, in feminist thinking, thinking no longer coincides with being disentangled from contingency, from material determinations; on the contrary, thinking is instead oriented toward the body, which, prior to being an object of knowledge, is the condition of thought's very unfolding.

The impossibility of identifying female identity with the generative body is, for feminist thought, a decisive theoretical theme. *Woman* has become a problematic concept not only because it is marked by the many differences among women, but also because it has to account for an excess that divides sexual (or gender) identity from female subjectivity. To give back a sexed body to the subject has meant assigning a body to that subject and a subject to that body. This is entirely different from defining the *objective truth* of the body. On this matter, in my opinion, feminist discourse diverges radically from the techno-scientific narrative. For women, the matter lies in overcoming the evidence, pinned onto the body, of what constitutes a woman without assuming the identity of the rational, disincarnate subject.

If one wants to avoid falling prey to the perennial conflict between nature and culture or, to say it in today's terminology, between essentialism and constructionism, one needs to renounce relying either on the authenticity of the "body which I am" or on the construction of the "body which I want." It is necessary and feasible to renounce both the idea of the body as a natural given, the cornerstone of any given discourse, and the idea that bodies, with all their differences, are a discursive construction. It is true that bodies are a constructed reality, yet this reality is such only if it is embodied in a concrete subject.

In other words, the body as the object of discourse is a (more or less effective) representation that *animates itself* in singular bodies. Briefly stated, the body is the material and symbolic place where the complex weave of relations that unites the self and the world is done and undone. It is thanks not so much to technology and science as to our body's plastic capacities for learning and modifying that we emancipate ourselves from nature's bonds. It is the body's permeability to the symbolic that makes it the place where the biological, psychical, and social intertwine within subjectivity.

As I said, embodied subjectivity, which is at the core of the thought of sexual difference, diverges radically from the representation of bodies and subjects implicit in reproductive technologies. With the biosciences, there has been a decisive turn, in body politics, toward the government of the living entities, with the possibility of deciding and orienting their forms starting from the various evolutionary stages. The body is dissected in discrete parts, each one is the object of studies and care, and the body-as-organism is dissolved. The unity of the living recedes to the pre-corporeal stage, and the genes become the core of identity. By operating on the biological stages, biotechnologies seem able to produce bodies' very existence.

The Biological Reductionism of Reproductive Technologies

Who is the reproductive couple in artificial fertilization? Is it the gametes' union obtained in the biologist's vial? Does this mean that, through fecundation, the biologist *creates* a parental couple? By taking sex out of the picture, reproductive technologies undo the relation between nature and culture in parental reproduction. In other words, the "natural" presupposition of the link between heterosexuality and reproduction and of the *supposed* coincidence of reproductive pair and spousal-parental couple crumbles to pieces. Assembling cells and organs and facilitating the genetic material's transit from one body to the other, ova, semen, and uterus are equated in a single, undifferentiated procreative contribution. From the dawn of times, the will to control the body is an integral part of the male fantasies to steal from women their primacy in the generative act, appropriating and expanding the maternal body's ability to do and undo bodies.

Technologies represent themselves as helping hands in men's and women's procreative projects and desires, indistinctly. This is so especially when their artificiality is underlined, to demonize it or value it or, in other words, when what is stressed is their ability to replace "nature," expanding the potentialities for the government of life. In fact, the end goal is to accomplish a *sexless reproduction* that not only does away with coitus (which happens in the most usual practices) or with sexed gametes (which happens when somatic cells are used) but that also, in the future, transfers gestation from the sexed female body onto a machine.

The use of reproductive technologies is legitimated through "therapeutic reasons." This is done by employing the reassuring image of reproductive technologies as a helping hand for the *normal* desire of *normal* couples to have a child to create a *normal* family and by stigmatizing "improper" practices and desires to have a child such as those entertained by homosexual couples or single mothers. If therapeutic reasons were however to be applied coherently, they should be allowed for all sterile individuals. Access to reproductive technologies should be granted to single, sterile women; recourse to artificial insemination would instead be unfeasible for sterile men because, to "cure" sterility, one would have to intervene on the female body. It is precisely the simplest and least controversial intervention though, namely homologous insemination, which openly contradicts the so-called therapeutic reasons. How can one justify an operation on a healthy body to cure another body's pathology?

Equally contradictory in terms of therapeutic reasons is the commonly accepted distinction between "homologous" and "heterologous" insemination, over which harsh debates occur regarding the licit status of the one and not the other. From a medical point of view, the operation is one and the same; it is the coupling of female and male gametes, strangers to one another. Yet the terminological distinction provides a scientific basis for the different legal and ethical legitimation of the operation.

Adopting the distinction between a "homologous" semen (belonging to the woman's legitimate partner) and a "heterologous" semen (given by an anonymous donor), it is assumed that the father "normally" corresponds with the biological parent. Yet the father is not at all identified through his biological contribution to conception but through the legal relation he holds with the woman and the child.

Talking of the sperm donor as of a "biological father" means endowing technology with the power to create a different form of parenthood, which will work as the standard for all social figures and practices, and not only for those directly implied in artificial reproduction.

If oocyte and sperm become the core not only of biomedical but also of social discourse, then the female body becomes a "way of transit like any other":[4] from the test tube to the ambience-uterus, to the world itself. Conception, pregnancy, birth, and the newborn become different stages of the same living process; they define moments of the same life.

Biological Parents and Parental Figures

Confronted with the only undisputable evidence, namely that one is born from a woman, man has always been faced with the need to establish a direct relationship both with the newborn and with the woman. The figures of the father and the mother do not coincide with reproductive biological functions, but with the primacy of men within sexual and parental relations. It is as father, and not as parent, that man recognizes his child and introduces the child into social relations. It is as father that man makes a woman his wife and the parental woman a mother. Today just as yesterday, far from corresponding to nature, the order of relationships grounded on patriarchal authority rests on controlling natural processes.

Yet for reproductive medicine, acquiring access to biological material is not enough to deliver what it promises. Whatever the technologies deployed for conceiving may be, there is no way to do away with pregnancy and the uterus. The result achieved in the lab can meet the demand for a child *if and only if* a woman's body welcomes it and, through pregnancy, carries it to birth.[5]

The irreplaceability of the maternal womb is the crucial problem that biotechnologies are yet to solve, even though there have been many experiments. This makes men's and women's position in terms of procreation asymmetric. As of today, becoming a mother and becoming a father are not the same thing. Whether as a scientist/doctor or as a potential father, man still depends on woman, as an individual and as a gender. Whereas, for women, technology opens up the possibility to do away with men and buy semen at a bank, men cannot just simply buy ova or embryos. There must be a woman who consents to a reimplantation and to give birth. Therefore, all conflictual tensions are amassed on the pregnant body, entangled in the dilemma of "generative power" versus the "thing" to be appropriated. Far from resolving contradictions, the apparent cancellation of the female body, made possible by shifting the focus from birth to conception, radicalizes such contradictions.

Because of reproductive technologies, who is a mother has, in fact, become an increasingly uncertain and controversial question. The mother has always been a symbolic mother, that is, "replaceable."[6] Being born from a woman does not guarantee that we are born from a mother. Who is (my) mother? What is the sense, the symbolic position we grant to being a mother? And what is the sense and the symbolic position we grant to being a woman? Mother and woman—these are two nouns, two meanings that have been brought to coincide. For a long time, women's thought instead has been striving toward their distinction, even though not their separation.

Biology seems to offer some ground for the issue of meaning. In other words, we seem to be able to extract some certainty concerning motherhood from science and reproductive technologies, which assess the "truth" of the mother based on one's genetic makeup. *Just the same* would occur for the certainty of fatherhood. If we claim that the "true" mother is the one who gives the egg-cell, or even just its nucleus, we are attributing to a lab test and to its administrative records the power to give meaning to—or, in other words, to speak not only the scientific or legal truth but also the symbolic truth of—parental figures and relationships.

Identifying the biological parent does not mean, however, identifying a mother or a father. There is an intertwining of possible combinations, and a more or less stable, *yet never certain* bond is established between the biophysical and the symbolic realms. For Jacques Derrida, "the assessment procedures" cannot define the bond because, from the symbolic point of view, "the history of law just follows."[7] The specter of a finally "proven" motherhood or fatherhood—meaning: having a child that I can claim to be "mine"—acts powerfully within medically assisted procreation. It sets out as the specter of genetics, but there is neither archive nor trace that can count as the evidence. There is no way of resolving, once and for all, the question of the signifier through a technical or administrative testing of the biological datum. On the contrary, we can *believe* in experience, in the possibility of recognizing it and recognizing ourselves in it.

Yet One Is Still Born from a Woman

Confronted with the new horizon of meaning that equates egg-cells and sperms and, therefore, mother and father, man and woman, as variants of a biological *unicum*, we must still acknowledge that it is a woman who gives birth. *One is still born from a woman.* The acknowledgement that one is born from a woman allows us to reconceptualize biotechnologies' forms of knowledge and interventions within a different horizon of sense. Yet we should not oppose the biological truth of the egg-cell with another, equally "objective" truth, namely, the truth of the natural mother. This would be a truth that defines the woman *objectively* by identifying her with her body. There is no doubt that the correspondence mother-woman-body rests on the real given, unmodified by biotechnologies, of female reproductive power. Neither the mother nor the woman can be reduced to this, though.

Acknowledging that one is born from a woman does not mean, therefore, defining the mother with certainty; this act would be the mirror image of techno-scientific knowledge. On the contrary, such an acknowledgement demands that we resignify knowledge, practices, and biotechnical interventions starting from the centrality of the woman in the act of procreation.

The Irreplaceable Womb

In fact, all problems raised by the most recent biomedical practices arise from the impossibility of accomplishing an essential part of that adventure—namely, the part that goes from conception to birth—in the absence of a woman. Between the new scenarios of medically assisted procreation and traditional sexual reproduction there lies the "irreplaceable womb." This is the name that, with Grazia Zuffa,[8] we have given to the woman who procreates: she who can do and undo the living human being. This woman can be replaced with a mother, but she cannot be replaced as a human-female womb—as a womb in the sense that the body is still unavoidable; as human-female because that womb is a woman, body and mind, undivided and indivisible. Without her, there is literally nothing other than an aggregate of cells resembling more an inert object, a dead thing, than a human being in its frozen state. And there is no doubt that the physical, intercorporeal relationship is the inevitable interface of the meaning we attribute to words such as "human being," "person," "individuality." Every birth is an event because that is what is implied in the detachment from the generative body. This is far from fusionality, or motherly omnipotence on the fetus; already in pregnancy, she is getting ready and makes the fetus ready for separation. Indeed, the woman who carries it to birth is not necessarily a mother, and this is far from being a novelty.

Giving meaning to the fact that we are born from a woman is necessary in order not to succumb to the impersonality of technology. It is also necessary so as to avoid paying for the *ethical guilt* of symbolic matricide, whether through the vampirism of universal values or through the cult of the Mother and the maternal, which is the sublimated and edifying version of the reduction of women to being the unaware and, therefore, terrifying creators of life.

That which is impossible with technology becomes irrelevant at a symbolic level because it is not birth but rather conception that is considered the inaugural moment of a new human being. In other words, the essential part happens outside and without a woman, and pregnancy would be nothing but a step in the biological continuum. Yet is it really like that? Precisely the freezing of embryos shows otherwise.

There will be no new human being without a woman welcoming him or her. There is a disparity, which is indeed "natural," that conditions the possibilities of intervention on human procreation. This should be recognized so as to bring some order at the symbolic, social, and legal levels. Frankenstein and his non-human and unhappy creatures are, not coincidentally, the creation of a woman who has anticipated the course of male science and has imagined its tragic results.[9]

Feminist Dissent on Surrogate Motherhood

The "irreplaceable womb" puts women at the center of procreation. Feminist readings have been diverging for a long time regarding this centrality, yet currently they oppose one another as if they were incompatible. If we understand "irreplaceable" to equate being a "mother," then the pregnant woman is an exclusive and excluding figure. From here descends the prohibition on surrogate motherhood. But, in fact, this exclusivity extends also to other experiences and relationships, reintroducing a distinction between the "real" mother (the biological one) and the acquired mother, that is, the social and legal one.

If, on the contrary, it is the pregnant woman who is "irreplaceable," then we can concede that this fact does not always turn her into a mother and that, nowadays, the range of such a possibility has increased. And we can recognize that a multiplicity of relationships can be organized around birth. That pregnant woman and mother do not coincide is not a new thing. Narratives of all kind attest to this fact, from the Bible to novels. And the history of maternity documents this.[10] A much more relevant matter is, however, the acknowledgment that the mother is a symbolic figure and not just a body. As a symbolic figure, she can be embodied in a (masculine or feminine) other who is not the pregnant woman.

Vice versa, if we make the mother and the pregnant woman coincide again, we are chasing after a completeness, an integrated figure, which was never there in the first place. It is the patriarchal construction of motherhood that presents it as such. Yet both in men and women, there is profound resistance, which is tied to ancestral fantasies and fears, to putting into question the certainty of the figure of the mother.

The newest aspect in all of this, still to be conceptualized and full of social and symbolic consequences, is the involvement of more than one woman in the process. Three, more often than just two, because there is also the donation of the egg-cell. But this novelty is seldom, if ever, named, even in feminist discourses. We usually discuss heterosexual or gay couples. And it is usually the latter's utilization of surrogate motherhood that sparks controversies. Surrogate motherhood gets classified as another form of men's traditional appropriation of female bodies and as an extreme, radicalized form of patriarchal power, because it cancels out the mother.

The possibility that the pregnant woman may refuse being designated as the mother is, however, excluded. This is a possibility that is absolutely legitimate, as far as civil rights are concerned, in the "normal" procreative practices. The frequent use of the Italian expression "*utero in affitto*" (literally, "uterus for rent") strongly names this fact. The woman is not, and cannot be under any circumstances, the subject acting in this practice. She is a body or, more precisely, an organ that is used to satisfy other subjects' desires and will.

There is no doubt that, within the practice of surrogate motherhood, the commodification of the body is a real tendency.[11] And it is a crucial problem that needs to be faced. I fail to understand how we are supposed to confront it if we erase the subjectivity of the woman involved in these practices. If the woman is identified with her uterus, we are not speaking to the woman, in her body and mind, and we are not listening to her experience; rather, we are excluding a priori and completely the fact that there could be a choice or, at least, a variety of conditions and experiences. We are excluding acknowledging that no choice is free in itself, and that experiential conditions, contexts, and relationships can change. And we are excluding recognizing that, anyway, there is always a subjectivity that expresses itself: for better or for worse, in a more or less recognizable manner. Even in the case of a commodified utilization of the body, of its expropriation, I cannot but refer it to a subjectivity, which is embodied and situated.

Beyond Parenthood

According to Derrida, to accept the plurality of relations that get to be organized around every birth, such relations must be desired prior to their being thought. We can mobilize desire toward plurality by breaking apart the rigid construction of identity and preestablished relationships. For Manuela Fraire, the decline of patriarchy opens up the scenario of "beyond parenthood."[12] This decline is facilitated, yet not caused, by technologies.

If this is the perspective toward which we are moving, how are we to begin this path? Which norms are necessary to create some order? The absence of law is, in fact, unthinkable because it would simply encourage market dynamics and, within them, the law of the strongest. Each and every woman who gets access to the practices of artificial reproduction should and ought to be able to give meaning to her act, to whether she wants to be recognized as the mother or not; and she ought to be able to indicate whom she wants to designate as the father and as the mother who will substitute her. The first fundamental consequence that follows from this principle is that the pregnant woman can change her mind about this choice, at least up to birth, whatever the reasons behind her choice to undergo the experience.

Just as much as we cannot force a woman to become a mother by completing a pregnancy, likewise we cannot force a woman not to be a mother even if, on the contrary, she has completed it. Every woman who accesses practices of artificial reproduction should and ought to be able to give meaning to her act, depending on whether she wants to be identified as a mother or not. And she ought to be able to indicate who shall be designated as the father and, in turn, who shall be designated as the mother in her own place. If she has undergone a surrogate motherhood, she ought to be able to reconsider it until after birth, whatever the reasons that convinced her to undergo such an experience might be. She cannot be forced, either by law or by contract, to abide an agreement made with others.

I am convinced that this is the strongest disincentive to the exploitation and commodification of women's bodies and their reproductive abilities, especially for women who find themselves in situations of socioeconomic inequality in the poorest parts of the world. And only the law can pose these limits by making illegitimate those agreements that have been made by a contract and that would force the woman to abide by them. Of course, this is not the only factor. We also have to exclude all regulations that pretend to control and discipline pregnancies.

The universal prohibition of surrogate motherhood only reinforces, like every prohibition, clandestine markets and deals. More importantly, it is a heavy stigma placed on the woman and the newborn. It is not the first time that, trying to protect possible victims, one ends up criminalizing them. Moreover, the prohibition hits women harder than men.

In surrogate motherhood, as in all changes that mark sexuality and procreation, what is at stake is female freedom, both the freedom of an individual woman and freedom among women. Freedom is, first and foremost, the freedom to resignify the experience and lived practice of procreating and welcoming a child, whether son or daughter.

Finally, the strongest and most dangerous specter is, as always, passed under silence so that we can exorcise it. Always caught in-between, between straight and homosexual couples, between who uses whom, the individual woman is never even mentioned. Nonetheless, she is the one accessing the technologies, and she is at the center of the relationships thus produced. Yet let us not represent the individual woman as a "single woman," as if lacking the permission that legitimates her choice, namely, traditionally the authority of a man or, on his behalf, of the state, of the entire society. To name the individual woman means not to ban her from getting access to medically assisted reproduction. More radically still, it means that all relationships are built on the basis of singularity. And it means that the subject of freedom is the individual woman, not "women" as a homogenous group equated with a figure, namely the mother, the oppressed, or some other, with whom we all must identify, as in the past.

Prior to technologies was the symbolic and social revolution of female subjectivity, which first of all upset the sexual and reproductive sphere. In front of this upheaval, there are no certainties we can latch onto. Not even the certainty of a mother.

Notes

1. Tamar Pitch, *Un diritto per due* (Milan: Il Saggiatore, 1998).

2. Barbara Duden, *Il corpo della donna come luogo pubblico* (Turin: Bollati Boringhieri, 1994).

3. Carla Lonzi, *Sputiamo su Hegel. La donna clitoridea e la donna vaginale* (Milan: Scritti di Rivolta femminile, 1974).

4. Duden, *Il corpo della donna come luogo pubblico.*

5. Caterina Botti, "Mettere al mondo. Il dibattito bioetico sull'inizio della vita," in *Il laboratorio della bioetica*, ed. Fabrizio Rufo (Rome: Ediesse, 2011).

6. Luisa Muraro, *The Symbolic Order of the Mother*, trans. Francesca Novello (Albany: State University of New York Press, 2018).

7. Jacques Derrida and Elizabeth Roudinesco, *Quale domani* (Turin: Bollati Boringhieri, 2004).

8. Maria Luisa Boccia and Grazia Zuffa, *L'eclissi della madre. Fecondazione artificale, tecniche, fantasie, norme* (Milan: Pratiche Editrici, 1998).

9. Mary Shelley, *Frankenstein* (New York: Norton, 2012).

10. Nadia Maria Filippini, *Generare, partorire, nascere. Una storia dall'antichità alla provetta* (Rome: Viella, 2017).

11. Melinda Cooper and Catherine Waldby, *Clinical Labor: Tissue Donors and Research Subjects in the Global Bioeconomy* (Durham, NC: Duke University Press, 2014).

12. Manuela Fraire, "Oltre la parentalità," in *Sofia* 2 (1998): 15–22.

Three

Aporias of the Maternal in the Women's Movement

Lea Melandri

The term "*aporia*" is used when conflicting lines of thought can be attributed to the same concept. In the specific context of the maternal, the word seems to me to be more appropriate than the term "contradiction."

The question from which I start is the following: in the way it has appeared in the women's movement, is the *maternal* (real or symbolic maternal; feminine or woman virtues [*doti femminili*], etc.) a *permanence*, an invariable, that is, an identity, a role that we inherit from what has been traditionally regarded as the "woman difference [*differenza femminile*]" (a difference more or less deriving from the biological ability to generate children) or is it a *factor of change*? Moreover—and here is where I think the *aporia* lies—is it possible to think that what has always been the ground for women's exclusion from public life—that is, their reduction to a homogeneous whole such as their kind [*genere*],[1] their self-identification through the sex to which they belong, the body, sexuality, the care that is needed for the preservation of life—can now become an opportunity for emancipation, for liberation, or for women's empowerment thanks to a simple *reversal* [*capovolgimento*] from negative to positive?

Why do I speak of a reversal?

At the origin of the process of *differentiation* that sees man reserve for himself the side of history (thought, language, the ability to make political decisions) and assign to woman the side of nature, animality, and the support needed for man's public destiny, there is something else—in addition to and more—than woman's generative abilities (with respect to which man has found himself in a position of marginality, envy, need for revenge). There is the experience of man's *birth from the woman's body*. That is, at the origin there is a lived experience of defenselessness, dependency, overestimation of the maternal power by the son-man [*uomo figlio*]. As Rousseau candidly notes, in the war between sexes, the one that ends up winning is the weaker, not the stronger sex.

Male dominance asserts itself as revenge, control, exploitation of the mother-woman [*donna madre*], who will therefore find herself at the center of an evident contradiction: that between, on the one hand, glorification and idealization at the imaginary level, to say it in Virginia Woolf's terms, and historical insignificance on the other. When we translate this into more contemporary terms, it means that in our current times we observe, on the one hand, the (at least verbal) recognition of "woman virtues" [*virtú femminili*] as an important resource for the economy and politics and, on the other hand, what Marina Piazza calls "the setback of maternity [*scacco della maternità*]," which she documents widely in a book by the same title.[2]

The *aporia*, which concerns the origin of the relation between the sexes, the construction of gender identity, and, moreover, the location of the maternal at the core of "woman difference" [*la differenza femminile*], of its alleged naturalness, was bound to surface in those women's movements that thought of using the real or symbolic figure of the mother as a way to attain emancipation. I deliberately use the term "emancipation" as a way to indicate the emancipatory movements between the nineteenth and twentieth centuries, the philosophical theories of the "thought of difference" that developed in the 1980s and 1990s, and what today is known as the "femininization" or womanization [*femminilizzazione*] of the public space, which some feminist movements too regard as an opportunity for women to gain power and bring significant changes to the world of work and politics. I use the word "liberation" to indicate instead that gap or discontinuity that, within the historical consciousness, produced 1970s feminism. In this form of feminism of the 1970s, what is made the object of critique and change is, at least in Italy, precisely the identification of the woman with the mother, of sexuality with procreation. What happens in those years is the realization that the deepest expropriation that women have undergone concerns, more than their parental role, their own *individuality*, that is, their being individuals first and foremost, ahead of their being wives and mothers. It is only once women recognize and vindicate their own sexuality that maternity can turn from destiny to choice.

In the 1970s, then, a new interpretative horizon appears, a horizon that is unprecedented and revolutionary when compared with the contemporary framework within which we currently live. In the 1970s, the *originary pair mother-child*—the pair we may consider as the foundation of the dualistic vision of the world that has endured until now—is replaced with the *relation between individuals of two different sexes.* One starts distinguishing femininity and masculinity as social, cultural, imaginary constructs different from the real being of men and women. It is a radical shift in perspective that translates into the anomalous practices of "consciousness-raising" [*autocoscienza*] and the "practice of the unconscious." These practices pursue a collective reflection on one's own personal lived experiences, the analysis of the *invisible* violence that occurs through the incorporation of power models that are in fact imposed, and the slow modification of the self as the presupposition for changing the world.

As Maria Luisa Boccia writes in her book *La differenza politica* [*The Political Difference*], consciousness-raising is the first form of "thinking politics differently." It implies shifting the focus on each woman's subjectivity through relationships with other women. It means understanding freedom as the process of liberation from (as becoming conscious of) one's profound complicity with male thinking.

> First of all, a woman must consume within herself the bonds with the identity that she has been given by male culture. The feminine identity produced by man is replaced with a self that does not conform to femininity, "a non-conforming self"; sexed subjectivity takes shape from out of this movement of relational singularity.[3]

The distancing of the 1970s feminist movement from the emancipatory movements of the early nineteenth century starts from such a critique of femininity as traditionally understood.

In her historical reconstruction found in the book *Questioni di cittadinanza* [*Questions of Citizenship*],[4] Annarita Buttafuoco clearly states that the maternal role is the "site" where what is at stake is both the exclusion of women from citizenship and the demand on the side of women that woman's "nature" should constitute "an essential element for the full assumption of rights." The generative body, which for centuries has been considered merely an object with specific functions and needs to be managed and disciplined, is brought onto the public stage as a *civic value*, capable of producing more humane forms of sociality and, in the case of colonialism, as material and psychological support for the nation. The motherly woman is then seen as the guardian of racial purity, educator of the colonized women, devoted to civilizing "savage" peoples.[5]

The contradiction is apparent. On the one hand, the extension of the "virtues" of the heart or "domestic virtues" to the public sphere produces important changes in the notions of politics and society. The women's groups that are born in those years prefigure the social welfare state. It is also true, though, that being so focused on the maternal, emancipation (as Boccia writes) "has strengthened the category of gender and given political relevance and dignity to a set of psychological, social, and cultural contents that are a shared presupposition of all women."[6] Maternity remains the distinctive feature of women's identity. What is proposed is a mere *reversal*, an inversion.

As Buttafuoco writes, "women invert the negative understanding of that model; they try to turn 'feminine' sensibility, unconditional generosity [*oblatività*], maternity into their points of strength by claiming that such a 'natural' attitude of theirs demands their full assumption of responsibility within politics and social life."[7]

In the 1980s and 1990s, the more original intuitions of the earlier Italian feminism concerning a plural feminine subjectivity seem to disappear. This happens precisely when the women's movement becomes widespread feminism. The difference between the sexes finds new terrain for elaboration, on the one hand, within sociological research—the so-called gender studies—and, on the other hand, within philosophy. What disappears, together with themes concerning the body, is psychoanalysis. Or better, psychoanalysis remains present in a minority group of Italian feminism, for example, in that minority group that in Milan begins reflecting on "sexuality and the symbolic" and then merges into the Libera Università delle Donne [Women's Free University] and the journal *Lapis*.

In those years, the women's movements begin a process of internal diversification, not without conflicts. The most prominent place, even at the media level, is held by the philosophical theories of the "thought of difference." I am referring especially to Luce Irigaray, Luisa Muraro, and the Libreria delle Donne [the Women's Bookstore] in Milan.

The thematization of the "feminine difference," which is once again made to coincide with the figure of the mother—a biological mother for Irigaray, a symbolic mother for Muraro—and is understood in terms of *positivity*, can be interpreted in some sense as a return to more reassuring positions, as the exit from practices that seem to distance women from the *polis* because they push politics to the edges of the unconscious (and these practices seem as interminable as Penelope's web).

In her book *Democracy Begins Between Two*, Irigaray proposes a reformulation of the pact of citizenship that grounds it on an *objective* foundation, namely, starting from the existence of *two subjects*, *two identities*, *two worldviews*. What the "feminine natural identity" is and where it comes from is said very clearly: women are the carriers of a culture of life, the body, and a sensibility that derives from their bodily *morphology* and from their procreative abilities. The founding of society anew would therefore start with "a dialogue in difference, a two that would be a couple not only within the intimacy of the home but would instead be a civil, political couple."[8]

In one of Irigaray's most recent books that has been translated into Italian, *Condividere il mondo* [*Sharing the World*],[9] it becomes clear that the dialogue between the two genders, whose identity remains substantially traditional despite being inverted and read in a positive key, reproduces the *love dream* as the dream of the harmonious reunification of complementary "natures" that can be "fecund" only in their encounter.

~

In Italy, the maternal takes up a specific theoretical (philosophical, logical, metaphysical, fideistic) formulation as ground of sexual difference in the positions of Luisa Muraro and the Milan's Women's Bookstore, the Libreria delle Donne.

In *The Symbolic Order of the Mother*, Luisa Muraro claims that to exist freely, women need a *symbolic order* that places *maternal power* at its center and does not deprive women of their qualities. In other words, the matter is that of coming to terms with a usurpation. Men have had "familiarity" with the matrix of life, "showing that they have attended to it and have learnt the art of it"; they have extolled the mother but have expropriated it of her power, thus inverting the order of things.

What needs to be done is to act anew on the ground of a *logical*, *metaphysical*, *linguistic* principle that is not subject to the "capricious domination of the real." This way, the mother can be given back the power and authority that have been stolen from her. According to Muraro, "knowing how to love the mother" must be understood in this sense also: "something that would be true simply by being said."[10]

The greatness and superiority of the mother are made to depend not on her biological ability to generate children but rather on the fact that the mother is the one who gives simultaneously the body and the word, that is, language [*la parola*]. This initial superiority must be recognized as a principle—a self-imposing truth, both logically and metaphysically.

In this situation too, as Muraro describes it, we are confronted with a *reversal*: through an inverted marker, the maternal shifts from the side of nature, where men confined it, to the side of philosophy, of logic. This shift proceeds by *analogy* with the move that has seen male thinking differentiate itself from its natural foundation, erase the body and psychic life. One could call this a *revenge within* the symbolic, a use of philosophy different from the way in which men have employed it. Yet this different use of philosophy is limited to the contents. For this reason, it does not escape the dualism body-mind from which philosophy itself, as freedom from "the capricious domination of the real," originates.

Wholeness, the unity of body and mind, would no longer be, as early feminism had thought, the result of a process of *self-modification* as disclosure of an interiorized vision of the world. Rather, it would be a logical truth warranted by "negotiation with the mother" and by a practice of "entrustment [*affidamento*]" that transfers into adult life "the ancient relationship with the mother so as to make it live again as the principle of symbolic authority."

In conclusion, maintaining the *centrality of the maternal* has the following implications.

It means to remain, although in ways different from the pre-1970s women's movements, within emancipatory logics; it means to confirm rather than challenge women's representation as "a kind [*genere*]," as bearers of an identity with which all should identify.

It means to remain within the dualistic structure that has construed masculine and feminine, male and female as complementary because it limits itself to a reversal of priorities and values. Thus, it does not exit the *dilemma between equality and difference*. That is, it oscillates between assimilation to the masculine, understood as neutral and universal, and the protection or valorization of feminine specificity.

It means to turn "gender" into the theoretical and political paradigm of a *collective subject*. The traditional meanings of femininity are thus "reproposed in an inverted manner and as no longer restricted to the domestic sphere," as Boccia argues. It means to take distance from practices such as consciousness-raising that focus on constructing sexed individualities along lines that remain autonomous from imposed models.

In our current times, for many women, maternity is no longer a destiny. Women can choose whether to generate children. Within public struggles, the temptation remains to turn the maternal into one's own "identity card," into the requisite that carries the value and authority to grant full citizenship.

For this reason, the *femininization of the public sphere*, that is, the extolling of traditional woman or feminine virtues as "resources" for the economy and politics, is seen as an opportunity even by some sectors of feminism.

I think that, confronted with the desire expressed by many women today "to count" within public life, what we need is an analysis of, and a confrontation between, two orientations that have characterized the women's movement so far, namely, emancipation and liberation. As I indicated earlier, emancipation is based on concepts (rights, equality, or difference) that find their origin in patriarchy, are in fact male constructs, and, even when they oppose it, confirm the system, which allows emancipation to exist as a form of self-inoculation. Liberation consists instead in one's exit, whether one is man or woman, from all complicity with the male, patriarchal way of thinking that operates through dualisms, that denies the other to assert itself, that asserts itself to deny the other, and that, ultimately, proceeds through a dialectic that denies the third because it considers it already implied in the one and the two, understood as standing in an opposition for which the notions of complementarity, harmony, and fusion of the sexes are simply the more peaceful (and yet devastating) aspect.[11] This confrontation between two different orientations should be carried out in an effort to leave behind abstract contrapositions and instead pay attention to relationships that have always been in place, especially if we look at the concrete life experiences of each individual woman.

(Translated by Silvia Benso)

Notes

1. The term "*genere*" in Italian can mean both "kind" (in the sense of the Latin *genus*) and "gender." Translator's note.

2. See *Attacco alla maternità. Donne, aziende, istituzioni*, ed. Marina Piazza (Portogruaro: Nuova Dimensione, 2009).

3. Maria Luisa Boccia, *La differenza politica. Donne e cittadinanza* (Milan: Il Saggiatore, 2002), 51.

4. Annarita Buttafuoco, *Questioni di cittadinanza. Donne e diritti sociali nell'Italia liberale* (Siena: Protagon, 1997).

5. Catia Papa, *Sotto altri cieli. L'oltremare nel movimento femminile italiano* (Rome: Viella, 2009).

6. Boccia, *La differenza politica*, 136.

7. Buttafuoco, *Questioni di cittadinanza*, 19.

8. Luce Irigaray, *Democracy Begins Between Two*, trans. Kirsten Anderson (New York: Routledge, 2001), 177.

9. Luce Irigaray, *Sharing the World* (London: Bloomsbury, 2008).

10. Luisa Muraro, *The Symbolic Order of the Mother*, trans. Francesca Novello (Albany: State University of New York Press, 2018), 24.

11. On this, see Lea Melandri, *Love and Violence: The Vexatious Factors of Civilization*, trans. Antonio Calcagno (Albany: State University of New York Press, 2019).

Part Two

Subjectivity, Power, and the Political

Four

Toward an Ethos of Freedom

Notes on Subjectivity and Power

Simona Forti

"Toward a Non-Fascist Way of Life"

I wish to start with a few simple and plain, almost naive statements. Nowadays perhaps more than ever, philosophy, particularly political and moral philosophy, acquires meaning only if it manages to turn itself into an exercise of anti-fascist practice. I do not mean this in the sense of a normative philosophy that a priori establishes the universal conditions of justice and prescribes the principles to which action must conform to avoid fascism. And I do not understand fascism simply as a historical category. By the term "fascism," I also mean an outcome that is always possible, that is intrinsic in all relations of power: namely, domination. This outcome is a possibility that traverses epochs and contexts, but in part depends on our way of becoming and remaining subjects. What I mean, in the title of this chapter, by the expression "toward an ethos of freedom," is then fundamentally nothing else but a way of saying "toward a non-fascist way of life."

As many readers will recall, in his preface to the English translation,[1] Michel Foucault describes the volume by Gilles Deleuze and Félix Guattari, *Anti-Oedipus*, with these words: "A book of ethics," of which the "major enemy" is fascism (Hitler and Stalin). As Foucault clarifies, "fascism" means not just the historical fascism of the two totalitarian leaders who managed to employ to perfection the desires of the masses, "*but also the fascism in us all, in our heads, in our everyday behavior, the fascism that causes us to love power, to desire the very thing that dominates* [. . .] *us*."[2] Foucault warns us that to combat the historical and political, past and present forms of fascism, one must first of all change oneself. For this reason, he argues, *Anti-Oedipus* must be read as a book of ethics. Just as the Christian moralists seek the traces of sin, of the flesh, within the most hidden folds of the soul, in the same way we have to "wash away" the fascism encrusted in our behavior. Using, already in this brief text, expressions that will become central in his later works and courses, Foucault associates the anti-fascist ethos of Deleuze and Guattari with the tradition of philosophy as "art of living," with a "philosophical life" with clear guiding principles to follow. Among them, he includes the disactivation of all unitary and totalizing forms of political action, the emancipation from the sacralization of law and limit, the discredit of the *gravitas* of commitment, and the questioning of sadness as a sign of good militancy.

In 1977, the year of the first English translation of *Anti-Oedipus*, Foucault seems to avow the Deleuzean mode of contrasting *all types* of "fascism," from the still solid representatives of the authoritarian-patriarchal society to the bureaucrats of revolution to the "functionaries of the truth." We should not, however, underestimate the hypothesis that it is precisely on the basis of his confrontation with *Anti-Oedipus* and in disagreement with its authors that Foucault radicalizes his own "positive" and non-repressive vision of power. Around this time, the theme of biopower, with its emphasis on the encompassing and productive force with respect to biological life, has already made its appearance at the center of Foucault's work.

Foucault is still interested in disciplinary power, subjected bodies, and the somatic singularities produced by various disciplines and particularly by medical knowledge. He seems to align with Gilles Deleuze in identifying the processes of de-subjectivation as a possible resistance to the practices of disciplinary power. To contrast any pyramidal hierarchization and allegiance to the "old categories" of the Negative—thus Foucault summarizes, with implicit approval, the intention of *Anti-Oedipus*—the Deleuzean key words are: "affirmation," "multiplicity," "difference," "fluxes," "disjunction," "juxtaposition," "proliferation," "nomadism," in a word, a joyful, positive process of "de-individualization."

We know that Deleuze will not abandon the project tied to these key words and will continue to carve its philosophical caliber until the end of his life. This occurs in *Mille Plateaux* (1980)[3] especially, but also in the more theoretical *Qu'est-ce que la philosophie?* (1991),[4] where philosophy is presented as one of the forms of knowledge that respond to the essential chaos of being, that try to *cut through chaos*, carving from it a portion of order and trying to create meaning. Nonetheless, the art of creating concepts (the realm proper to philosophy) does not reject the art of "making the subject collapse" so that a body, all bodies, may make themselves rhizomes with the rest of nature. In other words, so that "each individual be an infinite multiplicity."

De-subjectivation or Becoming Subjects?

To contrast the neoliberal view of the world, a good part of the continental philosophy of the last few decades has found in the Deleuze-Foucault pair its own theoretical weapon, yet without much dwelling on the enormous differences that divide the two authors precisely on the question of subjectivity and its relation to power. Flattening Foucault upon Deleuze and often relying on a simplified reading of the Deleuzian legacy, these forms of philosophy remain convinced that to practice *a non-fascist way of life*, it is indispensable to push the collapse of the subject ever further. As if the subject—this is the implicit assumption—could not escape the alternative of either the will to power and domination or the total passivity of the subjugated. The subject would then be either synonym with "sovereignty," with a thirst for domination and possession, or the victim of the will to power. In sum, as if a thought of freedom, a free way of life, and an ethos of freedom could not be conceived other than through a progressive de-subjectivation of the human being, a constant shedding of attributes, until the human being reaches the simple breath of that "bare life" that constitutes the only form of life in which power surrenders.[5]

I am certainly not alone in thinking that, beginning with the second half of the 1970s, Foucault considerably complicates his approach to the question of the subject, thus making it possible to think of a different access to a *non-fascist way of life*. It is indeed not by chance that the expression "modes of subjectivations"—which was absent from Foucault's work until the mid-1970s—gains increasing prominence over the years until it becomes the central theme of the last phase of Foucault's work.[6]

In light of the above observation, the question that has occupied me for a while is the following: How can we keep together the aspiration of philosophy understood as "a non-fascist way of life," as ethos of freedom, and a thought of "becoming subjects" that does not fall into the illusion of evading altogether either the relations of power or the drives toward identification? How can we think of a way of life that keeps open the space for freedom without capitulating to the idea that there can be only one alternative? This would be the alternative between, on the one hand, a free subject in the sense of the sovereign, proprietary subject, closed onto itself, and, on the other hand, a subject freed from subjectivity through a process of progressive de-subjectivation. The latter is the subject of an uncompromising nomadism that considers "becoming-animal," "becoming-stone," "becoming-grass," in other words, the impersonal as the only possibility of freedom from the cage of power and domination.

Socrates against Plato

To add my modest contribution to the construction or possibility of thinking an ethos of freedom, I deploy what amounts to a very common, and altogether immodest, gesture within philosophy. Borrowing from Deleuze, I use a "conceptual persona." In particular, I resort to that *conceptual persona*—the quintessential philosophical *dramatis persona*—that philosophy has never ceased considering, namely: Socrates. Here, Socrates certainly does not function as the reactivation of the legacy of a specific character in the history of philosophy per se. Here, Socrates rather becomes the name for a line of thought, which has remained submerged and neglected, that insists on the ethical *and, at the same time, political* importance of the relationship of the self with itself. Socrates becomes the name that allows me to name subjectivity beyond the substantial-subject, beyond the subject as substance. He also allows me to name the only place, inevitably immanent in all relations of power, from which a contemporary form of counter-conducts can begin. The point, then, is not the interpretation of one or the other of Plato's dialogues; rather, the issue is to seize one of the opportunities of a counterfactual figure offered by philosophy. Socrates, a certain way of reimagining Socrates, brings us beyond the separation between ethics and politics, between ethics and action.

My first reference is to those philosophies that, ever since the second half of the last century, have turned Socrates, his way of living and dying in Athens, into the paradigm of the true philosophical experience, often in contrast with Plato's doctrine of the ideas. The relation between the Socratic and the Platonic Socrates has often been understood in terms of a distinction, sometimes even an opposition, as powerfully reasserted in recent years by Pierre Hadot.[7] On the one hand, for Hadot, there is the Platonic Socrates of the doctrine of ideas, who founds philosophy as contemplation and logic of discourse, as a discourse on discourses. On the other hand, there is the Socratic Socrates—the one who, according to Hadot, emerges from Xenophon and the first Platonic dialogues—who is a witness to philosophy as art of living, as the quest for the best way of life.

This is not the place to dwell on the intricate map of different contemporary philosophies as they proclaim themselves the interpreters of

Socrates' "real" legacy, regardless of or against Plato and Platonism. I would like to look instead, among the protagonists and the texts of what we might call philosophy as "art of living" (a losing strand within modernity), for elements of a sub-tradition, of a marginal line that summons Socrates not only as the representative of philosophy as way of life but also as the conceptual persona who configures the critical and radical posture of thought and points to the permanent possibility of real dissidence.

By "dissidence," I do not primarily mean the actions of either a collective or a necessarily riotous, insurrectionist subject. Returning the term to its etymology, *dissidens* is, in Latin, the present participle of the verb *dissideo*, which literally means "I sit apart." The term "dissidence" thus delineates, more than an organized political movement, a position that requires the courage of firmness, even at the cost of solitude.

From Jacques Lacan[8] to Pierre Hadot, from Gregory Vlastos[9] to Peter Sloterdijk,[10] from Jonathan Lear[11] to Alexander Nehamas,[12] in the twentieth century many are those who, from diverse cultural traditions, have revived Socrates as the teacher of an irregular way of life, the one who shatters the foundations of social normativity with his irony. Borrowing again from a Deleuzean vocabulary, here I choose to be represented, so to speak, by those "friends in thought" who have accompanied me over the last few years, namely, Hannah Arendt, Michel Foucault, and, in some ways, Jan Patočka. These authors are so different one from the other, yet deep down they are all moved by the same philosophical and political restlessness, which in some ways can be seen as a legacy of their radical Socratism. I have to confess, however, that I pull these authors to my side, somewhat in the same way in which they themselves pulled Socrates and some Platonic dialogues to theirs.

Arendtian Socratism

Beginning already with the first half of the 1950s, Socrates is an important point of reference for Hannah Arendt. For her, Socrates represents a sort of original unity of *logos*, which does not yet know the metaphysical game of Platonic dualism. It is Plato who will betray some aspects of Socratism by decreeing a disagreement between philosophy, understood as the love of what is true and eternal, and politics as the realm of what is contingent and transient and the domain of opinion. Arendt's alter ego, Socrates—Plato's teacher whom Plato betrayed—emerges over the years as the only real example of "nonprofessional" thinker and the paradigm of a way of life that, with its actions, undermines all dichotomies, not just the one between thought and action, between philosophy and politics, but also that between private and public life.

It is particularly beginning with the Eichmann trial, held in Jerusalem between 1961 and 1962, that the figure of Socrates rises to the status of paradigm for a subjectivity that comes to attrition with the various faces of power.[13] I think that it is precisely in these years that the intuition comes to life, in Arendt, of pitting Eichmann and Socrates against each other as two antithetical ways of life, as typologies of always possible but alternative outcomes of subjectivity.[14] Eichmann too is somehow used by Arendt as a conceptual persona representing the functioning of a mind that in no way opposes the normative context in which it is immersed. It is not nihilism that brings Eichmann to Nazism. Eichmann's subjectivity is not possessed by the will to power. He does not want nothingness and destruction. Not only does he not transgress the positive law, he is even convinced of abiding by the moral law. In fact, as Arendt says, he listens attentively to the voice of his conscience, yet his conscience speaks the language of collectivity, in turn an expression of the content and standing of the new normative order.

The proper noun "Socrates," then, comes to gather a set of concepts that, in the essays and talks that Arendt writes and gives in the mid-1960s, is used to indict our moral tradition, both in its ordinary religious version and in its philosophical-Kantian articulation. Particularly in *Some Questions of Moral Philosophy*, a series of lectures held between 1965 and 1966,[15] the attack on Christian morality has more generally to do with an understanding of conscience as grounded on the command-obedience relation. This is not the place to retrace the various steps of Arendt's argument; suffice it to say that in the hetero-normative model of the Christian (moral) conscience, Arendt sees a mechanism of neutralization of the conflicts within the self so powerful and pervasive that it becomes the very matrix of all types of conformism.

The dynamic underlying the Socratic *daimon* is altogether different though, and it is obvious that Arendt bends it to suit her own purposes. The *daimon* does not work on the basis of a vertical and prescriptive relation. It commands of the Self one norm only, namely: never abide by what has already been judged. The *daimon*, which is, for Arendt, nothing but the collateral effect of the critical and negative power of thought, does not tell Socrates what to do; it simply says "no," but the effect of this "no" is the destabilization of dogmas, of established norms, of shared opinions. The *daimon* compels Socrates and his interlocutors ever again to problematize the context, to discern *every time* what is right and what is wrong, keeping *doxa* at a distance. The effect of social criticism of the Socratic teachings, which for Arendt is still detectable in the early Platonic dialogues, is for her strictly connected with a "plural" or rather "dual" conception of the Self, the only one that allows thought and judgment to create attrition with the context. This duality of the Self, Arendt seems to tell us, will be translated (and betrayed) by the Christian religious moral conscience into a Manichean struggle to death between the two contenders. Whether it is the struggle of the will against desire, the struggle of reason to bend the will, or the struggle of one part of the "good" Self against the other part of the "evil" Self, the struggle must end with the victory of only one of two.

In what we might call the Socratic conscience, on the contrary, thought *must* constantly flex in a double movement: it must immerse itself and let itself be entangled by the power of the outside, but then it must recoil, analyze, and parse the forces that, in that opening, modify the Self. Far from being self-referential, the Socratic exercise of "two-in-one," to use Arendt's exact words, is the point of departure from which the subject can become another, an alterity to itself. The act of thinking, for which Socrates is the metonymic noun, entails then a complex version of the principle of non-contradiction. When one thinks, one indeed becomes one's own interlocutor but also—and here lies the difference between Socratic and Platonic dialogue—one's own potential adversary. Far from being a call to the peace of the One, to the solipsism of the contemplation of being, the Socratic dialectic is a plea to respond, also in front of others, to the pressure and power of the context; it is an exhortation to bear with courage the solitude and even the risk of death that may come from refusing to fall in line. I may be forcing Arendt's text here, though not any more than Arendt is forcing Plato's. Becoming an ethos of freedom does not mean, for the Arendtian Socrates, to erase the differences within the Self in the harmony of the soul so as to receive the One (as it is in the late Platonic dialogues). It means, instead, to manage to remain a two within the Self, a field of forces that communicate yet are always potentially in contrast.[16]

Of course, these references do not solve the hermeneutic riddle involving the status of the Arendtian subject. As the author of *The Human Condition* tells us, the "*who*" is constituted by the web of relations in which it is always already caught. A subject, we could say, becomes such because it is, from the beginning, part of a game of recognition and reciprocal visibility with others. In non-Arendtian terms, one could say that the activity of thinking begins with the impact of the outside on the inside and lives of the perpetual movement of exiting from the Self and returning to it. This, however, does not fully clarify in what the "two-in-one" is rooted. At times, it almost appears as an inexplicable gift, potentially given to everyone.

Yet if we read these lectures together with some contemporary notes in Arendt's *Denktagebuch*,[17] in the retrospective light of *The Life of the Mind*, an altogether unsuspected path opens up. More than the product of a mysterious capacity, the Socratic *daimon*—the figure through which Arendt describes the dynamic split within the subject—seems to correspond to a conflict in the temporal perception of the I. It is a conflict between the part of the Self that experiences itself as finite, subject to time, change, and death and the part of the Self, called here by Arendt "the I of apperception," which, though inseparable from the vicissitudes of the corporeal and mortal I, cannot but perceive itself as eternal. *The Life of the Mind* will return to this perceptive illusion of eternity on which, according to Arendt, both metaphysical reason and the belief in the immortality of the soul are built. In this case, too, it is Plato who imposes a transcendent inflection to the movement of Socratic thought. It is interesting to note, though, that in the context of her reflections in the 1960s, and particularly of the 1966 *Denktagebuch*, the conflict within the Self is strictly related to the capacity to render thought ethically and politically resistant. Among the conditions that facilitate the absence of judgment and dissent, we can count the exclusive victory of one of the two perceptions over the other. It is as if Arendt were telling us that the type of subjectivity tied to the possible rise of domination, of political evil, emerges more easily when, among the perspectives of Self's self-perception, one demand affirms itself as hegemonic, as a demand that, absolutized, negates the other. Socrates accepts death as an integral part of his way of life precisely for this reason, that is, because throughout his existence, he has held the two conflicting parts in relation without ever silencing one in favor of the other; because the "two-in-one" is nothing but the constant exercise of putting in dialogue, in contrast, positive reality, which is affirmative of life, and the dis-identifying perspective of death.[18]

The Socratic ethos of freedom, as Arendt reconstructs it drawing from Socrates but also projecting onto Socrates, is, in other words, a way to exercise power on oneself that inevitably produces collateral effects in the city, unsettling the ethical and political positions of the actors on the scene. Bending Arendt's words in *The Life of the Mind: Thinking* for my own purposes, one might say that the capacity of Socrates's thought—"that wind that destroys opinions, values, doctrines, unreflected theories"—can, in some crucial instances, transform itself *immediately* into action.[19]

Socrates as Ethos of Freedom

Now, is it not something similar that Foucault seeks in the practices of Greek, Hellenistic, and Roman ethics? Does he not identify, in the ethos of the care of the self and *parrhesia* [frankness or fearlessness of speech], a force, a space of response and resistance to power, which does not coincide either with the interiority of the Self or with the expression of a collective political subject in the political realm? Perhaps it is precisely the meaning of this "in-between," never completely put into focus by Arendt, that we find in Foucault's reflections on "the hermeneutic of the subject" and the "courage of truth."[20] Certainly Foucault is not interested in an antiquarian history or an anachronistic repetition of the past. I rather believe that he wants to show us, as a counterfactual strategy, the possibility of an ethical way of life no longer perceptible in modernity. For Foucault, the matter is that of undertaking an untimely inquiry: to seek, in the folds of ancient ethics, a modality in which the relation of subject, truth, salvation, and power allows for the emergence of a constellation that is *different from the one structuring the geometry of the governed subject*.

Foucault's analysis of pastoral power, which precedes the early 1980s courses devoted to the notion of government, draws clear connections between the "Christian modality" of exercising power within the monastic and ecclesiastical institutions and the contemporary form of governmentality. In both cases, though obviously with different modalities, power works not so much through negation but rather, by taking care of human beings, it seeks to let them grow and prosper, it aims at their salvation or health, and, in this way, it structures subjectivity as conformity.[21]

The question obsessing Foucault during his last years is how to think a subjectivity that limits as much as possible the weight of subjugation, in the awareness of the inevitable persistence of relations of power, of the impossibility of escaping the hold of the government of conduct.

Perhaps a clear answer comes from Foucault himself, a year before his death, in a synthetic definition of *parrhesia* that, more than any other, sounds like a real call to "ethical resistance" that immediately becomes political. Democratic Athens thinks of *parrhesia* as "a kind of verbal activity in which the speaker has a specific relationship with truth through frankness, a certain relation to his own life through danger, a certain type of relation with himself and with others through criticism (self-criticism or the criticism of other people) and a specific relationship with moral law through freedom and duty [. . .]. In *parrhesia*, the speaker uses his own freedom and chooses to speak frankly instead of persuading, truth instead of falsity or silence, the risk of death instead of life and security, criticism instead of adulation and moral duty instead of his own advantage or moral apathy."[22]

In Foucault's 1982 course *The Hermeneutic of the Subject*, the ethics of *parrhesia* appears as a political praxis that stands against adulation and rhetoric. In that context, truth is not correspondence between a knowing subject and a known object. We are not in the realm of gnoseology or epistemology. The truth that the speaker activates has primarily an ethical effect. The term *parrhesia* refers to a relation between the speaking subject and that of which he or she speaks, so that the one who speaks makes clear and manifest that what he or she affirms is what he or she believes to be true. The subject is as much the subject of the enunciation as he or she is the subject of the *enunciandum* [that which is to be enunciated]. And he or she testifies directly to this truth in front of others with his or her own body, with his or her own life.

In the course that started in 1984 and was published with the title *The Courage of Truth*, after talking about the contradictions of *parrhesia* in democratic Athens and before addressing ancient cynicism, Foucault dwells on Socratic *parrhesia*. Socrates displays all the characteristics of the true *parrhesiastes*.[23] He proclaims truth in the form of a personal opinion, which is not a mere point of view. He testifies through his own person to the strength of the enunciation, applying his truth to his own way of living, risking his own life. In this sense, as any authentic *parrhesiastes*, he acquires legitimacy on the basis of the harmony between *logos* and *bios*. If the *daimon* pushes Socrates toward philosophy and not toward political participation, nevertheless Socratic "truth-telling" is no less useful to the city than the political speech pronounced on the public square. The ethos assumed by Socrates pushes him toward the "care of the Self" and *parrhesia*. And Foucault too, like Arendt, radically distinguishes between the "Socratic" Socrates, who practices the care of the Self and *parrhesia*, and the Platonic Socrates, who instead pursues "knowledge of the Self" as a transcendent truth.

This point is crucial, and it is not merely a choice in terms of Platonic hermeneutics. It is as if the character of Socrates turned into a philosophical category apt to redesign a different conceptual constellation to rethink autonomy. Being autonomous, according to the radical Socratism embraced by Foucault, does not mean indulging in the illusion of placing oneself, alone, at the opposite end of relations of power; even less does it mean claiming the ontological status of the Self's sovereignty and self-foundation. Giving oneself an ethos rather means thinking of the subject as a process that is shaped by the practices of power but, at the same time, thinking of it as a singular event—a singular event that, in the asymmetries of the process, may open the space within which to accept or reject pressures from the outside. If Foucault insists on the constitution of the Self, this is also to highlight the potentialities, ever present within subjectivity, to alter, dismantle, and overturn those power relations that have constituted and still constitute the subject itself. There is a constitutive asymmetry between Self and power relations from which the Self takes shape. In the gap produced by the disconnections lies the space for the exercise of freedom.

To my mind, what becomes absolutely clear in the mouth of Foucault-Socrates is the possibility of a double modality of becoming subjects, of two different and alternative modes of connecting ethics, truth, and power. The first modality is that of the knowledge of the authentic Self and the true Being, which from Pythagorism, Platonism, and neo-Platonism passes into Christianity. It envisages the necessary conduct that enables the move from the impure to the pure, from the contingent to the eternal so that the subject can become the recipient of a truth that will be revealed to it from the outside and to which it will have to conform its conduct. Along this itinerary, Foucault tells us, everything that is experiment, exam, and verification disappears from Socratism in favor of the search for the subject's ontological foundation in a divine creature or a supreme being endowed with reason. The other itinerary is instead that of the care of the Self and *parrhesia*, which are not doctrines, but practices. They are strategies of the continuous movement between identification and disidentification of the Self, without guarantees, and sustained exclusively by the courage of saying what one believes to be true—courage that demands constant surveillance of one's own judgment but also the capacity to problematize, again and again, one's own acquired identity.

In the *Laches*, which for Foucault is the exemplary text of *parrhesia*, Socrates is a *parrhesiastes* not only because of the speeches he makes, but also because of the life he lives. This is the "aesthetic of existence" of radical Socratism: the attempt to transform one's own life into the space of visibility of the truth through gestures, actions, and choices. Unlike the Stoic sage, Socrates exposes himself to unceasing restlessness, to that constant movement of self-interrogation that he cannot renounce, lest he die. Because a life without the practice of constant problematization is not worth living. Care of the Self, *parrhesia*, courage, constant questioning of one's own positions of power—these are all intimately connected elements that Foucault finds in a praxis that, besides being ethical, is also political. This is, simplifying in the extreme, the Socratic-Foucauldian ethos of freedom.

Foucault does not tire to return to the alternative internal to the Platonic dialogues. On the one hand, there are *Alcibiades I*, the *Phaedo*, and the *Republic*, where we find the power of the psyche as an ontological reality separate from the body; to this corresponds a way of self-knowledge as contemplation of a reality that lies beyond the contingence of the senses. This is the path of metaphysical subjectivity, of that discourse that reveals to human beings their own essence and what they must do to conform to it. In this perspective, ethics dictates the rules of conduct that human beings must follow to rejoin the ontological foundation that corresponds to them. On the other hand, the *Laches* and, in part, the *Apology* are the texts that show the way of the aesthetics of existence understood not in the aestheticizing sense of making one's life a work of art but in the sense of an art of living, a practice. Foucault constantly repeats this: the anti-Platonic Socrates is the one who chooses to give an ethos to his *bios*; who conceives of truth as questioning *doxa* and not as contemplation. In the perspective of the *Laches*, living in truth does not imply establishing the conditions under which a statement is verifiably true; rather, it means to take on the risk of telling human beings that they need courage to embody literally, in their own flesh, the ethos of freedom.

Though Foucault pushes us into a contraposition that sometimes may feel strained, the message he sends is clear. One does not become an ethical subject by receiving a truth that comes from the outside. Subjectivation is not only subjection to a power that "saves," eradicating, once and for all, the negative within us, the conflict and putting an end to the incessant movement of constitution and destitution of identities. On the contrary, one can become and remain a subject also through an uninterrupted athletics of contrasting forces, of courage and judgment.

The *Laches*, then, which is a bridge-text toward the radicalism of the cynics, offers us the onset of the submerged itinerary of a subject that ties itself to truth ethically. The subject does not submit to truth in the attempt to reach a more real world beyond the world; rather, it interrogates itself over what, in the city and in the relations with others, could be different from what the power of *doxa* dictates.

The Dissidence of Permanent Socratism

It is then not by chance that, during the 1984 course, Foucault refers to another author, Jan Patočka, and to his book on Plato and Europe, warmly recommending it to his students. Foucault points to the Czech author as the one who identifies, in the Socratic notion of *epimeleia*, care of the Self, the possibility of a practice of dissent or, as Foucault prefers to say, the tie with the practice of "counter-conducts."[24]

Unfortunately, there is no space to remark on the sometimes polemical confrontation that Michel Foucault undertakes with the thought of the Czech philosopher. To my mind, for example, Foucault is wrong in thinking of Patočka's notion of the soul as still tied to a dualistic vision of the human being. Instead, I am convinced that the "Socratic discovery of the soul," which Patočka invites us to rethink, does not reproduce metaphysical dualism and an idea of the soul as substance. The "care of the soul," as Jan Patočka understands it, is, once again—not unlike for Arendt and

Foucault—the choice of philosophy as a way of life and of a philosophical ethos capable of opening itself to praxis and, with it, to dissidence.

Then again, the very biography of the Prague philosopher seems to be the demonstration of how the philosophical appeal to a certain ethical conduct is not simply an exercise in hermeneutics. Patočka is the one who, for his *parrhesiastic* gesture, has become the example—not only in the Czech Republic—of a thought that manages to become *praxis* without becoming doctrine. Having become the speaker for *Charta 77*, he ends his philosophical life as an internal exile to make that life visible in the light of the *agorà*. Because of this, he dies after an exhausting series of interrogations that cause a cerebral hemorrhage.

In Patočka's 1973 book *Plato and Europe*,[25] which is the text Foucault uses and references, the soul as Socrates thinks of it is different from the soul as conceived by Plato. The text is interesting, but I cannot address it here. For the purpose of the current discourse, it is more interesting to turn to a series of writings from the mid-1950s that were never published by the author and were posthumously edited with the title *Negative Platonism*.[26] In these pages, more clearly than in the book on *Plato and Europe*, it is already without doubt that the "care of the soul" has to do with the soul not as substance and essence of the human being, but as the energy of a movement of overcoming that actually never comes to an end. The care of the soul indicates the "movement of distancing ourselves from that in which we are put." As Patočka states in the 1973 book, the soul is not an essence; rather, it is the space of "philosophizing," if by "philosophizing" we mean the action of an existence that exits itself and returns to itself. Socrates understands philosophy not as the guide for a soul en route toward eternal truth, but as a praxis of permanent interrogation of the demands that the forces of *doxa* make on the subject.

Socrates' is a "negative philosophy," Patočka never tires of repeating, not just because it refuses to assume any positive truth content, but because it appropriates negativity as a condition for freedom. To take care of the soul, then, means not putting an end to the movement, keeping up with the discovery of duplicity, of conflict, and of the mutual implication of the positive and the negative. It means maintaining the tension between what reassures and identifies us and the problematization of this belonging.

An-archic Subjectivity?

Now, to conclude and retrace my argument: what ties together the "two-in-one" of Arendt's Socrates, the "care of the Self" and *parrhesia* of

Foucault's Socrates, and the "care of the soul" of Patočka's Socrates? And, most importantly, what brings us to say that they all share an idea of philosophy as a way of living and an ethos of freedom? Why might they help us embrace that "non-fascist way of life" from which we started? If there is an element that really connects these references to Socrates (a Socrates so different and distant from Plato's), it is the conviction that, to prevent power from becoming domination or to disrupt a web of powers that constrains us until it becomes unbearable, political action cannot but be the visible manifestation of an ethics. That is to say, political action is the collateral effect of an ethos, a posture, a conduct of the Self toward itself that is rooted in the daily "way of life" of the individual but can, without a doubt, "contaminate" the public space. We may invoke all kinds of revolutionary change; if, however, our subjectivity remains unaltered, we will have nothing but a change among those who monopolize political action, without any change in the real structure of the exercise of power.

In which sense, then, can we inherit from Socrates, from *this* Socrates, the example of an ethos of freedom? If, for Plato in the *Republic*, the soul, the better part of the Self, is supremely unjust if it cannot become, to say it in Plato's words, "One out of many," the soul, the better part of the Self of Socrates, of *this* Socrates, remains free precisely if it manages not to become One. It insists on a "two" that cannot find peace in the One, so that it will live in a constant disidentification, dis-appropriation of the roles assigned to the Self. Certainly, as both Socrates and Plato say, the soul feeds on its relation with the city. It is inevitable that, living in the *polis*, it will seek integration and belonging. Yet it is only in its ability to disavow the key words of recognition within the political *doxa* that the soul can continue its movement of freedom.

The ethos of freedom does not express the will simply to overturn the social order because it knows that any overturning becomes unfailingly another order that simply substitutes the former. The ethos of freedom instead expresses the urgency of positing oneself in relation to the world by questioning the hierarchies of value that the world proclaims as natural, constantly deconstructing the self-sufficiency of the Self so that it never acquiesces to the pretenses of social identities.

Arendt's, Foucault's, and Patočka's Socrates is not the professional opponent but rather the one who manages to render strange every matter that, to others and sometimes to himself, seems obvious and familiar. He is the merciless critic of all those who think that they possess truth and justice; and, most of all, he is the one who bestows irony on those who presume to deduce absolute norms from *doxa*, from common opinion.

The ethos of freedom, "a non-fascist way of life," then, cannot ever conform to an injunction that is univocal and absolute and that, in the name of its own necessity, demands assent and compliance. In this sense, it is a radical exercise of constantly revoking the affirmative power of what surrounds us and presents itself as the only possible reality. If considered from a purely philosophical point of view, radical Socratism, unlike positive Platonism, which regards the full attainment of the idea as possible, never pretends to overcome the concrete historical experience. It simply remains faithful to the liberating awareness of contingency; it dwells in the transcendence of the given reality without ever coming to rest in a hypostasis.

Returning to Socrates, distancing him from Plato, and attributing to him an idea of the Self is, from a historical and philological point of view, a somewhat paradoxical enterprise. It is an untimely and, for this reason, courageous philosophical choice that aims at reappropriating words philosophy has used, while redefining their meaning radically. The dialogue of "the two-in-one" in Arendt, Foucault's *parrhesia*, Patočka's "care of the soul" do not appeal to Socrates to reactivate a lost nobility of thought, to revive Socrates' experience in order to contrast the desolation of modern politics. The Socratic *daimon*, which prompts us to take on the ethos of freedom, is the name for that which, in the subject, constantly resists, that which creates friction with the obvious force of circumstances: from the authoritarian injunctions of politics to the blackmail of violence, from the unilateral pressure of things to the imperious will to life. In short, the Socratic *daimon* is the name for the possibility, for the power that everyone has to resist another power.

The possibility of domination, of the "fascist way of life," is then also linked to the way in which one constitutes oneself as a subject, to how a subject responds, sustains, accepts, or reacts to relations of power. What is at stake in Foucault's search within the folds of tradition as well as in Plato's Socratic dialogues is the indication of an opening—certainly narrow and always at risk of being closed again—that enables us to reach the place of a possible interruption: the interruption of those *dispositifs* that establish a vicious circularity with power. The ethos of freedom is not the way for the construction of a collective subject that will reestablish the political good in history. Nor can it be reduced to the quest for an ever nomadic and multiple identity. It is, rather, the path of a possible "ethical revolution": the singular revolution of a *bios* that succeeds in becoming ethos and of an ethos that can become *praxis*, that is, the *praxis* of an exercise and continuous effort of appropriation and disappropriation. In this sense, as Foucault often said, "the revolution will be ethical or it won't be."

Notes

1. See Michel Foucault, "Preface," in Gilles Deleuze and Félix Guattari, *Anti-Oedipus: Capitalism and Schizophrenia* (New York: Viking Press, 1977), I–IX.

2. Foucault, "Preface," VI. Emphasis added.

3. Gilles Deleuze and Félix Guattari, *A Thousand Plateaus: Capitalism & Schizophrenia* (Minneapolis: University of Minnesota Press, 1987).

4. Gilles Deleuze and Félix Guattari, *What Is Philosophy?* (New York: Columbia University Press, 1994).

5. The obvious reference is to Giorgio Agamben, *Homo Sacer: Sovereign Power and Bare Life* (Stanford, CA: Stanford University Press, 1998).

6. For an overview on this position, see *Foucault and the Making of Subjects*, ed. L. Cremonesi, O. Irrera, D. Lorenzini, and M. Tazzioli (London-New York: Rowman & Littlefield, 2016) and especially the essay therein contained by J. Revel, "Between Politics and Ethics: The Question of Subjectivation," 164–74.

7. See, first of all, Pierre Hadot, *Philosophy as a Way of Life: Spiritual Exercises from Socrates to Foucault* (Oxford: Blackwell, 1995). See also Pierre Hadot, *Eloge de Socrate* (Paris: Ed. Allia, 1998).

8. See Jacques Lacan, *Le séminaire. Livre VIII. Le Transfert (1960–1961)* (Paris: Seuil, 1991).

9. Gregory Vlastos, *Socrates: Ironist and Moral Philosopher* (Ithaca, NY: Cornell University Press, 1991).

10. Peter Sloterdijk, *Du musst dein Leben ändern. Ueber Anthropotechnik* (Frankfurt am Main: Suhrkamp, 2009).

11. Jonathan Lear, *A Case for Irony* (Cambridge, MA: Harvard University Press, 2011); Jonathan Lear, *Wisdom Won from Illness: Essays in Philosophy and Psychoanalysis* (Cambridge, MA: Harvard University Press, 2017).

12. Alexander Nehamas, *The Art of Living: Socratic Reflections from Plato to Foucault* (Berkeley: University of California Press, 1998).

13. Hannah Arendt, *Eichmann in Jerusalem: A Report on the Banality of Evil* (New York: Viking Press, 1963).

14. See the essays collected in Hannah Arendt, *Responsibility and Judgment* (New York: Schocken Books, 2003).

15. This essay is collected in Arendt, *Responsibility and Judgment*, 49–146.

16. On the "Two in One," see also Hannah Arendt, *The Life of the Mind, One: Thinking* (New York: Harcourt, 1978).

17. Hannah Arendt, *Denktagebuch. Bd. 1: 1950–1973* (Munich: Piper, 2002).

18. Arendt, *Denktagebuch. Bd. 1*, 455–56.

19. Arendt, *The Life of the Mind*, 192.

20. Michel Foucault, *The Hermeneutics of the Subject: Lectures at the College de France 1981–82* (New York: Palgrave Macmillan, 2005); Michel Foucault, *The Courage of Truth: The Government of Self and Others II. Lectures at the College de France 1983–1984* (New York: Palgrave Macmillan, 2011).

21. Michel Foucault, *Security, Territory, Population: Lectures at the College de France 1977–1978* (New York: Palgrave Macmillan, 2007), 115–254.

22. Michel Foucault, *Fearless Speech* (Los Angeles: Semiotext(e), 2001), 18–19.

23. Foucault, *The Courage of Truth*, 141–76.

24. Foucault, *The Courage of Truth*; see the Lecture of February 22, 1984.

25. Jan Patočka, *Plato and Europe* (Stanford, CA: Stanford University Press, 2002). On Socrates, see also the series of lectures given by Patočka in Prague during the summer semester 1947: *Socrate. Lezioni di filosofia antica*, ed. G. Girgenti (Milan: Rusconi, 1999).

26. See Jan Patočka, *Pé e o duši. Sv. 2. Negativní platonismus*, ed. I. Chvatik and P. Kouba (Prague: Archivni Soubor, 1987); partial English translation, Jan Patočka, "Negative Platonism: Reflections Concerning the Rise, the Scope, and the Demise of Metaphysics and Whether Philosophy Can Survive It," in *Jan Patočka: Philosophy and Selected Writings*, ed. E. Kohàk (Chicago: University of Chicago Press, 1989), 175–206.

Five

Biopolitics and Economy

Between Self-Government Practices and New Forms of Control

Laura Bazzicalupo

Biopolitics

Nowadays, when languages and cultures are crossed by processes of planetary integration, it is difficult to identify specific philosophical positions. There are nevertheless trends within which one can highlight shared elements of specificity. This chapter partakes of that trend of studies known as biopolitical critique. Biopolitical critique finds its point of reference in the postfoundational and poststructuralist philosophies that emerged in the 1970s and coalesced around the ability to understand the profound transformations occurring within the contemporary individual and social experience.[1] These philosophies displayed great attention to difference as the effect of a radical deconstruction of the logocentric metaphysics of the mainstream Western tradition. This sensitivity to difference allows us to grasp the novelty of the neoliberal model of government, yet not without some ambiguous collateral outcomes. Within the line of research that self-identifies as biopolitics, the perspective I wish to advance focuses on the themes of economy and the critique of neoliberal governmentality.[2]

Biopolitics presents itself as a constellation of concepts and practices. It is therefore not surprising that this term designates very different experiences, events, practices, theoretical formulations, cultural imaginations, and forms of knowledge.

Overall, biopolitics recognizes the turn in the modern management of power. This occurs when power takes charge of the governed in their dimension of living beings, that is, as lives that are governed in order to increase their biophysical potentialities, their *bios*—that is, their life. Foucault defines biopolitics as power that, within modernity, shifts from power of death and withdrawal to power *to make live and to let die*. In the wake of Foucault's definition, the task of promoting and increasing biological life as a productive force, between survival and well-being, becomes the overall theme of politics.[3] The issue is therefore *life* and a politics *about* and *of* life. This shift presupposes processes of naturalization of the human beings now understood in their scientifically objectifiable, and therefore governable and optimizable, dimensions. The current neoliberal phase highlights the full completion of this biopolitical process.

The biopolitical paradigm seems better capable than the traditionally modern political-juridical framework of understanding crucial contemporary phenomena that focus on living bodies beyond their formal qualification. Agamben underlines, within biopolitics, the reduction of bodies to bare life with reference to migratory flows, terrorism, wars, hunger, and racist discrimination. In his reading, bodies are stripped of juridical and political characterization; they become defenseless human conditions, exposed to violence, physical stigma, or the silent horror of corpses beheaded by terrorists.[4]

Agamben's perspective is persuasive. Yet one needs to consider that the biopolitical paradigm as government over living bodies is also, and perhaps above all, characterized in terms of an expansion of life.[5] The paradigm is therefore ambivalent. It also sheds light on the governmental techniques that initially had a disciplinary nature aimed at forming docile and adequate bodies for factory work and then, later, assumed a neoliberal aspect urging individuals to organize their lives as human capital to be invested, increased, and enhanced in market competition.

Grasping the epochal dimension of biopolitics means repositioning the perspective of analysis in light of the immanence of effective, *concrete life*, in the cruel richness of its contradictions: life is governed and organized even in its innermost spaces, and yet life is also capable of resistance, self-organization, and freedom.

This aspect of biopolitics emerges in the studies that Foucault devoted to the transformation of sovereign power into governmental power in correspondence with modern society. In modern society, the emergence of capitalism required a disciplined but free, productive population safeguarded from risks and deviations.[6] Within this context, the attention to biopolitics was closely connected with the practice of government. This practice is very different from sovereign command. Its model goes back to the pastoral activities of the Christian bishop, who operates by supervising and caring for the souls and lives of his flock "in their interest." The bishop's activities are based on a truth—the divine Providence and its plan of salvation—which is the competence, the *expertise* of the bishop, and such truth matches the internal norm of each individual creature. Thus, alongside the political theology of sovereignty, imposing on the subject a command that is external to the subject and to which the subject subjects itself, there exists an economic theology of management, of administrative power urging the subjective growth of the governed.[7] Governmental dispositifs direct living beings toward the pursuit of what is thought to be a development inscribed in their internal, natural norm because this is the only possible way to enhance people's lives, that is, by regulating them. This is therefore a process of subjugation aimed at subjectivation; that is, it is aimed at the production of a docile subject, adapted to its natural characteristics, and capable of contributing *freely* to social productivity. To be effective, the government works differently on the various groups and populations, linked by similar potentialities or risks. Currently, this process of governmentalization shifts from the disciplinary model, which was still prevalent in Fordist capitalism, to a neoliberal form.[8] My attention focuses on this latter form of life management and its ambivalence.

Evaluated Lives

The neoliberal governmental technique—which we qualify as bio-economy because the mode of governmental management follows an economic logic of organization and its goal is the production of forms of life suitable to economic production—would seem to have nothing in common with Fordist and welfarist disciplinary management. In a libertarian way, it deprecates every intrusion of state law into private lives. Its rhetoric attacks disciplinary practices and dispositifs because they produce docile, passive, compliant subjects. Its mantra is the promotion of freedom, of individuals' self-government, and of the race for self-empowerment that makes individuals responsible for their own wealth, for investing in the right education, a good job, and their own existential success. Nonetheless (or precisely because of this), this is a particularly effective technique of life government.[9] So how does it work?

First of all, we need to refer to the role of *expertise* within governmental management. This is the contemporary version of the pastoral care of the bishop who was an expert on the topic of Providence and the true nature of human beings. Currently, the new and pervasive *expertise* is based on the un-questionability of the "natural" (both biological and economic) sciences, which modernity has placed at the center of the knowledge about the living humans.[10] The program of scientificization of the entire anthropological universe is a project articulated on two levels: on the level of the sciences that, through statistics, provide hypotheses and propositions for objective and mathematizable knowledge of the living human beings and on the level of *doxa* or opinion that, using that scientific knowledge, builds dispositifs and norms for everyday life—norms that evade debate and remain unavailable to the intervention of politics. To think of behaviors and meanings in terms of regularities that make them predictable and governable implies a certain reductionism, yet not an absolute one. It is rather a need for classifications that aggregate data dispersion—classifications based not on identity but on difference, that is, on the differential deviation of meaning that does not exclude any term, yet subjects them all to an inclusive taxonomy.

Attention to differences—their release from a normative criterion that assimilates and annihilates them—was the core of the 1970s stream of protests against representation and delegation to authority. This vindication of differences, which are rooted in the body as the place that preserves one's absolute singularity (each body feels pain and desires in a different way), aimed to legitimize all differences and forms of life, regardless of any normative criterion. Yet the insertion of existential differences into a naturalistic paradigm (provided by both biology and economics) subjects them to the hierarchy that is inherent in the concept of *zoe*, and human animal life is evaluated in terms of its greater or lesser degree of adjustment to the highest *humanist* form, that is, *bios*.[11] Existential differences are included into living nature, into *zoe*, which in turn involves an internal, selective hierarchy and a differential management.

The Law, shaped by the universalism of Justice or Order, produces effects of exclusion and inclusion through judgment. Conversely, naturalistic classifications link similarities and associations to form identifiable groups of differences that will demand different forms of *management*. These expert, technical-scientific classifications—free from the arbitrariness of sovereign and artificial decisions—*authorize* working unequally on differences. Christian pastoral theology too worked in a nonegalitarian way, according to the weaknesses and risks of each living soul: *omnes et singulatim* [all and each one]. Expert and technical-scientific knowledge, however, not only guarantees effectiveness of action, but also obtains the consent and collaboration of the governed—this only happens when the *rule* is objective, *natural*. The normative power of nature therefore applies to political, social, and juridical sciences, which until recently were tied to ethics and political reason.

The goal is to attain living beings' best performance and adaptation to the environment of which they are part and, at the same time, the utmost indisputability of governmental decisions.

In neoliberal bioeconomy, the control of the living beings is no longer practiced, as in disciplinary governmentality, *ex ante*, by homologating and assimilating behaviors to a norm presupposed as optimal; rather, it occurs *ex post*, downstream, using standards and evaluative markers to guide classifications and orient the *decision makers*. It works according to a strategic and competitive logic, which is believed to be the natural logic of the living being itself.

Thus, living beings self-govern and self-regulate precisely when they follow the logic of the market. From a political point of view, this government/self-government transfers the space of the conflict between desire and control into the subjective psyche, into the mind of each individual. The goal is not compliance with a transcendent model of Law but adaptation, *fitness*. That is, the goal is a behavior that is appropriate to living beings' competitive nature and to the environment: the norm or standard of behavior is derived from widespread and "regular" conducts. The term "fitness," which through a social-Darwinian trivialization of evolutionary biologism has spread beyond its scientific meaning, indicates the living beings' adoption of a "fitting" behavior, adequate for survival and for strengthening the vitality of an organism in a given environment. It is a regulatory criterion, an ethos rather than an *eidos*, an idea or model: it leads to more efficient behavior.[12]

The human living being, which, to use Deleuze's terms, can be thought of as a desiring, anarchic productive machine,[13] on the one hand is left to itself, to its own self-government, but, on the other, finds itself regulated by a strategic-competitive natural logic, immanent to life itself.

Expert knowledge supplies the strategy of self-empowerment and realization with the technique of organization, with the ethos to optimize potentialities and manage risks wisely. The neoliberal hegemony of economics over politics is highlighted, more than by the prevalence of the economic field over other spheres of life, by this organizational economy. The organizational economy is extended to all aspects of life because the entire life of each individual is implicated in the race to adaptation and optimization.

Competition means agonism, differentiation, and hierarchization. It should be stressed that this hierarchy is unstable, nonidentifying; it does not refer to an identity status but to the position someone takes in the scale of productive performances, a position that is always precarious and unstable.

Precarious Transcendence in an Ontology of Immanence

What criterion organizes the hierarchy of the living beings? Which standard arranges social inequality in the race to self-optimization? Within neoliberal bioeconomy, the standard "arises" from the interplay of different behaviors, and its *value* is determined a posteriori by the contingent outcome of the competition. The standard (which, in the market, is price) that guides choices and investments in terms of one's self-subjectivation is nothing more than a contingent and precarious transcendence. It is according to this that individuals organize their own competitive conduct. The neoliberal standards are certainly not so solid and durable as the laws or the Constitution. Rather, they are points of partial and temporary social transcendence, the contingent products of the expectations and choices of each competitor. And yet they are experienced as systemic necessities.

Therefore, within the neoliberal economy, the paradoxical outcome of self-government and autonomy is a heteronomous power without mastery, headless. This power refers to a rule of conduct that is imposed on everyone as external. Yet it is not such. It is not possible to attribute this power to anyone because it emerges from the intersecting of the choices of everyone and no one. Yet it is a power that can totally govern society.[14]

The new forms of life are processes of subjectivation rather than subjects. They are routes of self-building according to the *Imaginary* of self-valorization whose *Reality* is to be subordinate to the market. Subjectivation floats around aggregation nodes rather than building itself on an interdict, as in the disciplinary way. Differences vary according to a minimum and a maximum, within loose, random, and virtual frames. These variations affect institutions and subjects in the form of permeability and transaction. There is no opposition or assimilation; rather, there is openness to the event.

The subjects that adopt the neoliberal Imaginary are driven to self-govern, self-manage their own talents and productivity—they identify their own success with the success of the business. Conversely, failure is perceived as their own individual inadequacy. The responsibility for the defeat falls on the agent and penalizes the agent in the forms of frustration, of exclusion from social communication. These forms appear as more severe precisely because they are forms of self-exclusion, of self-depreciation. The conflict, the antagonism that built the modern subject through the subject's confrontation with Law and authority, which were held responsible for any possible defeat, is now pushed inward, inside the subject itself.

What remains external yet immanent is the space where success and failure are evaluated, namely, the market. The market becomes the measure and truth of society.[15] We must clarify, though. The market as a truth-test does not mean the total commodification lamented by the Frankfurt *Kulturkritik*. Market test means that the market is the place for the verification of competitiveness, for a differential, never egalitarian valuation; the market provides the standard, "the value." This logic of evaluation, needless to say, is heterogeneous to the legal and political egalitarian logic of rights and democracy. The logic of rights and democracy is ontologically dualist, is tied to negation and normative transcendence. The market, instead, is the bearer of a paradoxical form of immanent normativity, emerging through intersections.

It is important to stress that, in a neoliberal economy, the deciding element in terms of value is not some sovereign subject. Rather, it is the crossing of multiple choice vectors that are asymmetrical, far from equal, and marking the market trend by combining complex factors that include psychological data (expectations, rumors), speculations, and geopolitical considerations as well as institutional powers, aggregations of random and idiosyncratic wills, collective reactions to noneconomic phenomena. The market is acephalous, headless, without a head: there is no decision-making center or a project program. This totally immanent ontology has a great influence on the subjectivation process.

Uncertainty strengthens mimetic and contagious rather than antagonistic behaviors. Because it is impossible to know a priori which human potentialities may be the most functional and which to train as the most suitable, it becomes more profitable to allow creative potentialities to develop freely and then drop those rejected by the instability of the market truth. An a posteriori check seems more convenient. All this makes the subjects' positions and the human capital of their competence entirely precarious. The truth of competition has nothing to do with Adam Smith's spontaneous harmony and invisible hand. It is, simply, the market trend. There is no objective and measurable parameter. There is only a play of resonances among various vectors and communications that finds a point of unstable equilibrium between claims and expectations. All this is as unstable as the market trends or the opinion polls. The cost of all this is the dwindling uncertainty of the labor market as well as the weakness of the political associations, which lack a stable foundation for their struggles.[16] Each actor, individual, company, or institution will try to integrate strategically into the market flows to earn, each time, the maximum gain possible.

Governmental biopower, in fact, no longer guides or disciplines conducts. It does not transmit contents that could become rapidly outdated. Rather, it aims at making psychologies more flexible, mimetic toward external needs, pliable, and able to adapt and unlearn.

An additional vantage point capable of better explaining the gigantic capture device at work in this stage of immanent libertarian powers is given by focusing on neoliberal subjectivities, which are presumed to be monads in perennial "natural" competition.

Within an ontology of differences and variations without transcendence, how can we still talk about subjects? Because there is not a pregiven subject but rather a tendency toward optimal implementation of one's virtual potentialities, the differential gap (which coincides with the subject) will consist in the ability to exceed, to produce a *novum*; it will amount to creativity that goes beyond mere repetition.[17] Hume's empiricism and American pragmatism provide conceptual tools for thinking this ability for the *novum* that coincides with the (collective rather than individual) subject. The task is thinking the *novum* not as a solitary and brilliant creation from nothing, but as the production of differences within a social brain or a productive Marxian *general intellect*. The *novum* becomes variation in repetitions and, as scientific communities attest, a "coordination" of forces, a power of cooperation among singularities and groups.[18]

The market economy intervenes then at a later time to select, within this spontaneous and social coproduction of the *novum*, the products that may be appreciated by the public and will be reproduced in a standardized form. On the one hand, the capitalist valorization process works a posteriori on the creativity of the desiring social machine and *general intellect* by selecting products that it is statistically predictable that an audience (better, a target) will appreciate. On the other hand, though, it will not limit itself to presupposing the social validation of products but rather will try to organize and govern it. Indeed, this *management* becomes its most strategic function. Thus, capitalist valorization confers economic value and power "effect" to a virtuality/potentiality immanent in the social. It channels words and images, which have been spontaneously and anarchically invented, into industrial reproduction.

The decline of the repressive, disciplinary, and oedipal building of subjectivities has indeed freed up creative waves that spread horizontally by imitation, by contagion, and that mark nonrigid and nonstable subjections. Yet these creative waves are selected and filtered so that they can enter the competitive market validation.

Antonio Negri emphasizes the Dionysian power and fruitfulness of social productivity, of "common thought" or the Marxian *general intellect*. According to Negri, this is a creative living force that is not immediately economic or appropriating because it expresses purely affirmative "outputs of growth," as economists would say, rather than founding them on rarity and sacrifice as work does.[19] It is hard to think, however, that this spontaneous and widespread productivity of everyone and no one may evade capitalist management and be enjoyed as a common good. The strategic and competitive principle, which structures the individual and social imaginary and its truth-value, will indeed push the *novum* into the realm of market valorization. Creativity will be measured in terms of competition, equivalent exchange, and general commensurability.

The antagonism and struggle that marked modern subjectivity have no place within neoliberal, functional, differential subjectivities. Their only remaining albeit distorted trace is in the competition for the best evaluation. This competition is a very different matter, though, from the dynamics of subjectivation through antagonistic confrontation that were so important for modern politics.

Populism, Nonantagonistic Political Subjects, Commons: Biopolitical Forms of Doing Politics?

The *displacement* of politics from the canonical places of struggle among groups and interests to the acephalous, headless mechanism of competition among different individuals within the market marks the decline of frontal clashes. When social unease finds a way to express itself, what we now have are forms of situated, partial resistances, linked to local contexts. The Leibnizian monads of the new, neoliberal governmentality, lacking both political synthesis and Smith's optimistic harmonization of interests, hardly reach the cohesion required for political struggle.

The fact that even aggressive forms of populism arise should not be interpreted as the revival of feelings of identifying with and belonging to a *people*. Unlike the classical nineteenth- or early twentieth-century versions, the new populism does not build a mass people-subject that achieves its identity through a strong ideology or monocratic party and an idealized leader. The old populism, full of heavy risks and therefore condemned by liberal-democratic constitutionalism, was linked to a political project and an identity myth that had deeper roots than just rhetorical evocation.

The current populism, which is postideological and born out of the deconstruction of traditional parties, coexists in a specular manner with the neoliberal and proprietary management of power. This populism operates within a very strong media and rhetorical context that operates beyond the classic national-popular channels (such as radio and TV). It works on the web level, where horizontal, rhizomatic connections spread the contagion of opinions according to discontinuous and rhythmic, mostly virtual, modulations. People's concrete lives have important yet intermittent, fleeting, partial contacts with these modalities. This populism aggregates multitudes of individuals around empty signifiers that are functional to giving one and the same relevance to different social, identitarian, utilitarian questions and heterogeneous discomforts. It gives up defining "the *people*" except in a rhetorically antagonistic way.[20] Because differences are not transcended in a common project or in an alternative and socially rooted socioeconomic program, all aggregation is transversal and bereft of roots; therefore, it is precarious and frail. Even the rhetorical use of antagonism shows the inconsistency and crypto-nihilist frailty of the populist front, which lacks a foundation in some shared subordination or in the asymmetry of power and class.

Instead, single individuals find multiple precarious places of aggregation and disaggregation that are intermediate between the monad's loneliness and the people's or class' fusion.[21] There is nothing else. An alternative politics must rely on these intermediate, specific, and contingent places. It often arises from grassroots local situations, such as a territorial issue of pollution (for example, a landfill project), a management problem of a semiabandoned and degraded public space, or, on the opposite front, hostility toward migrants and widespread petty criminality.

These *bottom-up* aggregations systematically avoid universal keywords (citizenship, rights) and punctiliously reject depreciated transcendent values, proudly claiming a pragmatic and anti-ideological style. Yet they are still "symbolic" forms. They arise from precarious positioning but are, nevertheless, capable of generating power outcomes, hence political effects. These precarious positional points (such as the financial trend, a survey's outcome, or the contingent protest movement for a denied right) can govern aggregations while remaining on a plane of social immanence, without transcending them.

What I intend to emphasize is that here, there is no repetition of the modern (and so radically resisted) process of forming a political subject (for example, a party) via a synthesis or an *overcoming* of differences. The top-down process, typical of modernity, in which partial powers and collective identities derive from the Universal, is not replicated here. These precarious aggregations can produce new forms of highly pragmatic political subjectivities, being themselves determined, so often unintentionally, from the synergy of behaviors.[22]

The case of the Commons (or shared goods) highlights this reversal of the point of view. The movement of the Commons is firmly determined to avoid legally defining the status of the (real) common good, in its intermediate status between private and public good.[23] It is very interesting that even the juridical definition of this interesting experiment refers to the *management* of the Commons, to good practices of governance, directly exercised by the stakeholders who, by governing and taking care of a good in a direct way, transform a private or public good into a common good, that is, the Commons.

This is the golden side of the ambivalent biopolitical governmentality from which we started. These new subjects exercise their social productive power without locking themselves in an exclusive identity/status. They transform the selective inclusion of neoliberal governance into self-government processes that escape competitive market control, which is countered with practices of cooperation.[24]

They prefer to fluctuate within functional and pragmatic aggregations rather than being organized by some hegemonic political subject that would sacrifice their inventive and differential freedom—something unbearable. Rather than political subjects structured by representation and representativeness, these subjectivities, which are political in a different way—Chatterjee speaks of a politics of the Governed[25]—are experiments of situational, local self-management. Those who engage from the bottom up are pragmatic, functional entities: "*essences opératoires*," Deleuze would say.[26] And they also avoid being captured by the nonidentitarian yet commercial, competitive neoliberal logic.

These subjects are not in opposition either to the typically modern representative and institutional state or to postmodern neoliberal governance. They are *infra-governmental* subjects, integrated into the loose network of neoliberal governance in an unexpected and alternative way, able to negotiate with other powers and to open new spaces of self-government.

Doubts remain. The key question we must not cease considering is the political problem of the coexistence of these bottom-up experiments and institutions with other, much stronger social and economic institutions. In the long and painful economic crisis, for example, which still has governmental effects on lives, the self-governed, bottom-up institutions (NGOs, Commons, and so on) are overwhelmed by financial institutions or corporations that, in the general demise of universal and public safeguards, are strong enough to affect the lives of many.

We must therefore support these valuable molecular and rhizomatic experiments[27] with a broader front of relentless struggle that links together alternative and subordinate powers and thereby reactivates the antagonistic form of politics.

Notes

1. Oliver Marchart, *Post-foundational Political Thought* (Edinburgh: Edinburgh University Press, 2007). For an introduction to biopolitical thinking, see Laura

Bazzicalupo, *Biopolitica. Una mappa concettuale* (Rome: Carocci, 2013); also translated into Spanish and Portuguese.

2. Laura Bazzicalupo, *Il governo delle vite. Biopolitica e economia* (Rome-Bari: Laterza, 2006).

3. Michel Foucault, *La volonté de savoir* (Paris: Gallimard 1976), 187; *Il faut defendre la société* (Paris: Seuil Gallimard, 1997), 206.

4. Giorgio Agamben, *Homo Sacer. Edizione integrale* (Macerata: Quodlibet, 2018).

5. Mitchell Dean, *Governmentality: Power and Rule in Modern Society* (London: Sage, 1999); Nikolas Rose, *Powers of Freedom: Reframing Political Thought* (Cambridge: Cambridge University Press, 1999).

6. Michel Foucault, "La gourvernementalité," *Dits et Écrits, 1980–1988* (Paris: Gallimard 1994), vol. IV, 641–42; *Sécurité, territoire, population* (Paris: Gallimard Seuil, 2004); *Naissance de la biopolitique* (Paris: Gallimard Seuil, 2004).

7. Laura Bazzicalupo, "Economy as Logic of Government," *Paragraph* 39, no. 1 (2016): 36–48.

8. Thomas Lemke, *Eine Kritik der politischen Vernunft: Foucaults Analyse der modernen Gouvernementalität* (Berlin and Hamburg: Argument, 1997); "Neoliberalismus, Staat und Selbsttechnologien: Ein kritischer Überblick über die governmentality studies," *Politische Vierteljahresschrift* 41, no. 1 (2000): 31–47; Nancy Fraser, "From Discipline to Flexibilization? Rereading Foucault in the Shadow of Globalization," *Costellations* 2 (2003): 160–71.

9. Graham Burchell, Colin Gordon, and Peter Miller, eds., *The Foucault Effect: Studies in Governmentality* (Chicago: University of Chicago Press, 1991); Graham Burchell, "Liberal Government and Techniques of the Self," *Economy and Society* 22, no. 3 (1993): 267–82; Barbara Cruikshank, "Revolutions Within: Self-Government and Self-Esteem," in *Foucault and Political Reason: Liberalism, Neo-Liberalism and Rationalities of Government*, ed. Andrew Barry, Thomas Osborne, and Nikolas Rose (Chicago: University of Chicago Press, 1996), 231–52.

10. Nikolas Rose, "Government, Authority and Expertise in Advanced Liberalism," *Economy and Society* 22, no. 3 (1993): 283–99, line 2006.

11. Roberto Esposito, *Bìos: Biopolitics and Philosophy* (Minneapolis: University of Minnesota Press, 2008); Alessandro Pandolfi, *Natura umana* (Bologna: Il Mulino, 2006).

12. Bazzicalupo, "Economy as Logic of Government."

13. Gilles Deleuze and Félix Guattari, *L'Anti-Oedipe. Capitalisme et schizophrénie* (Paris: Minuit, 1995); Arnault Skornicki, "Le Biopouvoir: détournement des puissances vitales ou invention de la vie?," *Labyrinthe* 22, no. 3 (2005).

14. Gilles Deleuze, "Postscripum sur les sociétés du contrôle," in *Pourparlers* (Paris: Minuit, 1990), 240–47.

15. Michel Foucault, *Naissance de la Biopolitique*, 249; Thomas Lemke, "Foucault, Governamentality and Critique," *Rethinking Marxism* 14, no. 3 (2002); Alessandro Arienzo, "Governo, governamentalità, governance. Riflessioni sul neo-liberalismo contemporaneo," in *Biopolitica e democrazia*, ed. Adriano Vinale (Milan: Mimesis, 2007), 253–79.

16. Maurizio Lazzarato, *Le Gouvernement des inégalités. Critique de l'insécurité néolibérale* (Paris: Éditions Amsterdam, 2008).

17. Maurizio Lazzarato, "Biopolitique/bioéconomie," *Multitudes* 3, 22 (2005).

18. Gabriel Tarde, *La logique sociale* (Paris: Alcan, 1904).

19. Michael Hardt and Antonio Negri, *Il lavoro di Dioniso. Per la critica dello Stato postmoderno* (Rome: Manifestolibri, 2001).

20. Ernesto Laclau, *On Populist Reason* (London: Verso, 2005).

21. Antonio Tucci, ed., *Disaggregazioni. Forme e spazi di governance* (Milan: Mimesis 2013).

22. Michael Hardt and Antonio Negri, *Assembly* (Oxford: Oxford University Press, 2017).

23. Peter Linebaugh, *The Magna Carta Manifesto. Liberties and Commons for All* (Berkeley: University of California Press, 2008).

24. Massimo de Angelis, "Crises, Capital and Cooptation: Does Capital Need a Commons Fix?," in *The Wealth of the Commons: A World Beyond Market and State*, ed. David Bollier and Silke Helfrich (Amherst, MA: Levellers Press, 2013).

25. Partha Chatterjee, *The Politics of the Governed: Popular Politics in Most of the World* (New York: Columbia University Press, 2004).

26. Gilles Deleuze, *Le Pli. Leibniz et le baroque* (Paris: Minuit, 1988), 4.

Six

Immunitary Politics

Caterina Resta

The Janus Head of Globalization

On November 9, 1989, the Berlin Wall, the emblem of the world's division into two opposing blocks, suddenly ceased to be a barrier. In addition to confirming the end of the Cold War between Russia and the United States, the two superpowers that won the Second World War, this date also marks the beginning of globalization. The wall was in fact perhaps the most eloquent symbol of the "Iron Curtain" set in the heart of Europe to separate two Empires, two worlds, and two irreconcilable ideological horizons after the catastrophe of Nazi-fascism, namely, Soviet communism in the East and liberal democracies in the West.

Even the wall's name embodied the *polemical* nature of its construction. Baptized by the German Democratic Republic *Antifaschistischer Schutzwall*, "anti-fascist protection barrier" (as if Hitler's Third Reich, and not the authentically democratic German Federal Republic, were on the other side), in West Berlin it was called *Schandmauer*, the wall of shame—two names divided by an impassable frontier, even though spoken in the same language, which hosted two irreconcilable meanings. That collapse signaled the first tremor of the catastrophic earthquake that would soon lead to the disintegration of the Soviet Communist Empire.

This end to the great bipartition of the world announced, with an overwhelming and irresistible force, the beginning of a new age. This new period has become known as the Global Era[1] precisely because, when the Wall that had divided the globe into two hemispheres fell, the world seemed to be in the position to rediscover its *global* geopolitical unity. In the general euphoria surrounding this epochal event, many thought that the fall of the Berlin Wall not so much marked the resumption of history, which had remained frozen during the years of the "Cold War," as it announced its end[2] and the beginning of a new posthistorical and postmodern phase, in which all borders would soon be erased. The shockwaves of the Wall's collapse caused excessive optimism insofar as they seemed to presage the "fulfillment" of the promises of modernity through the opening up of a "smooth" space, in which free markets and democratic freedoms would rapidly spread across the whole planet. Neoliberal ideology for years propagandized this "messianic" version of globalization, which was dramatically shattered on September 11, 2001, along with the Twin Towers of the World Trade Center. For this reason, it can be said that the triumphal march of globalization, which began with the collapse of the Berlin Wall, came to an abrupt halt twelve years later with another collapse, that of the Twin Towers in Manhattan. Whereas the first collapse, that of the Berlin Wall, nourished the hope for a world finally free from the grip of Nuclear Terror and the Ideological Enemy, the second collapse, that of the Twin Towers, threw the whole of humanity into the nightmare of Global Terrorism[3] and the Theological Enemy.

The attack on the Twin Towers marked a setback in the rapid process of world unification and showed for the first time the unsuspected vulnerability of the North American superpower, seriously wounded *within* its own territory. At the same time, the demands for security and protection began to be all the more insistent and peremptory as the absolute permeability of the borders and the difficulty of a timely defense became more evident. Compounding the increasingly widespread sense of precariousness and insecurity was the financial and economic crisis that exploded in the United States in 2007 and spread rapidly, like a contagion, to a global level, affecting the most fragile countries of the European continent in a particularly severe, lasting manner and also triggering the sovereign debt crisis. It should be noted that the austerity policies adopted in Europe to deal with the crisis were a worse cure than the disease. They strangled the poorer classes, increasing the gap between rich and poor to an intolerable extent and destroying the middle class. This widespread social unease was also at the root of the extraordinary success of neonationalist and populist movements, which are seriously questioning the European Union project itself. The coup de grace in what is already a worrying situation is provided by growing migratory flows, fueled by the proliferation of "glocal" wars as well as by the worsening effects of climate change. Moreover, since the fall of the Berlin Wall, the process of world unification has not yet succeeded in achieving a new global order. Instead we see widespread anomy reigniting conflicts in hot spots of geopolitical friction. Old and new divisions have reemerged, and wounds that had never fully healed have started to bleed again, while the most defenseless individuals are subjected to brutal violence.

The interaction of all these factors of crisis was bound to produce a climate of widespread distrust and insecurity and a peremptory request for greater protection in every respect. It is not surprising, then, that the migrant has become the new Enemy, the one who, in many ways, is even more threatening and destabilizing than Islamic terrorists. The migrant is the new scapegoat, the new barbarian invader to be repelled as the bearer of all evil. This is why the growing need for security focuses on migrants, and the only defensive measure against their intrusion seems to be the *theatrical* raising of new walls,[4] which not by chance are being built again all over the world, while those already built some time ago are being extended and reinforced. The walls do not represent the *end* of globalization, as one might hastily conclude. Rather, they constitute an *internal* reaction to it as well, as they display an aspect that is mistakenly underestimated and overlooked. Alongside the demolition of walls and the removal of borders, globalization in fact involves, as a *backlash*, an equally powerful push in the opposite direction. We see, once more, a desire for fences, for a sense of belonging, and for a protective shelter within *walled* borders. Globalization is not only deterritorialization and delocalization. It is also, and at the same time, always reterritorialization, a search for *closed* spaces in which to find shelter, in the face of uprooting forces that *tear people away* from every place and prevent them from feeling at home where they are. Out of this need for *fenced-in* spaces and protective barriers, new walls are erected to mark boundaries, separate spaces, and build new fences.[5] Their dissuasive power, which is more symbolic than real, tells people to stop, it prohibits movement, and it deceives us into thinking that we can stop the unstoppable flow of human beings driven by war or hunger to look elsewhere for a hope of survival.

A list of walls could be very long, and we do not need to reproduce such a list here. Particularly significant, also symbolically, is the Great Wall of America, the border fence that Trump intended to expand and strengthen, as if he were setting up a *cordon sanitaire* to protect the healthy body of wealthy North America from the dangerous contagion of miseries coming from the Latin American South. Of even greater symbolic relevance is the "Security Fence" between Israel and the West Bank, a large defensive-offensive barrier that separates Jews and Palestinians, a separation wall that excludes (literally "closes out," from the Latin *ex-claudere*) the latter, relegating them to the open-air prison of the Gaza strip. This "Apartheid Wall" certainly does nothing to encourage the peace process between the two neighboring peoples. Walls not only protect but also condition the way a community represents itself as besieged and enclosed within a fortress, surrounded on all sides by hostility, which these defensive barriers in turn contribute to fomenting. Finally, I would like to mention another wall, this time invisible, which has been erected in the middle of the Mediterranean and divides its banks as a new impassable frontier, like new columns of Hercules guarding the entry gate into Europe, a space that has become inaccessible for all those desperate people who risk their lives at sea.

Boundaries[6] are devices for circumscribing, defining, and protecting spaces, and the identity and sense of belonging of those who reside within them also depend on them. Precisely for this reason, the demand for their drastic cancellation, as it was taken up in the first unsettling phase of globalization, was bound to generate insecurity due to the loss of protective banks, anxiety due to the risk of losing one's own identity, and fear due to new kinds of precariousness that arise everywhere in new forms. When it is no longer possible to distinguish clearly between Inside and Outside, then the immediate contact among different peoples and cultures, inside and outside state borders, causes conflicts and new wars that are at the same time both local and global, as is eloquently attested by the current global disorder.

Globalization is therefore characterized by two opposing driving forces, which mutually fuel each other. One pushes for the overcoming and demolition of barriers, above all from an economic point of view, and encourages the expansive logic of capital; the other reacts to this overwhelming force by pushing in the opposite direction, and resorts to the oldest of barriers, the wall, to try to make the boundaries impassable.[7] As we have seen, this results in the resurgence of *real* walls all over the world with significant dissuasive symbolic value and designed to stem migratory flows from poor to richer areas. Or it results in greater border surveillance, or also in the restoration of *symbolic* barriers through a return to protectionist economic policies, which in turn cause destabilizing tensions and retaliations.

Like the two-faced Janus, who was the god of doorways and transition, globalization has two faces. On the one hand, as it impetuously forges ahead, it tends to cancel boundaries; on the other, by way of reaction, it causes borders to spring up more numerous than before,[8] driven by the imperious need to reestablish the protective barriers that have been lost. Globalization must therefore be understood in its entirety and in its intrinsic contradiction as an incessant movement of deterritorialization and reterritorialization. It would be a mistake to consider only one of its two faces. One thing seems to be clear, though: the dream of neoliberal globalization, of being able to break down borders in the name of an uncontrolled freedom, that is, freedom devoid of all rules and constraints, has de facto led to the disastrous, explosive growth of social inequalities. These inequalities no longer concern only the gap between rich and poor countries, but also affect wealthy Western societies from within, in the form of intolerably unfair distributions of wealth: a growing number of poor, marginalized people, and an ever smaller number of enormously rich. New borders of exclusion become more and more visible and controversial, such as those between *residents* and *migrants*, between *citizens* and *illegal immigrants*. These borders fuel increasingly devastating conflicts concerning not only the sphere of economic requests and social protection, but also affecting the fundamental rights of the person because they reject from humanity those who find themselves, for various reasons, marginalized.[9] The dream of a world without borders is floundering in the face of new impenetrable walls, both visible and invisible, whose violent power of exclusion far exceeds the defensive intent behind their construction. As Jacques Derrida noted, "borders are no longer places of passage, they are places of interdiction, thresholds that one regrets having opened, limits towards which one hastens to return people, menacing figures of ostracism, expulsion, banishment, and persecution. We now live in shelters under surveillance, high-security neighborhoods."[10]

A border is not just an impassable barrier, though. As the Latin language attests, in addition to being a *limes*, that is, the perimeter of a space that takes shape and is determined precisely by its outline, a border is also a *limen*, a threshold, a liminal space of crossing and passage, which not only separates two distinct spaces, but also creates a relation between the two and connects them. The border is a line of demarcation that separates, divides, and *defines* different spaces; at the same time, though, it allows them to relate to each other and facilitates movement between them. The border is a line of tangency along which two different spaces come into contact, where the familiar and the unknown meet, without necessarily clashing or fighting each other as enemies; it is a place of transit, of incessant *trans-lation*. It is therefore completely misleading to think that borders necessarily only serve the function of *barrier* and *exclusion*. A border may be closed, reinforced, or walled, but it can also be porous, containing the openings formed by doorways.

Without the possibility of establishing borders and crossing them, in fact, there simply would be no world; what would be there would be the undifferentiated surface of a desert or the liquid expanse of an ocean without a horizon.[11] A world, on the other hand, only arises from the possibility of *qualitatively* delimiting different spaces, which host *different* languages, cultures, and peoples. The globe of globalization cannot be reduced to a tabula rasa, a clean slate on whose smooth surface everything flows together and all differentiation is lost. The Earth hosts a variety of worlds, civilizations, and cultures. Their boundaries, while indispensable to defining them, do not necessarily have to be insurmountable walls and defensive barriers whose inevitable, fatal consequence is that of becoming exclusive, offensive closures that give rise to endemic "clashes of civilizations."[12] We need to keep many doors open along the border, to encourage exchange, dialogue, confrontation, trans-lation, the passage between sides, mutual knowledge and recognition, even living in the *other's land*, not "at one's own home," and being welcomed, experiencing new forms of nonconflictual coexistence, based on the principle that we are all guests and migrants.

The Crisis of Modern Topolitics

As we have said, by breaking down boundaries, the process of globalization causes, as a reaction, the raising of insurmountable barriers, thereby producing an irremediable contradiction. Given this situation, all we can do is to try to interrupt the violent dynamic between the *cancellation of every delimitation*, which produces homologation and indistinctness, and the *enclosure of closed, impenetrable spaces*, which produces rejection and exclusion.

The State, born in the modern period to end the religious wars by means of clear territorial delimitation, adopts a *spatial* conception of the political, which Jacques Derrida called "topolitics" and which is based on the principle of a "sovereignty tied to the control of a territory."[13] Across borders, this form of sovereignty clearly marks the perimeter of an *ordered* space within which to exercise an *autonomous* power, which does not admit any external interference. Starting with the first two World Wars, but especially after the end of the second, in particular with the establishment of supranational bodies such as the United Nations and the promulgation, in 1948, of the Universal Declaration of Human Rights, the territorial sovereignty of states is for the first time seriously put into question. The process of globalization confirms its irreversible crisis.[14] In the absence of a new global order, capable of giving an adequate political and legal form to global challenges that escape the logic of borders, the state-form is no longer able, except marginally, to exercise its territorial sovereignty and ensure protection and order. We are therefore in an anomic interregnum characterized by a dual lack of power. On the one hand, transnational dynamics, above all those of an economic nature, cause a progressive erosion of state sovereignty; on the other, the supranational institutions are not yet strong enough to impose their supranational power on the languishing sovereignty of states. In turn, the more states feel that their sovereignty is threatened and de facto limited, the more they try to entrench themselves, to enclose themselves defensively within their frontiers, fortifying their borders, in a desperate attempt to safeguard a sovereignty on which they now have clearly lost the monopoly. Rather than addressing the new global challenges that emerge on the horizon and require the ability to invent a new global geopolitical structure and new postnational institutions capable of guaranteeing it and bringing order to the present anomy,[15] the only (merely reactive and regressive) response of the declining sovereign states has been to "wall up" borders, to exorcise their evanescence through the construction of new solid barriers that are only capable of stopping and exasperating, rather than resolving, the problems posed by globalization. The term "sovereignism" indicates this form of exasperated neonationalism,[16] a reactive manifestation of a sovereignty that senses its own impotence.

The loss of sovereignty on the part of states also entails greater difficulty in guaranteeing protection. Precisely for this reason, then, the feeling of growing insecurity strengthens the *regressive* desire for a nostalgic return to the ancient refuge of territorial sovereignty, to forms of defensive closure, often harbingers of new violent exclusions. Everywhere there is an attempt to erect *immunitary barriers* against all that comes from the *outside*, which is perceived as a dangerous threat to the integrity of the *inside*. Never before have we witnessed such a veritable *obsession* with frontiers. The relentless defense of borders turns them into trenches. The more state sovereignty appears to be weakened, overwhelmed by disruptive forces, the more states feel the need to resurrect old, anachronistic, and useless fortification systems. The more the real ability of political sovereignty to exercise power within its territory declines—eroded because of transnational flows of capital, labor, and information—the more its violent and theological side reemerges.[17]

From this point of view, the old European continent represents a paradigmatic example. The reason for its exemplarity lies in the fact that it is made of autonomous state entities that, for centuries, have fought one another or have established contingent alliances. Each state is endowed with a specific physiognomy, yet nevertheless they all share a *common* history. It is on the European soil where the state-form was "invented" and where, for at least four hundred years, it produced a Eurocentric *nomos* of the interstate and international Earth, namely the *Jus publicum Europaeum*,[18] on the basis of which the world was "ordered." Not surprisingly, it is again on the European soil that the states' territorial sovereignty *resists* its inevitable waning with the most vigor to the point of radically challenging the very project of unification into a single, large continental space.

A new specter is wandering around Europe, namely sovereignism. This notion is the hyperbole of a theological-political ghost of sovereignty that is reappearing just when the state has irretrievably lost its sovereign character. This neo-nationalism regressively attempts to resurrect the ancient sovereign power, instead of elaborating new forms of *shared* sovereignty reflecting the interrelations of a world that has become global. Caught in the collapse of the old interstate *nomos* and still unable, today more than ever, to achieve a different, fully federal *political* order, Europe is the epicenter of this earthquake and the political workshop of this epochal crisis that concerns the new world order. Reactionary forces, driven by the illusion of a possible return to autonomous and independent forms of sovereignty, are seriously threatening the federal project of Europe. In this interregnum, where xenophobic sovereignists and neoliberal marketers confront each other, the states' objective weakness exposes the most fragile among them to all the repercussions of the political inability to find adequate answers to the difficulties of the current situation—that is, answers capable of moving beyond both neo-nationalistic entrenchments and uncontrolled globalization, where the law of the (economically) strongest prevails.

The more a state's sovereignty appears to be weakened, the more obsessively the state tries to withdraw into itself and resort to all forms of protective barriers to exorcise its own vulnerability. This goes as far as inventing ever new enemies to consolidate internal cohesion and feeding old and new forms of racism along with widespread xenophobia. Enclosures are back in fashion as the theological-political foundation of territorial sovereignty. The sacred impassable furrow marks the beginning of state's history, but it also marks its end. We need to look *beyond* the claustrophobic perimeter drawn by the borders of nation-states, *beyond* their moribund sovereignty. Only by going beyond the neo-nationalisms that today are tearing it apart can Europe perhaps overcome the difficult moment it is going through and offer the globalized world the paradigm of a different way of uniting—without canceling—the linguistic, cultural, and religious differences of which it is composed, also welcoming those who come from outside and cross its borders. Confronted with the smooth, borderless space that an anomic globalization would like to impose and that is met, in a totally reactive way, with the raising of new fences, we instead need to return to thinking of borders as *thresholds*. That is, not as dividing walls but rather as spaces of interconnection and crossing, designed to facilitate the passage between inside and outside, between one's own and the space of others. Rather than builders of walls, we need builders of doors and bridges, capable of creating and unlocking openings that allow transit and *trans-lation*, encounters with those who, being from the outside and foreign, precisely because of their *otherness* introduce something different and thus prevent us from dying as a result of being suffocated by *sameness*.

Immunitary Sovereignism and the Right to Citizenship

The crisis of the state-form as territorially defined sovereignty, as we have seen, *reactively* generates, as a defense mechanism, the desire for protective closures and the rejection of any interference that comes from the outside, perceived as such as threatening. This response, which we can define as *immunitary*, concerns all forms of sovereignty in their insistence on being absolute and unconditional. It concerns even the sovereignty of an ipseity that thinks it can exist regardless of any relation with the other. Inherently connected to the demand for sovereignty is the demand to preserve an *identity* with clearly defined borders, an identity that is pure, intact, not contaminated with any foreign element, and constantly on guard against anything that could threaten it. Sovereignism and identitarianism are united in the common strategy of immunitary defense against any pathogenic agent that would like to enter *from the outside*, threatening the autarchy of a subject that wrongly thinks of itself as sovereign, autonomous, and identical to itself in its own self-mirroring. This is why the foreigner, the migrant who wants to breach the immunitary barriers of the sovereign nation, attacking the supposed integrity and homogeneity of its people, is the mortal Enemy to be "rejected," repelled, expelled, and *excluded* at all costs. The more permeable the frontiers are, the more we see a reaction as new protective banks are raised and exposed areas are strengthened to contain the threat of this "invasion" and the fear of this "contagion." At the same time, the obsession with security increases and the immunitary response is triggered, resulting in xenophobia. The *identity drive*, which acts behind all phantoms of sovereignty, becomes increasingly paranoid and persecutory the more the subject refuses to acknowledge and denies the other *within itself* on the basis of which every ipseity is constituted. The subject thus sets in motion an immunitary machine of annihilation of the other by whom it feels endangered. We therefore need to deconstruct the immunitary-identity device—which is the basis of all sovereignisms, both political and ipseological—which generates exclusion and rejection. We need to try to understand how it works and not to underestimate the fear that fuels it.

What is at stake is precisely identity, that is, the integrity and indemnity of a subject as well as a community. For this reason, the immunitary paradigm[19] is the one that best lends itself to understanding how the annihilation of all foreign bodies is necessary so that one's own body remains healthy. We need, however, to consider the interweaving of immunity and autoimmunity, because the latter is not to be understood as the simple reverse or opposite of the former, but rather as its radicalization. This is why Derrida spoke of a "terrifying but fatal logic of the *autoimmunity of the unscathed*"[20] and of the community as *auto-co-immunity* insofar as it is a "*common auto-immunity*: no community [is possible] that would not cultivate its own auto-immunity, a principle of sacrificial self-destruction ruining the principle of self-protection (that of maintaining its self-integrity intact). . . . This self-contesting attestation keeps the auto-immune community alive, which is to say, open to something other and more than itself."[21]

In its constitution as well as in its preservation, any community identity as well as any subjective identity is therefore traversed by a process that, at the same time, protects and threatens it, constructs and deconstructs it. This process annihilates the *external* enemies that threaten the self. Yet it may even reach a point where, taking its defensive intent to the extreme, it no longer acknowledges the enemies as *internal* to itself, as part of itself. Thus, it self-destructs at the very moment when it believes it is saving itself. At the same time, though, it can save itself only when it seems on the verge of self-destruction. As Derrida suggests, it is in fact precisely when, because of excessive closure, the immunitary aggression directed outward turns inwards to become auto-immunitary aggression and attacks the very protective system of self-defense; it is precisely at this moment that the collapse of the immunitary barriers, rather than destroying the community or ipseity, turns into the only condition capable of ensuring the "survival" of the community or ipseity. This occurs by letting in and hosting the other within oneself, without any longer destroying the other and thereby simultaneously suspending also one's own self-destruction. This is the hetero-auto-sacrificial logic that lies both at the basis of any ipseity and behind all desires for identity, sovereignty, and self-appropriation. For this reason, the more absolute and hyperbolic the identity drive is, the more it reveals its hetero- and self-destructive character; the more it protects itself, annihilating the other outside itself, the more it harms itself. It is only by lowering the immunitary defenses and allowing the stranger to come within oneself, recognizing him or her as part of oneself, that one can escape one's own self-destruction. The same is *in itself* different. For this reason, autoimmunity is not just something threatening and negative. As Derrida writes, "autoimmunity is not an absolute ill or evil. It enables an exposure to the other, to *what* and to *who* comes—which means that it must remain incalculable. Without autoimmunity, with absolute immunity, nothing would ever happen or arrive."[22]

Immunity and autoimmunity must therefore be thought together, in their indissoluble relation. Both are, at the same time, threat and promise. If absolute immunity results in the annihilation of the other, and absolute autoimmunity turns into self-destruction, lowering one's immunitary defenses is the only way, certainly not without risks, to interrupt this device of hetero-self-annihilation. Ipseity—be it of the self or of a community—is constitutively exposed to the other outside itself because it has always *hosted* the other within itself. More generally, this hospitality means the opening to the event of the other,[23] as it enshrines the very possibility that there may be a future.

Borders are not only the trench, though, along which the identity-immunitary politics of the new forms of sovereignism clash with everything that would like to transgress them. By territorially circumscribing the political space of sovereignty, borders end up defining the limits of *citizenship*. This is the case even though, starting with the 1789 *Declaration of the Rights of Man and of the Citizen*, citizenship should be recognized as a fundamental right that belongs to all human beings, regardless of whether they are part of a political community. Whether the right of citizenship is determined by *ius sanguinis* [right of blood or citizenship by bloodline] or *ius soli* [right of soil or birthright citizenship], these are measures that apply to those who intend to reside within a specific *territory*. This right, together with all the other rights connected to it, has validity and coincides with its borders, just as it *ends* beyond them. Although the 1948 *Universal Declaration of Human Rights*, promulgated by the United Nations—that is, by an *extraterritorial* and *supranational* body—sanctions the right of each individual to citizenship (Article 5), nevertheless the constant lack *not* of the legal recognition of extraterritorial and supranational citizenship (this is promulgated, in fact, in the *Declaration*, which retains the value of a *legal* and not only *moral* document) but of the guarantee of its actual observance, de facto assigns exclusively to the state the power to attribute—but also to *deny* as well as to limit—this right.[24] We thus need to break the link between citizenship, state, and territory, which enables immunitary politics of rejection and exclusion, and must instead give greater strength and power to supranational and extraterritorial institutions, including nongovernmental organizations.[25]

In the current phase of globalization, we see a clash between pushes, dictated by prevailing neoliberalism, toward unregulated economic-financial unification and regressive pressures to seek refuge and protection in xenophobic forms of sovereignism that call for closed borders and demand unconditional sovereignty over their own territory. In this context, the *decisive* clash is no longer, as in the past, the class conflict between workers and capital. Now, even more radically, the clash is between *residents* and *migrants*, *citizens* and *illegal immigrants*, those who feel "masters in their own home" and the sole holders of rights and those who, unable to take advantage of the refugee status, are de facto deprived of all rights, forced to assume an illegal status, *cast outside* by the law that considers them to be *out-laws*, and expelled from humanity itself. The epochal clash, which causes an irremediable contradiction, is therefore between the *global mobilization* of the flows of money, goods, information, and so on and the demand for the *total immobilization* of migratory flows. Only those who are citizens are allowed to move freely around the planet, not so much by virtue of a passport but rather by the power of a credit card. Those who do not have one and intend to transgress the implicit prohibition of mobility; those who, above all, demand the right not only to *e*-migrate, but also to *im*-migrate to a place other than the one they left should realize that, except in those rare cases in which the right to asylum is applied (and which is granted in an increasingly restrictive way), thirst, hunger, and the complete poverty that put their very survival at risk every day will not be considered sufficient reasons even to acquire refugee status. The only condition that global *zoo-politics* offers to these refugees is that of *illegal immigrant*,[26] that is, the one who is no longer considered even a person but only an invisible "naked life," exposed to the violence of those who exploit it as cheap labor or use it for illegal trafficking. It is on this border, namely, the border between *citizen* and *illegal immigrant*, that currently a world civil war is being fought between those who are *inside* and those who must be kept *outside*, those who have a future and those who see it denied to them, those who have the right to live and those who can be let to die, those who have rights and those who have none, those who are part of humanity and those who are excluded from it.

In the dramatic historical period in which we are living, when not only the right to citizenship is denied and the conditions to benefit from the right to asylum become increasingly restrictive but also the individuals' right to *emigration* and movement is criminalized and denied, the appeal to human rights is the *only*, the sole resort to prevent all forms of dehumanization affecting unarmed victims,[27] precarious lives,[28] discarded existences[29]—that is, those individuals who are not always able to fight personally to claim those rights. Universal human rights are not rights pertaining to human "nature," therefore *pre*-political or even *anti*-political or depoliticizing. They constitute a counter-*power* against the *zoo*-politics of a sovereign state that intends to make a discriminatory and, ultimately, *racist* use of *national* and *territorial* citizenship, thereby perverting what should have been an instrument of inclusion into an arrogant right to *exclusion* against other people, sealing borders and *artificially* (that is, legally) transforming those who are "out-cast" into non-humans. Far from representing an instance of depoliticization, universal human rights affirm the constitutively *political* principle of human life and force us to think differently about the political and the legal, on the basis of the fundamental "right to have rights."[30]

Taking the rights proclaimed in the 1948 Declaration seriously means "having the courage today to detach them from citizenship in the sense of *belonging* (to a particular state community) and therefore from statehood. [. . .] To recognize their supra-state character [. . .] and therefore protect them not only inside, but also outside and against States."[31] The figure of the "resident foreigner" testifies to a different way of cohabiting, finally free from demands for exclusive possession of the land.[32] If so, the figure of the migrant embodies the possibility of imagining a future humanity for which citizenship will no longer have limits or boundaries, constraints or conditions. Rather, it will correspond to our being, all of us, coinhabitants of the same land that hosts us.

(Translated by Simon Tanner;
revised by Silvia Benso and Elvira Roncalli)

Notes

1. The literature on globalization is now vast. I mention here only some texts, which have become benchmarks: Zygmunt Bauman, *Globalization: The Human Consequences* (Cambridge: Polity Press, 1998); *Society under Siege* (Cambridge: Polity Press, 2002); and *Collateral Damage: Social Inequalities in a Global Age* (Cambridge: Polity Press, 2011); Ulrich Beck, *Risk Society: Towards a New Modernity*, trans. Mark Ritter (London: Sage, 1992); *What Is Globalization?*, trans. Patrick Camiller (Cambridge: Polity Press, 2000); and *World Risk Society* (Cambridge: Polity Press, 1999).

2. Francis Fukuyama, *The End of History and the Last Man* (New York: Free Press, 1992).

3. Particularly illuminating are the analyses by Jean Baudrillard, *The Spirit of Terrorism and Other Essays*, trans. Chris Turner (London-New York: Verso, 2012) and Donatella Di Cesare, *Terror and Modernity*, trans. Murtha Baca (Cambridge: Polity Press, 2019).

4. As observed by Wendy Brown, *Walled States, Waning Sovereignty* (New York: Zone Books, 2010), 20: "nation-states, rich and poor, exhibit a passion for wall building."

5. On the political use of walls and barriers, see Claude Quétel, *Murs. Une autre histoire des hommes* (Paris: Perrin, 2012); Olivier Razac, *Barbed Wire: A Political History*, trans. Jonathan Kneight (New York: The New Press, 2003); Elisabeth Vallet, ed., *Borders, Fences and Walls: State of Insecurity?* (London: Routledge, 2014).

6. On the meaning and role of borders, see Gian Primo Cella, *Tracciare confini. Realtà e metafore della distinzione* (Bologna: Il Mulino, 2006); Manlio Graziano, *Frontiere* (Bologna: Il Mulino, 2017); Piero Zanini, *Significati del confine. I limiti*

naturali, storici, mentali (Milan: Bruno Mondadori, 1997). The dynamics of globalization are responsible for renewed attention to the geopolitical, anthropological, and sociological role played by borders, as evidenced by the vitality of "Border Studies"; see Doris Wastl-Walter, ed., *The Ashgate Research Companion to Border Studies* (Farnham: Ashgate, 2011); Thomas M. Wilson and Hastings Donnan, eds., *A Companion to Border Studies* (Malden: J. Wiley & Son, 2012).

7. On the contrasting dynamics triggered by globalization with respect to the modern concept of territorial sovereignty, see Bertrand Badie, *La fin des territoires. Essai sur le désordre international et sur l'utilité social du respect* (Paris: Fayard, 1995).

8. Michel Foucher, *L'obsession des frontières* (Paris: Perrin, 2007) and *Le retour des frontières* (Paris: CNRS Ed., 2016). My translation.

9. Alessandro Dal Lago, *Non-persons: The Exclusion of Migrants in a Global Society* (Milan: Ipoc Press, 2009); Sandro Mezzadra, *Diritto di fuga. Migrazioni, cittadinanza, globalizzazione* (Verona: Ombre Corte, 2001); Sandro Mezzadra, ed., *I confini della libertà. Per un'analisi politica delle migrazioni contemporanee* (Roma: DeriveApprodi, 2004).

10. Jacques Derrida, "Manquements du droit à la justice," in Jacques Derrida, Marc Guillaume, Jean-Pierre Vincent, *Marx en jeu* (Paris: Descartes & Cie, 1997), 74. Author's translation.

11. Zygmunt Bauman has insisted on the "liquid" nature of globalization; see Zygmunt Bauman, *Liquid Modernity* (Cambridge: Polity Press, 2000) and *Liquid Life* (Cambridge: Polity Press, 2005).

12. This perspective becomes inescapable only to the extent that large, strongly identifying and *closed* spaces clash, as argued by Samuel P. Huntington, *The Clash of Civilizations and the Remaking of World Order* (New York: Simon & Schuster, 1996).

13. Jacques Derrida and Bernard Stiegler, *Echographies of Television: Filmed Interviews*, trans. Jennifer Bajorek (Cambridge: Polity Press, 2002), 79.

14. On the crisis of the relationship between sovereignty, territory, and citizenship, which led to the decline of modern topolitics, a fundamental analysis of the period between the two World Wars remains that by Hannah Arendt, "The Decline of the Nation-State and the End of the Rights of Man," in *The Origins of Totalitarianism* (New York: Harcourt, Brace & World, 1966). In this regard, see the interesting discussion of Judith Butler and Gayatri Chakravorty Spivak, *Who Sings the Nation-State?* (Calcutta: Seagull Books, 2007). More generally, in relation to the dynamics of globalization, see Kenichi Ohmae, *The End of the Nation State: The Rise of Regional Economies* (London: Harper Collins, 1995).

15. On the need for a new global order in a cosmopolitan direction, see Seyla Benhabib, *Another Cosmopolitanism* (Oxford: Oxford University Press, 2006); Jürgen Habermas, *The Postnational Constellation: Political Essays*, trans. and ed. Max Pensky (Cambridge: Polity Press, 2001); and David Held, *Democracy and the Global Order* (Cambridge: Polity Press, 1995).

16. On the conflict generated by the tension between the erosion of territorial sovereignty and the desire to reaffirm it through new forms of nationalism,

see the interesting discussion in Bernard Badie and Michel Foucher, *Vers un monde néo-national?* (Paris: CNRS Ed., 2017).

17. As observed by Brown, *Walled States, Waning Sovereignty*, 64: "In the course of its waning, nation-state sovereignty becomes more intensively and openly theological."

18. Carl Schmitt, *The Nomos of the Earth in the International Law of the Jus Publicum Europaeum*, trans. Gary L. Ulmen (New York: Telos Press, 2003). On the issues set forth in this work, of fundamental importance in reconstructing the genealogy of globalization, see Caterina Resta, *Stato mondiale o* Nomos *della terra. Carl Schmitt tra universo e pluriverso* (Reggio Emilia: Diabasis, 2009).

19. For the immunitary paradigm, see above all Jacques Derrida, "Faith and Knowledge: The Two Sources of 'Religion' at the Limits of Reason Alone," trans. Samuel Weber, in *Religion*, ed. Jacques Derrida and Gianni Vattimo (Cambridge: Polity Press, 1998); "Autoimmunity: Real and Symbolic Suicides," in Giovanna Borradori, *Philosophy in a Time of Terror: Dialogues with Jürgen Habermas and Jacques Derrida* (Chicago: University of Chicago Press, 2003); and Roberto Esposito, *Immunitas: The Protection and Negation of Life*, trans. Zakiya Hanafi (Cambridge: Polity Press, 2011).

20. Derrida, "Faith and Knowledge," 44.

21. Derrida, "Faith and Knowledge," 51.

22. Jacques Derrida, *Rogues: Two Essays on Reason*, trans. Pascale-Anne Brault and Michael Naas (Stanford: Stanford University Press, 2005), 152.

23. For a deeper discussion of this issue, see Caterina Resta, *L'evento dell'altro. Etica e politica in Jacques Derrida* (Torino: Bollati Boringhieri, 2003).

24. The risks related to the violent will of this *political* power had not escaped Hannah Arendt; in the new European order following the end of World War I, because of the loss of their original citizenship, huge masses of refugees found themselves in the condition of being stateless persons without any rights (see Arendt, *The Decline of the Nation-State and the End of the Rights of Man*).

25. For a deeper understanding of these issues, see Caterina Resta, "Il diritto di essere umani," in Carmine Di Martino, ed., *I diritti umani e il "proprio" dell'uomo nell'età globale. Diritto Etica Politica* (Roma: Inschibboleth, 2017). On the tension between *national* recognition and the *supranational* enactment of rights, see Seyla Benhabib, *The Rights of Others: Aliens, Residents and Citizens* (New York: Cambridge University Press, 2004). More generally, see Étienne Balibar, *Citizen Subject: Foundations for Philosophical Anthropology*, trans. Steven Miller (New York: Fordham University Press, 2017); Stephen Castles and Alastair Davidson, *Citizenship and Migration: Globalization and the Politics of Belonging* (New York: Routledge, 2000).

26. On the figure of the illegal immigrant and their invisibility, see Donatella Di Cesare, *Resident Foreigners: A Philosophy of Migration*, trans. David Broder (Cambridge: Polity Press, 2019).

27. On the growing violence to which unarmed victims are subjected in our time, see Adriana Cavarero, *Horrorism: Naming Contemporary Violence*, trans. William McCuaig (New York: Columbia University Press, 2009).

28. Judith Butler, *Precarious Life: The Powers of Mourning and Violence* (London: Verso, 2004); "Introduction: Precarious Life, Grievable Life," in *Frames of War: When Is Life Grievable?* (London: Verso, 2009).

29. Zygmunt Bauman, *Wasted Lives: Modernity and Its Outcasts* (Cambridge: Polity Press, 2004).

30. Criticizing in this regard the position of Arendt, to whom we owe this famous expression, Butler has rightly observed: "The right to have rights is one that depends on no existing particular political organization for its legitimacy. Like the space of appearance, the right to have rights predates and precedes any political institution that might codify or seek to guarantee that right; at the same time, it is derived from no natural set of laws"; see Judith Butler, "Bodies in Alliance and the Politics of the Street," in *Notes Toward a Performative Theory of Assembly* (Cambridge: Harvard University Press, 2015), 80.

31. Luigi Ferrajoli, "Dai diritti del cittadino ai diritti della persona," in Dario Ippolito and Fabrizio Mastromartino, eds., *Iura paria. I fondamenti della democrazia costituzionale* (Naples: Editoriale scientifica, 2017), 144–45.

32. Di Cesare, *Resident Foreigners*, revolves entirely around this perspective.

Part Three

Responsibility, Emotions, Time

Seven

Responsibility as Being Here in Our Own Time[1]

Laura Boella

Responsibility for What We Are Not Responsible for

In contemporary thought, responsibility has become the generative root of ethics, particularly within reflections on the destructive consequences of our abilities to interfere with human life and the environment. Rethinking responsibility has been the answer to the individual and collective crisis caused by the historical-political catastrophes of the twentieth century and by the deep transformations of the moral agenda linked to technological development. Thus, the *aporias* of freedom and the autonomy of the subject have come to light, together with the risks of actions that are taken away from the agent's control, the fragility of human life and nature, and the presence of the other as a fundamental dimension of individual existence. If we look at the contemporary existential and social situation, we notice a shrinking space for freedom and, at the same time, a flight from freedom; an unlimited responsibility and a de-responsibility; the rejection of bodily constraints and the desire for the impossible (eternal youth, reading the other's mind, and so on). Free acts, if and when they are carried out, bring into the open various forms of freedom with no obligations or ties to others and nature. The outcome of this upheaval of thought can be summarized in terms of a contradictory figure: responsibility today calls us *to be responsible for what we are not responsible for.*[2]

Science, first and foremost experimental brain research, attests to the enormous expansion of the range of actions that are not under our control and rule. We know that a significant part of the basic processes related to conscious actions is triggered in ways that are not only unconscious, but also subpersonal. The vast debate on free will that occupies the cognitive sciences and the philosophy of mind seems to be essentially concerned with fending off the consequences of the "illusion" of free will.[3] The question of responsibility is consequently addressed by resorting to emotions, to historical and social constructs, or, finally, to commonsense strategies implemented to guarantee a minimal order to social life.[4] One wonders whether the antithesis between the subject's sovereignty (that is, free will) and its dismissal by brain mechanisms ("it wasn't me, my brain did it") replicates the ancient debate on determinism and indeterminism, remaining on an exclusively theoretical level.

The idea of a responsibility linked to what we are not responsible for allows us to go deeper. We know the extent to which our decision-making processes and even our emotions and intentions are linked to automatic and involuntary mechanisms, to bodily interactions, and to affective resonances. The task then becomes precisely the integration of this knowledge and awareness into our actions. The doses of free will that are necessary to make a will, kill our partner, or take drugs differ. Their variations modify the traditional notion of responsibility, but they do not eliminate it. Rather, they relaunch it as the task of a critical reappropriation of the results of experimental research, starting from those reported as pop science or under the aegis of famous biologists and neuroscientists. Such a reappropriation is a question of competence and information. Above all, though, it is everyone's duty to integrate into our experience the new knowledge regarding neurobiological functioning, which first of all works on our own identity. The problem, which also arises in relation to the new digital technologies that, in the communication and information fields, "enhance" human capacities, basically consists in not taking for granted the anthropological transformations produced by science and its applications.

The contemporary epoch is the age not only of big data and big science, but also of the shadows that the historical-political catastrophes of the twentieth century still project on the new millennium. In rethinking responsibility, philosophy has been attuned to the social and political tragedies of the last century and to the impact of technology on human existence. A difference must be noted, however, with respect to what has happened in the scientific fields. The acknowledgment of the *aporias* of freedom has gone hand in hand with a radical redefinition of responsibility so that the relation between freedom and responsibility has been overturned: responsibility comes before freedom (will, conscience, decision). In the words of Emmanuel Levinas, "responsibility for others could not have originated in my commitment, in my decision. [It is] a debt contracted before all freedom, before all conscience, before every present."[5] This is a well-trodden path of thought, which includes the contributions of some of the greatest thinkers of the twentieth century.

My attention in this chapter focuses on a specific configuration, one for which responsibility, which speaks the language of constitutive human relationality, takes on the *aporias* of freedom by, on the one hand, sharing freedom's destiny and, on the other, proposing itself as freedom embodied in the contradictory scene of contemporaneity.

The widespread appeal to responsibility we experience today is an expression of the need to make human freedom conditional whenever freedom attempts to affirm itself as an unlimited power to act, as uncontrolled individualism. Yet the "limits" of freedom are not simply a restriction of the sovereignty of the ego. Rather, they correspond to the ego's manifestation against the background of its involvement in lives that are not our own, to use Judith Butler's expression that echoes Levinasian and Arendtian themes. We are not free except on the stage of a world that is inhabited by others, in which our words are listened to, are accepted or contradicted, and our actions are measured on what they do (or do not) provoke in others and in the surrounding world.[6] Here, a fundamental effect produced by rethinking responsibility emerges. The autonomous, self-mastering, and world-transforming subject is replaced with a subject aware of being a force field of power; of operating through unconscious, genetic, and neurobiological mechanisms; of having unchosen ethnic and cultural affiliations; of partaking of global processes not under the subject's control, and of being related to others in the first instance. In other words, the responsibility that comes before freedom deals with a relational and, at the same time, vulnerable subject, which is exposed not so much to a collision with the others' freedom, but rather to the risk of abandonment, to the need for others, and, eventually, to the related violence.

Responsibility carries with itself the burden of a "difficult freedom"[7] that implies a demanding ethical commitment. This is the complete opposite of the disengagement that results from relying on ungovernable processes and forces. At the same time, responsibility is placed at the core of conflicts and dilemmas because we will never be able to untie the knot of opacity and darkness that binds us to others. No reference to a bodily interdependence understood as instinctive emotional resonance and spontaneous empathy can solve this problem.[8]

From an ethical point of view, the responsibility for what we are not responsible for can in fact be a very heavy load that risks turning into a feeling of powerlessness. It is true that one is responsible for one's own body, for one's emotions, for one's face, for what one has (or has not) become, for one's actions and omissions, for the genetic makeup and the environment bequeathed to one's own grandchildren. As Paul Ricœur noted, the proliferating uses of the term "responsibility" cover such a vast range of occurrences that it could turn it into fatalism.[9]

History in the I

If responsibility means "responding" and neither the subject's freedom nor its autonomy can remain unaffected by others and nature, then the disruptive force of this awareness leads to questioning the commitment of a subject who is implicated in biological processes, in relations of power and violence, but who also assumes the risk of acting, of saying "Here I am!" (following Ricœur and Levinas). Nowadays, individual actions present themselves in their most elusive and difficult dimension, namely, that of a conflict and disproportion with respect to historical-political events, impersonal processes, the "world" of techno-science, and the global economy—in a word, the present we live in. Responsibility calls for the search for new figures of experience, in relation with the historical times.

One of the deepest changes that individuals have experienced in the twentieth century is that the I "no longer resides in history; rather, lately history resides in the I."[10] This statement by Ingeborg Bachmann corresponds to the experience of those who did not "make" history as leaders or great personalities but rather suffered in their bones the revolutions, world wars, persecutions, and totalitarian regimes that marked the history of the past century. History entered "the subject" because it singularly targeted individuals' body and soul, depriving them of the ground beneath their feet, making them a battlefield between past and future. Succumbing to the "spirit of the time" or challenging it in the forms prescribed by political and cultural ideologies seemed the only alternatives.

There is another possibility, though. Accepting that history enters the I could also mean to refuse to live one's own time as a fatal event or an ideology, to let oneself be completely unsettled in order to discover the messages of guilt, decadence, faith, cynicism, exhaustion, innocence, and love with which every age addresses every human being. In this case, historical time concentrates in one's personal experience and becomes a way of living the present that discloses relevant perspectives for anyone who now wonders about how to live.

What does "living the present" mean? Our present is punctuated by the "after" (modernity, the Berlin Wall, the Industrial Revolution), by the "never again" (Auschwitz), by the various "ends" (of Communism, of

Marxism, of the idea of progress). In fact, though, history did not terminate. What was apparently finished continued to end; what appeared as turning points and ultimate closures revealed themselves to be evanescent, fading events. The present turns out to be a trap where history plays cat and mouse with our desire for resolution (which, for many, has been a living generational experience; for example, the resistance against fascism or the events of 1968). A whirling motion turns out to be a *sur place*, an in-place, onsite, without movement; the new immediately becomes old, the future becomes past. Feeling contemporary often means remaining on the visible, tragic surface of the present, seeing only the façade even though it is full of cracks. We believe that we are contemporary simply because we hastily marshal the present in a contiguity of actual, albeit disparate, phenomena. We let famines in Africa coexist with Western overproduction and food waste; police background checks and terrorist acts go hand in hand with sophisticated art exhibitions in big cities; religious fundamentalism cohabits with the polytheism of image devotees. Heartbreaking current phenomena remain unrelated and, when they clash materially, become a matter of domestic or international security. Contemporary times are often embodied in the walls that are built in Europe and the United States on the routes of migrants and that rise in the metropoles to separate the districts inhabited by non-EU citizens, rich people's gated communities, and downtown shopping areas. The same applies to the social divide between employed and unemployed workers, young people and adults, women from non-European countries and European women, impoverished petty bourgeoisie and huge asset holders. This is a way of looking at the present that describes its contradictions and can partly explain them. Yet it does not move it from its fixity, giving it a profile of confused instability, of quicksand, of indifference and impotence. Christa Wolf has recognized the "horrible secret" of the men and women of our age when she describes it as a "being there and not there at the same time."[11]

The present and its elusive actuality are nevertheless also inhabited by other times: shreds of the past that come back or remain suspended and manifest themselves in the form of obsessions, fears, anxieties, unpaid debts, uncollected credits, unaccomplished gestures, unspoken words, and unthought thoughts. There is something that secretly misaligns the present and renders it both ardent and miserable. There is something noncontemporary in the present,[12] something that is grafted on economic and political events but that corresponds to a way of experiencing and interpreting them in the form of emotions and the imaginary, of omens and nostalgia, of poetic invocation and existential discomfort, of doubt, anger, and resistance. The present contains unrealized ideals, betrayed dreams, images of a vanished or illusory past (such as one's childhood or the mythical idea of nature). The sense is that something is missing, does not work, but hovers on the edge of the present, on the fleeting borders that divide it from the past and the future. It would be wrong to consider this kind of experience as the other side of the coin, the subjective experience of the economic and social reality, or the spiritual or philosophical interpretation that we can give of it. On the contrary, this is a decisive component of the present; it corresponds to the powerful contrasting forces that operate within it, which are memory, the aspiration to the absolute, dreams, but also our dark inner sides.

Noncontemporaneity allows one to read an opening to unexpected experiences and knowledge even within the painful and destructive experiences of the present. We must wonder how many fantasies, ghosts, chimeras, anxieties, nostalgia, frustrations, and resentments the present can contain without losing its concreteness and its existential and responsible commitment, without trimming it into a place of aesthetic or political adventure, with no distinction between good and evil, truth and falsehood, or without transfiguring it into an abstract, ideal realm. To what extent can noncontemporaneity be experienced and thought of without heroic, aristocratic, or adventurous traits? Without requiring a vocation for the extreme or an inclination toward all that remains unfulfilled? These questions remind us that noncontemporaneity is the place of the tormented, meditative, unquenched, and unquenchable imagination. It is the place of the anxiety about salvation and the destructive impulses, but is also the place of the quest for meaning, of the effort to make what happens understandable, working to find new words and feelings even for those who cannot or do not want to. In the absence of an experience of noncontemporaneity, it is impossible to decipher the impurity and confusion of the present, to move it from its expressionless and brutal fixity, to animate it along with its shadows and tragic ambiguity, returning to it the voice of memory and expectation.

Noncontemporaneity is a lived experience of the present. It is contradictory and disturbing, studded with wounds and mourning, but, in any case, it is lucidly aware of the contemporary condition of disproportion between individuals and historical-political processes. Noncontemporaneity means not only exposing oneself to imbalance, but also offering one's own life experience as a way of processing the relation with a time out of joint.

History as Responsibility and the Ethical-Political Transformation of Phenomenology

Derrida reads in Jan Patočka the idea of "responsibility as history and as history of Europe."[13] The Czech philosopher has bequeathed to us an ethical-political legacy of high symbolic value centered on the thesis that "history is not a vision, but a responsibility."[14] In his *Heretical Essays on the Philosophy of History* (1975), he speaks of the "experiences on the front" during World War I where, between enemies, the struggle for life and death created a "solidarity of the shaken," of those who had experienced, through their lives constantly at risk, the collapse of day-to-day stability, the "stumbling" into nothingness. For Patočka, such an experience could potentially pull humanity away from war and the rule of force. Even the bitterest foes can recognize a common horizon in the mortal finitude that binds them.[15] Derrida correctly deduces from these reflections the idea of a problematic history, in which darkness and light, openness to meaning and nonsense are tossed, and he focuses his attention on the nexus of death and responsibility that springs from such experiences of extreme commitment. In fact, only death can sanction the irreplaceability of the individual at the dreadful intersection of opposites in which modern individuals find themselves. This interpretation is confirmed by the fate of Patočka himself, who died in 1977 after having undergone a police interrogation as a spokesman for the *Charta '77* opposition movement.

Patočka's legacy has a symbolic value that is not only existential but also theoretical. Despite the emphasis on death and on a sort of zero point of existence, the demanding "sacrifice" mentioned in many of the Czech philosopher's writings is rethought outside its heroic meaning and can be read as a gesture to reopen the possibility of a renewal of moral and political life.

The idea of "history as responsibility" should not be interpreted simply as laudable participation in the tragic events of the contemporary era. It proposes the figure of responsibility as a personal assumption of the relation between historical-political events and one's own life. It is the exercise of freedom as preservation of the even minimal, yet real possibility of acting in order to prevent reality from closing off the horizon of the world and reducing it to one's own backyard; of acting in order to prevent the mind from becoming a prisoner.

What is the origin of Patočka's responsibility? First of all, it should be pointed out that in their own distinctive way, Jan Patočka and Hannah Arendt, together with Emmanuel Levinas, Maurice Merleau-Ponty, and Karel Kosík, belong to the generation that has been the protagonist of the transformation of phenomenology in an ethical and political direction. There is still no precise picture of the work of the phenomenologists who personally confronted Husserl and Scheler—Edith Stein first, then Patočka and Levinas—or explored the research pathways that the founding fathers had opened, and who were attuned to the great twentieth-century crises taking place outside academia.[16] Husserl's lesson was in some cases criticized and compared with Heidegger's thought, although with an awareness of its deep innovative value. The phenomenological perspective was then applied to a world out of joint, that is, the world of Europe between the two World Wars and during the postwar period when two systems, Western technocratic capitalism and Eastern bureaucratic and authoritarian socialism, showed many traits in common. In times of crisis, during a century in which human beings became self-estranged in the crowd and were subjected to authoritarian and bureaucratic mechanisms, phenomenology appeared as a tragic attempt to restore the bond between individuals and their surrounding world. So phenomenology offered a new method for approaching ethical and social issues. This method was based on the strong link between experience and responsibility.

The world is given to us not as an object but in lived experiences—this is what phenomenology teaches. Experience is one's emotional, cognitive, practical commitment in the world. Lived experiences, beginning with the horror and fear of which the twentieth century was so generous, do not involve only the individual; they are also experiences of being together that bring into play freedom and individual dignity (and their opposite) within the common life. In the phenomenological perspective, world and subject are linked by different and particular moves—which are carried out in the first person—of actualization, involvement, and implementation of their relation. Various are the activities that relate to the world: perception, memory, and imagination are linked to the way in which different phenomena manifest themselves—a thing, another individual, an emotion, a work of art, a physical law, a fantasy, a desire. The reality that is encountered in different profiles and in various possible styles of manifestation has therefore a generative structure open to intersubjective verification, and it brings into play a certain understanding of oneself, the world, and others. Experience is the presence of an individual to the world and the presence of the world to that same individual. It is not the production of mental states caused by the reception of external stimuli on the psychophysical setup. The world is a constant call to actions, a system of perspectives that attests closeness to the self and distance from other points of view. In the entanglement of subject and world, what is therefore fundamental is the "here" of the bodily experience in which subject and object, near and far, the I and the other are involved in moving exploration and expansion, as reciprocal obstacles, and commensuration. Starting from the "zero point" of orientation of the living body located in the surrounding space, the world and its objects manifest themselves as possibilities that extend individual freedom and the corresponding responsibility beyond the limits of the I—first of all, toward the existence of other individuals and toward nature. In other words, impersonal instances and processes bounce back on the subjective life and "conditions" of human life. That is, space and time, birth and mortality are experienced within a state of activity, of bodily movements, gestures, and words performing our presence in the world.[17]

The phenomenological picture we just outlined is not unified in any way, as it encloses contrasting insights. Its disruptive force comes from the fact that it suggests the possibility of an expansion of experience, of an opening to encounters and activities beyond the divide between subject and object and based on the "here" of the embodied self that perceives things and people and acquires knowledge through acquaintance with the world. The consequences for responsibility are crucial. Through the body, all individuals insert themselves in the world as a "zero point" of orientation, as a "personal element in an impersonal situation," without however delimiting an inviolable "thing" called the "I" or automatically immersing the individual in the intersubjective dimension.[18] Things and people are partners in a series of worldly movements and actualizations, from practical commitment to reflection to aesthetic sensibility. At this point, subjectivity and intersubjectivity are profoundly transformed. The individual must "act" the intersubjective dimension, actualizing it in the space of the world, within the plurality of one's own and others' perspectives, each of which puts into effect one's own interaction with oneself, the world, and others.

Following the phenomenological inspiration, responsibility becomes responsibility to be here, to be present, responsibility for intersubjective interaction as opposed to a body in the crowd but also as opposed to the ambitious isolation of the sovereign individual. The empathic act, for example, which acknowledges the presence in the world of other human beings who are different from the I, involves the responsibility of their recognition as beings who act, think, and move in the world from an autonomous perspective.[19] The transformation of phenomenology in an ethical and political sense offers a method for dealing with the historical-political experience, not reducing it to a biographical-existential element but rather interpreting and making it significant within the lived experience and the agent's multiple perspectives. The active relation with reality in its manifestations is already its preunderstanding, which is often emotionally loaded. Through the impact with historical events, the present shows itself as constituted by possibilities of experience that are never guaranteed, are always unfinished. Here is where an understanding, a rethinking, and a commitment whose characteristics are ethical and political begin.

Starting from the relational constitution of the I and of reality, history and politics enter the subjective experience in the form of a responsibility to be here, to speak, to act, to think while preserving the importance of the individual against the logic of the crowd.

Patočka carried out the implications of the phenomenological perspective radically and to the end, rendering its ethical-political sense explicit through an original language. Going back to the common origin of philosophy, politics, and history within the Greek *polis*, the Czech philosopher incorporated Arendt's intuition of the *vita activa* as the actualization, again and again, of the novelty introduced by every single human being into the incessant flow of becoming. He placed a particularly tragic emphasis on what, in his view, represents the fundamental element in the historical experience of the modern individual, namely, the cultivation of the difference between life understood as survival and life understood as opening to the world. The life lived "not in the mode of *acceptance*, but of *initiative and preparation*, ever seeking the opportunities for action, for the possibilities that present themselves; it means a life in active tension, of extreme risk and unceasing upward striving."[20] Such is, in other terms, the life of freedom.

Patočka deems decisive the transition from being spectators to becoming actors on the stage of history; that is, becoming beings who act and decide. In a statement that leaves no possibility for misunderstanding, the Czech philosopher claims that this means the responsibility to "seize those possibilities of relationship with oneself, in the middle and by means of things that must be somehow already open to us, as they can only be in a real situation, in the factual 'here' that is different for each of us and at any time [. . .]."[21]

The Responsibility to Be Here

The figure of the responsibility to be here, in which the present is not "an object, but [. . .] 'what is up for us to grasp,' "[22] discloses history as the responsibility of our freedom. Taking into account the breadth of articulations of Patočka's thought, I focus on the fact that this responsibility cannot be read only as a struggle between war and peace, death and life, strength and freedom in which the individuals sacrifice themselves and die. Patočka speaks indeed of "adversaries" in a Heraclitean *polemos*,[23] yet the phenomenological perspective mentioned above suggests that the stage of the clash between opposites derives its political and moral meaning from the presence of a single actual subject that contends with two forces. The adversaries have the aspect of the past and the future, that is, two equally destructive forces that, in the image taken from Kafka's 1920 text "He" and commented on by Hannah Arendt, represent the fury of the event threatening to crush the small and fragile body of an anonymous being.[24] In Patočka, in addition to the figure of the "two adversaries," we find expressions such as the "front," which recalls the *Kampflinie*, and the "fight with *no holds barred*" of Kafka's piece. The same applies to the theme of the night, which refers to Kafka's "darkest night."[25] Without neglecting the elements of his critical discussion with Arendt, which is staged by Patočka in his *Heretical Essays*,[26] the figure of the responsibility to be here indisputably means suffering and acting at the intersection of one's own singularity and power, violence, history, and politics. For Arendt, the "diagonal of thought," which originates from the meeting of the two divergent vectors of past and future in the "gap of the present" occupied by "He," corresponds to the endless exercise of "understanding what happens."[27] Kafka's image, however, allows us to go beyond Arendt's commentary. Exercising the ability to think is an ethical gesture because it is practiced by every individual whose background is the anonymity of bodies reduced to bare life and the consequent destruction of the criteria of moral and political action.

It is important to note that, in the heart of the contradiction, one may be crushed. Yet one may also trust the protective barriers of group membership, income, and complicity with power, and one may survive. It is also possible to have the courage to recognize that we are the target of forces that violently collide, and admit that they are aimed at every single individual and are part of the lived experience. The one who has this courage acknowledges being here, and, by his or her mere existence, he or she becomes therefore a force of contrast that occupies the gap between the individual and the processes that dominate him or her.

Central to the idea of history as responsibility is a defenseless, anonymous subject that does not coincide with the figure of the victim, of the specter that hovers, simplifies, sometimes even reduces the ethical and political tragedies of the twentieth century and of the new millennium to a macabre accounting of corpses and, eventually, of indemnities. The responsible subject's defenselessness and anonymity refer not only to the subject's risking death but also to its being in a situation where it is displaced with respect to profession, social role, skills, and knowledge. Patočka and Arendt were led to think of this figure of responsibility by extreme experiences. From them, we can draw inspiration to direct our gaze toward less exceptional, yet equally urgent situations.

Milena Jesenská writes: "These days I realized that in human life, politics is just as important as love. It penetrates under the skin, sticks to the body like a shirt that is too tight, and lurks in the heart like the most intimate feelings. [. . .] So long as completely apolitical individuals will not consider 'politics,' i.e., what occurs to us, at least as important for themselves as private events, the big crowd will let itself be taken away by the events with indifference, without taking into consideration that those will head their way into their apartments and take a place at their own table in front of the bowl that is filled at noon."[28]

Jesenská's intuition takes us directly to Karel Kosík, the Czech philosopher who released Jesenská from Kafka's shadow in a wonderful 1992 essay.[29] Kosík is the author of *Dialectics of the Concrete* (1960),[30] a seminal book for the ethical-political transformation of phenomenology, in which Marx, Husserl, and Heidegger are rethought in an innovative framework. Twenty years younger than Patočka, Kosík discussed intensely with him; he lived a buried life in Prague after 1968 and even after 1989, having forgone exile to be there, to stay in his homeland and teach his students. In a 1997 paper, the theme of "sacrifice" is taken up in multiple variations.[31] Kosík refers to the canonical examples of the sacrifice of Prometheus, Socrates, Abraham, Jesus, Jan Hus, and to some more recent ones: the sacrifice of Father Kolbe, who, in the summer of 1941, asked the German commander of the camp where he was a prisoner to take the place of another prisoner sentenced to execution; and the gesture of Marianne Fabianová, an employee of the Third Reich's railways who "offers" Kosík the possibility of sending news to his family when in captivity during the war. Last, Kosík remembers the sacrifice of Jan Palach, the young man who set himself on fire in Wenceslas Square in 1969 to protest against the Soviet invasion. These gestures occupy the wide and often ambiguous space of human existence tragically contended between suffering, lamentation, and misfortune on the one side and courage, pride, and resistance against evil on the other. In the three latter examples, the following movements need to be noted: Father Kolbe leaves the line of prisoners without foreseeing the outcome of his action and risking "practically everything";[32] with her "offer," Marianne Fabianová assumes "all the risk of her friendly gesture";[33] and the young Jan Palach shows "the courage of the leap, not the safety of fitting in," reversing the relation between the generations as the son reminds the fathers that they failed and did not do their duty.[34]

The terms "risk" and "leap" must be understood in the sense of an interruption, a break through which one's own presence in the world produces a structural difference—the difference of being able to decide. An interruption is not the same thing as "doing otherwise." Rather, an interruption introduces an element that cannot fit in the general scheme and therefore disrupts the apparently monolithic structure. This is the birth of a new practice, of an oblique movement (leaving the line, going in the opposite direction, but also doing nothing, standing still) that diverges from the direction of the macroprocesses.

Such gestures testify to the polysemic character of the word "sacrifice," which, in some languages, designates not only the victim but also the offerings. Working on the contradictory richness of "sacrifice," Kosík interprets it as putting in motion both sides of the contradiction that defines the human condition. The philosopher does not use euphemisms to describe the situation in the Eastern and Western blocks in the 1990s, when individuals were caught in a grotesque game between winners and losers, were held hostages by a power that flattered them with the promise of a dispensation from the "creative acknowledgement of what is happening in the present and of what the age requires."[35] The century of the Shoah and of totalitarianisms ends in the confusion of good and evil, mediocrity and banality, in the absence of limits and the replaceability of everything.

In this scenario, we find again Patočka's theme of the antithesis between "mere living" and openness to the possibility of realizing one's freedom. In the sacrifice that "does not bring profit, but generously gives everything," Kosík sees the reactivation of the "productive dispute over the meaning of life," the affirmation of its "non-obviousness."[36] In the stories of Abraham's sacrifice and of Jan Palach's death, which was "speechless, silent," which did not proclaim a political program, did not ask for penitence nor wanted to be an accusation but only intended to be an act of "remembering and begging," we witness the birth of conscience and of moral action.[37] At the same time, it is essential to note, a "moral element of the *polis*" is founded, namely: the community of free human beings, of those who, walking, talking, eating together, creatively reactivate the difference between daily life and festivities, between life and death, between the eternal and time.[38]

This brief outline cannot exhaust the complexity of a model of moral and political responsibility that implies a concrete rewriting of the forms of human action and suggests the possibility of changing the rules of the relation between the individual and the historical events. The limit, the interruption, the deviation that is produced by the intersection of a single life and the global processes replaces the sheer disproportion that is at work between the smallness of the individual and a limitless globalization, the infinity without boundaries of the web, of the speed of flows. Instead of the clash between two absolutes—individualism versus global powers—what occurs is a movement within reality that opens it to other possibilities. Through the distinction of its different levels, which the great mechanisms force into a gigantic *reductio ad unum* [reduction to one], reality regains its richness and stratification. This means the possibility of talking about victims who do not allow themselves to be degraded through pure passivity, who refuse the counting of corpses, of hungry people, of unemployed workers, and of the defeated, thereby escaping the logic of suffering and humiliation but also that of saints and heroes, and acting as a force of contrast, leaving out the totalization of both evil and good.

There are many ways to reshuffle the cards, to rotate on its axis the plane of the reality of power, its language, its opacity, and the anaesthetics that make reality unrecognizable, and to open it onto a further plane where the space for other values and behaviors may emerge.

Notes

1. For the expression "here in our own time," see Jeanne Hersch, *Eclairer l'obscur: entretiens avec Gabrielle et Alfred Dufour* (Paris: L'Age d'Homme, 1986), 89.

2. Laura Boella, *Neuroetica. La morale prima della morale* (Milan: Cortina, 2008), 79–86; "Natura e morale," in *Neuroetica*, ed. Andrea Lavazza and Giuseppe Sartori (Bologna: Il Mulino, 2011), 85–107.

3. Daniel M. Wegner, *The Illusion of Conscious Will* (Cambridge, MA: MIT Press, 2018).

4. Daniel A. Dennett, *Freedom Evolves* (London: Penguin Books, 2004); Robert M. Sapolsky, *Behave: The Biology of Humans and Our Best and Worst* (New York: Penguin Press, 2017).

5. Emmanuel Levinas, *Autrement qu'être ou au-delà de l'essence* (La Haye: Martinus Nijhoff, 1974), 12.

6. Judith Butler, *Giving an Account of Oneself* (New York: Fordham University Press, 2005), 90.

7. Emmanuel Levinas, *Difficile liberté* (Paris: Albin Michel, 1986).

8. Laura Boella, *Empatie. L'esperienza empatica nella società del conflitto* (Milan: Cortina, 2018).

9. Paul Ricœur, "Le concept de responsabilité. Essai d'analyse sémantique," *Esprit* (1994): 28–48.

10. Ingeborg Bachmann, "Das schreibende Ich," in *Frankfurter Vorlesungen. Probleme zeitgenössischer Dichtung* (Munich: Piper Verlag, 1980), 54: "*es sich nicht mehr in der Geschichte aufhält; sonder dass sich neuerdings der Geschichte im Ich aufhält.*"

11. Christa Wolf, *Kindheitsmuster* (Berlin und Weimar: Aufbau Verlag, 1976), 52; English translation, *A Modern Childhood* (London: Virago Press, 1982).

12. See E. Bloch, *Erbschaft dieser Zeit*, in *Gesamtausgabe*, Bd. 4 (Frankfurt a.M.: Suhrkamp, 1977), 104–25.

13. Jacques Derrida, *Donner la mort* (Paris: Galilée, 1999), 85.

14. Jan Patočka, *Saggi eretici sulla filosofia della storia*, trans. Davide Stimilli (Turin: Einaudi, 2008), 56. English translation, *Heretical Essays in the Philosophy of History* (Chicago: Open Court, 1996).

15. Patočka, *Saggi eretici*, 138–47.

16. For a first historical reconstruction, see Mike Gubser, *The Far Reaches: Phenomenology, Ethics, and Social Renewal in Central Europe* (Stanford, CA: Stanford University Press, 2014).

17. See Edith Stein, *Zum Problem der Einfühlung*, ESGA 5 (Wien-Leipzig: Herder Verlag, 2010); Maurice Merleau-Ponty, *Phénoménologie de la perception* (Paris: Gallimard, 1976); Hannah Arendt, *The Human Condition* (Chicago: University of Chicago Press, 1998). See also Laura Boella, "Hannah Arendt fenomenologa," *aut-aut* 239–40 (1990): 83–110; Sophie Loidolt, *Phenomenology of Plurality: Hannah Arendt on Political Intersubjectivity* (New York: Routledge, 2018).

18. Jan Patočka, *Body, Community, Language, Word* (Chicago: Open Court, 1998), 5, 27, cit. in Gubser, *The Far Reaches*, 158.

19. Boella, *Empatie*, 109–18.

20. Patočka, *Saggi eretici*, 43.

21. Patočka, *Saggi eretici*, 54.

22. Patočka, *Saggi eretici*, 55.

23. Patočka, *Saggi eretici*, 49–50.

24. Franz Kafka, *Confessioni e diari*, trans. Ervino Pocar (Milan: Mondadori, 1972), 811–12. For a longer commentary of this text, see Laura Boella, *Il coraggio dell'etica. Per una nuova immaginazione morale* (Milan: Cortina, 2012), 110–17.

25. Patočka, *Saggi eretici*, 142.

26. See Laura Boella, "Ripensare la condizione umana," *Studium* 114, no. 6 (2018): 20–38.

27. Hannah Arendt, *La vita della mente*, trans. Giorgio Zanetti (Bologna: Il Mulino, 1987), 296–305.

28. Milena Jesenská, "Adieu, Jules Romain!" *Přítomnost*, 1 Februar 1939, in «*Alles ist Leben*». *Feuilletons und Reportagen 1919–1939*, trans. Dorothea Rein (Frankfurt a.M.: Verlag Neue Kritik, 1984), 200–1.

29. Karel Kosík, "Il secolo di Grete Samsa," trans. Jitka Křesálková, in *Un filosofo in tempi di farsa e di tragedia. Saggi di pensiero critico 1964–2000*, ed. Gabriella Fusi and Francesco Tava (Milan: Mimesis, 2013), 201–11. See Laura Boella, "Milena Jesenská," in *Le imperdonabili. Milena Jesenská, Etty Hillesum, Marina Cvetaeva, Ingeborg Bachmann, Cristina Campo* (Milan: Mimesis, 2013), 37–67.

30. Karel Kosík, *Dialettica del concreto. Studio sulla problematica dell'uomo e del mondo*, trans. Gianlorenzo Pacini (Milan: Mimesis, 2014).

31. Karel Kosík, "Il ragazzo e la morte," trans. Francesco Tava, in *Un filosofo in tempi di farsa e di tragedia.*

32. Kosík, "Il ragazzo e la morte," 146.

33. Kosík, "Il ragazzo e la morte," 132.

34. Kosík, "Il ragazzo e la morte," 148, 150.

35. Kosík, "Il ragazzo e la morte," 143.

36. Kosík, "Il ragazzo e la morte," 15, 150.

37. Kosík, "Il ragazzo e la morte," 150–51, 153.

38. Kosík, "Il ragazzo e la morte," 161.

Eight

Emotional Subjects

For the Care of the Future

Elena Pulcini

A Philosophy for the World

The global challenges threatening the future of the living world (such as the ecological crisis, forced migrations, and new poverties) impose a radical *restyling* on philosophy if it wants to avert the risk of being reduced to a wordless philosophy, a philosophy *without a world*, as seems to be prevalent on the international stage today. What we must hope for is a *living thought* in direct contact with the world.[1] This is a thought that knows how to deal critically with events, face the challenges of reality, and recognize the priorities and urgencies of the present times to be able to imagine alternative scenarios.

The task is not easy. It requires that we understand why, at these times, the *human condition* is once again displaying not only some of the usual aspects of evil but also an unprecedented version of it, which cannot be traced back to any of the traditional ontological images: namely, the risk of self-destruction. Paradoxically, humankind seems exposed to a "loss of the world"[2] that goes far beyond its existential meaning to become a concrete and planetary threat imposing a mortgage upon the future of the entire living world. We must therefore refine the tools to interpret the absolute radicalism of the "new" that still catches us unprepared, despite the looming, ever more visible, and frequent signals of an epochal change. "Here, everything is new." Hans Jonas had already sensed this in the second half of the twentieth century,[3] ushering in what I would call a philosophy *for the world*.

To manage to attain this understanding, a critical thought is evidently required. As things stand, however, critical thought does not seem to be enjoying good health, relegated as it is to the sidelines by the bloodless and abstract hegemonic philosophy. To say it with Foucault and his proposal of an "ontology of actuality," what we need to ask ourselves is which "events . . . lead us to constitute ourselves and to recognize ourselves as subjects of what we are doing, thinking, saying."[4] This question must be reinforced with the pathos inherent in Adorno's bewilderment when he tried to "understand why humanity, instead of entering a truly human state, is sinking into a new kind of barbarism."[5] This question can be asked, however, only if we allow the reawakening of that generative passion to which Descartes, after Socrates and Aristotle, assigned a supreme position, inaugurating the transition to modernity. That passion is curiosity. Curiosity or, rather, wonder is indeed what can move us today not only to break the tyranny of the obvious, imposed by the mere fact of enjoying a universal *audience* and *mimesis*, but also to be scandalized by what is subtly accepted as normal and inevitable.

Critical thought means cutting through the narcotic fog of the mentality of the *così fan (pensan) tutti* [that is what they all do (think)] to regain not only the freedom to disagree, perhaps with the inexorable tenacity of Melville's Bartleby and his "I would rather not,"[6] but also the freedom to discover that *there is something else*, that there could be something else—that is to say, traces of removed, or even unexplored ideas, images, and paths—behind the axiomatic violence of *TINA—There Is No Alternative*. It means to recuperate the freedom to be willing not only to be amazed by unexpected findings that could come to light in a meticulous archaeological excavation, but also to recognize the unexpected budding of new images of the world, which are hidden in the shapeless crevices of the realm of possibility, like the finished statue that already exists in Michelangelo's sketches.

We need an "occasional philosophy," as Günther Anders called it,[7] which leads us to select events, to choose, in the deafening crowd of media information and social chat, those that actually and symbolically mark our contemporaneity and hence reveal, crucially in my opinion, not only the pathologies[8] but also the chances, not only the regressions but also the promises. Indeed, philosophy cannot be satisfied with the nonetheless essential results of critical thinking. It cannot stop at the diagnosis of *evil*. It must also dare to go into the *good*, think of it, name it, and love it, on the one hand, challenging its much acclaimed indefinability and, on the other, avoiding its rhetoric. Despite its presumed outdatedness for the sophisticated paradigms of a normativism too preoccupied with respecting pluralisms and formal procedures, today the concept of the good is more than ever clamoring to return to the scene. It will certainly not—let it be clear—play the role of an essentialist and universally shared perspective. Rather, it will work as an ideal tension that asks us to have the courage to establish priorities, to formulate radical questions. These questions appear ever more legitimate in the face of the holistic twist produced by the global age and its challenges, and increasingly unavoidable if we really want to, or even have to, "change our lives," as Sloterdijk suggests. We could define these questions as real questions of meaning: Do we still want to preserve the world in which we live? What aspects of the human do we want to save and enhance? Do we consider life on earth a value? A critical thought that does not make these questions explicit and instead entrenches itself, as for example in some aspects of the otherwise illuminating biopolitics, in the altogether reassuring boundaries of realism risks failing to grasp fully the novelty of the global age and its challenges. We must therefore venture into what I would like to call a *thought of metamorphosis*. This is a way of thinking that knows how to draw emancipatory perspectives and a culture of responsibility from the awareness of the catastrophe weighing upon the world[9] and is able to complete criticism with a utopian-normative proposal, provided that it is renewed and faithful to the spirit of the time.

The task is that of rehabilitating the utopia that, in times of adaptation to the world like ours,[10] seems set to be buried in the attic of useless and cumbersome tools or, at most, condemned without appeal by a skepticism that is all the more shared as it is justified by the failures of the great utopian projects of the twentieth century.[11] Once freed from the ideological ballast, utopia can once again become what it was at the dawn of modernity. That is to say, it can return to being the courageous trust in a possible horizon where to overcome the deficiencies and pathologies of the present while at the same time exploiting the potential of the current times (as in Bacon's *New Atlantis*). This potential is immanent in our time and in the subjects that inhabit it. It is perhaps nestled in the dark areas of what is repressed, and is waiting to be brought to light by a gaze that is not afraid of emancipating itself from the present and transforming it by looking at the future. We must try to find out *what we can count on*, which more or less visible realities, parallel to or slotted into the existent, we can work on so that we can hope for different and better *images of the world*.[12]

This undoubtedly means starting from the *negative*, from everything that generates suffering, humiliation, and unhappiness. It also implies taking advantage of the contradictoriness of the negative and its illegitimacy, as recently reproposed in a refined Marxist perspective,[13] and as had already been suggested by the interesting paradigm of negative justice.[14] But it also means identifying and enhancing the positive aspects that reality offers us, despite everything, in the direction of a richer and broader vision of life, freed from the miserable goals imposed by pure self-preservation and utilitarianism, by unlimited individualism and the "sad passions,"[15] and returned to its "flourishing."[16] We can grasp this vision through empathic relations and solidarity actions, care of the environment and virtuous projectuality, gratuitousness and disinterested action, as is stressed by the underground or dissonant paths of modernity (from moral sentimentalism to the ethics of care, from the paradigm of the gift to many voices of feminism). But I come back to all of this later.

Utopia must feed on what I have called a *heretical normativism*[17] that can indicate to us, on the basis of criticism, which possible resources, which potential sources of the good are available, *hic et nunc*, here and now, be they individual or collective. To recover utopia is not to cradle oneself in the insipid dream of the perfect and ideal city. Rather, it means not to renounce imagining "Neverland," to regain confidence in the future and the ability to reimagine the future while still counting, despite everything, on the fact that, as Adam Smith claimed, our basic drive is the "desire to improve our condition."[18] Reactivating the imagination, escaping from the tyrannical opacity of a present orphaned of the depth of time means recovering the projectuality that, although inscribed in the DNA of modernity since its origins, has been lost in the quicksand of a "liquid"[19] and inconclusive postmodernity. Currently, this projectuality cannot, however, be limited to Hobbesian foresight, when the future was still given despite the scarcity of its resources. Rather, it must supply itself with a surplus of creativity and the unyielding courage of a decision without guarantees, in the face of the mortgage that is weighing upon the world.

Which Subject?

At this point, the question seems inevitable: Which subject can be up to this task? Are there figures of subjectivity, today, that can meet the challenges of our time?

The answer is far from easy because the subject has always been, for better or for worse, the undisputed protagonist of modernity and its self-legitimization. In fact, that of the subject is a long or, rather, interminable and complex parable. From the beginning, the subject has shared the constitutive ambivalence of modernity, its conquests and pathologies, its triumphal successes and recurring declines. Yet we refuse to acknowledge this ambivalence because of our enlightened pride and our crude and superficial trust in progress, still basking in the fake idea of humanity's "magnificent and progressive fate" toward which Italian poet Giacomo Leopardi directed his solitary, melancholic sarcasm. Were we aware of this though, then, within the cyclical alternation of successes and regressions that characterizes modernity, we could better understand and follow the adventures and misadventures of the subject, propose *less naive* diagnoses of the now tired idea of the death or end of the subject, and open the shrine of the realm of *possibility*.

If we want to delve into the maze of images created in different times to define this phoenix, we must equip ourselves with one of the few compasses we have available, that is, the compass that can guide us through the passage from the modern (from a sovereign, rational, Promethean, patriarchal, atomistic subject) to the postmodern (to a fragmented, multiple, nomadic, expressive, narcissistic subject).[20] While it is perhaps a bit coarse, this compass is undoubtedly useful for tracing at least some boundary lines on a jagged and sometimes fuzzy map; provided, however, that we manage not to fall into the trap of opposing sides in favor of one or the other. What I would in fact unhesitatingly like to argue is that ambivalence pertains to *both* figures, as each of them has positive and negative aspects.

If, on the one hand, the very idea of the subject (and the individual) is the flagship of modernity, its Rosetta Stone, as it represents the proud conquest of the values with which we can decipher it—autonomy, freedom, and rationality—on the other hand, its unilaterality and pathologies emerge right from the start.[21] One can just think of the three forms that have marked its path at least until the first half of the 1900s, which all share a sort of perverse alliance between selfish-acquisitive passions and instrumental reason. First, on the epistemological level, we have a strong and unitary *sovereign subject*, as Descartes conceptualized it, *maître de soi* [master of itself], firmly anchored in consciousness, and guided by reassuring dualisms. This subject, however, hides the dark face of its domination over devalued polarities (the body, passions, the feminine), as women's critical thinking has wisely revealed to us. Second, on the anthropological level, we have the *homo oeconomicus*, who places his egoism and calculating rationality at the service of growth and progress and who however is ready, in return, for that sacrificial asceticism of which the Weberian Franklin represents the most eloquent image;[22] he is a methodical Prometheus, disciplined and capable of renouncing any enjoyment in the present for the sake of the future, destined to end up behind the bars of the "steel cage" of an increasingly rapacious and unlimited capitalism that decrees his alienation. Third and finally, on the level of praxis, we have the *homo faber*, who uses and transforms nature and the environment to build a useful and lasting world but who soon turns, thanks to the vertiginous developments of technology, into a potential, and actual, destroyer of nature, as Arendt says,[23] or even perverts himself into the *homo creator*, as Günther Anders calls it,[24] alluding to a subject possessed by *hybris*, who has lost the meaning and purpose of action, exposing the world, and itself, to unprecedented pathologies and fatal drifts.

It does not seem difficult, then, to share the spirit of postmodern thought, which, starting from the second half of the twentieth century, took leave from the ultimate values and the tyranny of the universal;[25] and which—on the wave of a world crossed by the delusions of bourgeois society, the contradictions of capitalism, and the new challenges that struck a blow to modern rationalist optimism—indeed invited us to open the cage, free the emotions, and enjoy the present. This postmodern spirit is already present in the restless tones of early twentieth-century thought, from Nietzsche's nihilism to the shattering of codes and certainties represented by the enigmatic characters of Joyce, Musil, and Pirandello, returning, with trustingly antagonistic overtones, in Marcuse's critique of the Promethean Self and his *plaidoyer* in favor of a narcissistic Self.[26] In its passivity, anchorage to the present, and hedonism, this is a Self that contrasts with Prometheus, the "culture-hero of toil, productivity, and progress" moved solely by the instrumental perspective of acquisition and profit. Narcissus becomes the image of the Great Refusal of a world that demands self-sacrifice. He opposes it with a "comprehensive existential order" in which it is possible to free what has been sacrificed, that is to say, imagination, pleasure, the feeling of a deep alliance with nature, and the fullness of an existence no longer subject to the blackmail of unlimited appropriation and the capitalist "performance principle."

Thus, together with an epochal shift from the solid world of our fathers to the "liquid" world in which we are still immersed,[27] a figure takes shape that seems to blast the rocky and granitic substance of the modern subject, to recognize decentralization and fragmentation as a fresh promise of liberation. Fragmented or multiple like in Andy Warhol's paintings, nomadic or fluid, hybrid or patchwork:[28] the linguistic creativity with which the postmodern subject is defined evidently reflects the euphoric density of this shift. It so happens that, even in the dizzying feeling of bewilderment that does not always lead to clear and convincing results, the postmodern wave takes leave from the disciplinary and Promethean paradigm, from the strong, rational and unitary, gloomy image and identity, open to sacrifice and waiting for the future fruits of the tree of plenty [*albero della cuccagna*]. And it opposes it with the inebriation of the Dionysian, of a prismatic figure, open to difference, proud of its unlimited expressive and creative potential, stubbornly determined to reclaim the right to the present and its promises of instant lightness.

And yet, into this rosy identikit creep specular shadows, which soon become consolidated as real pathologies of the postmodern subject.[29]

The *consumerist* transformation of mass society feeds and multiplies selfish hedonism, accentuating the self-affirming anxiety that is not only intolerant of any ethical and social bond but also finds no fulfillment except in the unlimited multiplication of desires. Induced by the infinite availability of goods, fluctuating and objectless desires are increasingly freed from real needs to pursue the conformist and standardizing logic of mimetic desire.[30] As Christopher Lasch had already noted in the 1970s,[31] consumer society builds false needs through the unprejudiced complicity of the media, producing a process of spectacularization of the real that even surpasses the gloomy predictions of Guy Debord, who nevertheless was still confident in the existence of a content behind the mask.[32] This process reduces individuals to being passive users of persuasive and seductive representations, separated from real needs and goals. In losing touch with its inner being, with its own deeper contents, the Self loses its center and becomes not only "other-directed,"[33] that is, exposed to the tyranny of mimetic compulsion exerted by the image of the other, but also *superficial* in the disturbing sense of identification with the surface, with what is seen, with appearance, flat and homologating. The Self becomes "the man without unconscious,"[34] endowed with the chameleon-like ability of Woody Allen's Zelig, who, lacking the deep core of a Self, is able to adapt to different roles or masks without identifying with anyone. Like Goffman's "hanger," this Self is careful to execute the most appropriate performance each time, to present itself to the others, persuading them and studying their expectations.[35]

This fragile and insecure Self, who only exists by being mirrored in the gaze of the other, from whom it awaits confirmation and recognition, is at the same time omnipotent and "grandiose"[36] and is as intolerant of any limit as it is inclined to underestimate reality and its obstacles. Like Narcissus as immortalized in Ovid's *Metamorphoses*, who pays the blunder that makes him fall in love with his own image with his death, the postmodern Self is animated by an entropic *self-love* that makes it incapable of distinguishing between itself and the other. This condemns the subject to a lethal and unlimited solitude not because, like the Marcusian Narcissus, it rejects an oppressive and eros-free world, but rather because an impenetrable opacity and a profound indifference separate it from the world *tout court*.[37] Indeed, this subject no longer suffers from that modern alienation that nonetheless presupposes the unity of the subject. Instead, it suffers from a sort of euphoric "schizophrenia"[38] that pushes it to adapt to the fragmentation and multiplicity strongly demanded by the new social codes and by a flexible capitalism that does not know what to do with integrity, stability, and durability.[39]

Now, this transition from the modern to the postmodern—which, it should be emphasized, in no way means the replacement of one paradigm with another—still took place in the name of a climate of diffused lightness and liberating relief in which the subject, despite running into that unprecedented post-Freudian emotion that is anxiety,[40] perceives more gains than costs, more gratifications than losses.

Quite different instead is the atmosphere that is established in the following phase, the one that, starting from the last decade of the twentieth century, leads to the global age, whose coordinates we still struggle to define also because we are ensnared in its dense opacity and complexity. Indeed, there is no doubt that the global age has produced a radicalization of the characteristics of the postmodern subject, making it free to fluctuate at will in the liquid substance of an (at least apparently) borderless world. Today, says Bauman, identity becomes a game freely chosen by "a man without essence,"[41] who is well suited to the reticular society as he privileges transitory and contingent bonds. A "tourist" in a world that does not concern it, except as a shining promise of commitment-free experiences and futile pleasures, as an expert "collector of sensations,"[42] the "modular self" anxiously chases object-less desires, casually adopting or abandoning situations and things that can excite it. Commonly baptized as disposable, this logic even dominates as sovereign in the sphere of relations, where the narcissism of the global Self takes up ever more instrumental and manipulative modalities toward the other, who is desired (or rejected) for his or her usefulness, power, and prestige.

However, as I mentioned earlier, much more obscure shadows are gathering on the irritating futility of this image, marking the distance between the postmodern and the global Self, the latter being enveloped in the amniotic fluid of a pervasive insecurity that corrodes the fabric of its day-to-day existence. Global risks cause the erosion of the feeling of immunity that individuals of early modernity still enjoyed in their reliance on state protection[43] and provoke the perception of being exposed to challenges that escape our capacity for decision and control. The result is a self-defensive closure that, in the face of the disappearance of objectively immunitary defenses, pushes the Self to erect, mostly unconsciously, areas of *inner immunity* that are all the more tenacious the more they are illusory, and to oppose the obscure perception of its own impotence with the double, now schizophrenic, face of the Janus of the "sad passions." That is, on the one hand, there are walls of individual apathy and indifference and, on the other, there are unexpected revivals of resentment and collective violence.

It seems, then, that the current figure of subjectivity is not up to the challenges of the present. Beyond its transformations—from a sacrificial vision of the future to the absence of the future, from productivism to hedonism, from limitlessness to insecurity, from indifference to violence—there is evidently a leitmotif that recurs in the different configurations of the subject and, in particular, in its pathological torsions, starting from its modern genesis. This leitmotif is its inexorable *self-referentiality*. Today, this quality can no longer be tolerated not only because it is ethically lacking or spiritually limited, but also because it appears doubly inadequate and dangerous. On the one hand, it is responsible for the destructive drifts that threaten the living world, and, on the other, it is incapable of finding the resources and the answers to keep them in check.

A Subject in Relation: With Whom, Though?

We must therefore think and hope for a real *metamorphosis* of the subject. This metamorphosis would be a process that takes seriously the valuable intuition of twentieth-century philosophy concerning the human being as incomplete and therefore always potentially open to a "new beginning."[44] This would be a metamorphosis in Elias Canetti's sense, that is, a metamorphosis that not only is limited to the physiological and involuntary transformation that always affects our lives, but also becomes a conscious change, capable of actively exploiting incompleteness as an opportunity and a *chance*—a chance to renew ourselves.[45]

Actually, we already have a figure that responds to this now unavoidable need. It is a figure that emerged some time ago from partly hidden traditions alternative to the hegemonic paradigm of modernity, whose unlimited atomism and egoism, acquisitive *hybris* and immunitary logic, patriarchal vocation for domination and narcissistic twist they denounce. From the ethics of sympathy to phenomenology, from the theory of the gift to some voices of feminism, from relational sociology to the paradigm of recognition, the image of a *subject in relation*, in its multiple variants, is taking on more and more consistency. This is the very promising image of a connected, bonded Self, aware of the ontologically constitutive link with the other, destined to fill the *black hole* of the modern individualistic subject. Nevertheless, this image only reveals all its fruitfulness if we inflect it on the basis of the questions: In relation to whom? And based on what? Only if we let ourselves be guided by an intelligent compass that knows how to point us in the right direction do we discover that, despite the diversity of the multiple perspectives that today combine to form a rather tangled skein, there is, however, an answer that all of them have in common. This shared answer is that the subject in relation is the one that opens up to the other, exposing its vulnerability, leaving open the *vulnus*, the constitutive wound of the human condition that has been removed from the modern fiction of the sovereign subject.[46] It is a subject dismissed from its claims of sovereignty, expropriated from its own foundations. It is a subject that is constituted as such, according to Levinas' radical lexicon, only starting from the ethical rupture of the absoluteness of its identity and *hybris*.[47]

Far from decreeing the "death of the subject" *tout court*, the subject in relation rather requires the death of a Self-without-*Autrui*, toward which it invokes what Judith Butler, in her loving imaginary dialogue with Levinas, calls a "necessary grief."[48] We must let the perverse fantasy of a self-referential Self die to allow that "intrusion" of the other that inaugurates the subject at the very moment in which the other violates it.[49] Vulnerability is a primary, original condition, with the very sign of the *human* engraved on it. It is therefore something we cannot avoid, something that "one cannot will away without ceasing to be human,"[50] whose origins it would be vain to seek because it precedes the subject's very formation. As Butler writes, "that we are impinged upon primarily and against our will is the sign of a vulnerability and a beholdenness that we cannot will away."[51] It is the trace not only of our insufficiency, but of the existence of the other whom we carry within us and who, so to speak, does not cease to challenge us from within,[52] allowing the chrysalis of the Self to open up and give birth to the butterfly, so as to complete its life cycle.

It is therefore evident: vulnerability is, can be, a *resource* as long as we grasp and know how to exploit its fruitful relational potential. This goal, which is anything but automatic, however requires the clear awareness of our condition, the ability to remove it from a secular process of repression caused by a dangerously Faustian modernity or by a postmodernity gratified by the unlimited fluidity and abundance of things. For vulnerability to resurface to consciousness, it therefore must become *experience*: the experience of failure, loss, suffering, or simply of one's own fragility and precariousness.[53] These experiences evidently are far from being new because they are inscribed in humankind's very DNA. Confronted with challenges that evoke the specter of our powerlessness, the global age can prevent their repression by opening the Pandora's box of the pathologies of modernity. And it can also transform such challenges into shared experiences at the global level, promoting the whole of humankind as a new subject of collective action and transforming vulnerability into an opportunity for community and mutual interdependence. "But where danger is, grows the saving power also": today, Hölderlin's words, evoked by Heidegger,[54] seem to take on a prophetic flavor. Whereas it is true that we are threatened by the risk, produced by ourselves, of the destruction of the living world, it is also true that there lurks the chance to bring to light that ontological bond, betrayed by history and society, that consecrates us as subjects in relation, bound to each other by one destiny. This destiny, let it be clear, is now devoid of any residue of fatality because it is predominantly in our hands.

At this point, a question imposes itself, identical and specular to the one posed above regarding the subject: Who is *the other* today? This question becomes inevitable and urgent from the moment we realize that the process of globalization produces an *extension* of the very idea of the other, rendering *significant* to us hitherto unknown, indifferent, and remote figures, to which it is difficult to even give a name.[55] These figures become the additional, provocative occasion for our metamorphosis. There is indeed *the other* who is *distant in space*, that is, the one who is different, the migrant who, previously separated by a border, suddenly crosses the threshold of our country, territory, or *oikòs* asking for justice, compassion, and hospitality and contesting the legitimacy of our privileges. And there is the other who is *distant in time*, who directs a mute appeal to us from the future,[56] asking us to pay attention to those who will follow us and who will inherit the world as we have left it. Attention is to be paid not only to our children and grandchildren, but also to future generations to whom we are not bound by affections or interests but by the awareness that the damage caused by our unlimited power places us in a position of *debt* toward them. This debt, it is important to point out, loses any negative meaning to assume instead the connotation of a "positive mutual debt"[57] and requires, here and now, an unconditional responsibility. Last but not least, there is one further figure of alterity that quite rightfully enters our "circle of concern":[58] namely, *nature*, or what we can still define as such. This is so not only because of the ontological debt we have always had toward it, but because our anthropocentric *hybris* has plundered its resources and upset its balance, endangering the life of the planet of which, in a striking paradox, we ourselves are part. This paradox should make us ask questions and shake us much more than it does. If it is true that our destiny is inextricably bound to that of the planet, this means that "we are all in the same boat," as Marina Abramovic recently reminded us with her flag waving over the sea of Trieste, revealing the renewed and provocative truth of a worn-out cliché. Being all in the same boat means, objectively, being *beyond the very idea of otherness*, whether this is understood as the negative polarity of a conflicting relationship (the subject versus the other) or, on the contrary, as the object of a rhetorical altruism (the subject for the other). Even, or perhaps especially, in its threatening realities, that is to say, in the planetary risks to which it exposes us, the global age gives us the chance to recognize ourselves as being in a condition of ontological sociality, in the "*être avec* [being-with]"[59] that has constituted us right from the start despite the fact that we have sacrificed ourselves to the idols of modern individualism.

Yet we seem unable to grasp the chance *subjectively*. Frightened by the danger of contamination with that which is different, we are entrenched in the immunitary citadels of a muscular and violent "We." Jealous of our privileges, we take refuge in the indifference toward a future from whose dark destiny we proclaim ourselves acquitted by making claims of powerlessness. Between violence and indifference, between excess and absence of pathos, the global Self is increasingly losing contact with the emotional sources that inspire its choices, motivations, and decisions; instead, it identifies with a purely egoic surface, detached from the deep regions of interiority and the unconscious. The reduction of the other to the residual and exclusive reality of an enemy or phantom therefore coincides—confirming the paradox that, unbeknown to us, swallows us up—with blindness to ourselves, as marked by that Promethean split between doing and imagining, knowing and feeling that worried Günther Anders so much.

The Emotional Relationship and the Metamorphosis of the Self

Being a *subject in relation* also means being in relation *to oneself*, in contact with one's own passions, which are the foremost and eloquent expressions of our *vulnerability*[60] and the essential sources of *motivations* for our action. To get back in touch with one's own passions is not only to recover that capacity to feel that has been lost in the schizophrenic drifts of the Promethean *hybris* of the modern subject and in the narcissistic apathy of the postmodern subject. It also means to return to understanding the reasons and meaning of what we do and think. This undoubtedly implies that some prejudices that nevertheless still persist in Western thought and common sense need to be overcome. Perhaps, thanks to progress in psychology, neuroscience, and psychoanalysis, no one any longer believes that passions are pure irrational forces, producing chaos and excess, undermining will and reason. Thus, the doors seem to have been opened for the idea of the cognitive function of passions as meaningful constructs through which we learn, communicate, and shape our relation with the world. Yet this does not translate *tout court* into the unanimous conviction that it is possible to *understand* passions, illuminate their dynamics and goals, and grasp their innermost meaning. Fearing that this understanding may remove from our emotional life that aura of elusiveness and mystery with which we try childishly to compensate for our unbending rationalism, we are still reluctant to accept the invitation extended by Spinoza—and subsequently by Rousseau and Freud—to embark on a path to understand our emotional life.[61]

And yet there is no transformation without awareness, and there is no awareness unless we rebind our diurnal world with the dark regions of the *Es* from which the search for meaning imperiously begins. An emotional subject is, therefore, one capable of *feeling*, thus already marking a victory over the pathologically affective illiteracy of our time; but it is also a subject capable of self-understanding and, like the sympathetic Smithian spectator, of positioning itself as an impartial observer of its own feelings and ensuing actions.[62] It is thus a subject capable of a reflective dynamic. This does not remove the possibility of abandoning oneself to the "normal chaos" of emotions;[63] nevertheless, it allows the Self, when it wants not only to be a witness of itself but also to change its own life, to engage in a *paideia* of its own affective life.

Understanding the passions is a prelude to the possibility of *educating*[64] and cultivating them.[65] And so we have to leave behind perfunctory and obsolete indistinctions and distinguish instead between positive passions that promote the flourishing of the Self and negative passions that lead to destructive and regressive results. Cultivating the passions is, in turn, what foreshadows the possibility of *transforming* ourselves.

This process of Platonic "conversion" (*periagoge*) cannot however take place in the self-sufficient solitude of a sovereign subject and *maître de soi*, as Sloterdijk proposes in his invitation to listen, as Rilke did at the Louvre Museum, to the voice authoritatively whispering that "you must change your life." Perhaps we are still able to respond to an imperative that springs from the inner depths of the Self as dictated by the urgent need to get out of the darkest *cave* of all times. Yet it is illusory to think that this can be the work of an ascetic subject that, in its self-sufficient solitude, can break its passivity and disassociate itself from the inertia of now suicidal habits in order to rise acrobatically toward the salvific regions of an *acropolis* where it achieves its *autopoiesis*. It is illusory to think so because this subject, strong and alone, simply does not exist except in the sublime fantasies of a virile metaphysics that, although irreducible to the mainstream figure of the "upright" or "vertical" subject,[66] nevertheless returns to invoke the myth of the solitary hero. This is an untarnished myth that, undoubtedly, we like more than the lifeless image of a utilitarian and rational Self. We especially like it when, as in our times, the hero takes on the murky and misty shades of the fascinating "true detective," like the one created by Nic Pizzolatto, who, mindful of his own demons, struggles with disenchantment, corruption, and disorder of the world.

And yet we cannot celebrate it because it remains inscribed in a path *without otherness*. The transformation can in fact only take place through an emotional dynamic with the other or, rather, with the multiple figures of the other we come across in our lives, starting from that first amazement or *wonder* before our mother's face, which inaugurates our entry into the world and, after the trauma of birth, reestablishes the relationship with otherness. It is a constitutive and original relationship: not only because we are not born alone as we do not suddenly sprout, as Hobbes would have it, like mushrooms from the earth but from a mother who has desired and imagined us;[67] but also because birth is only the beginning of an interminable body-to-body relationship with the other through which we test each other in the confrontation-clash of emotions.

The emotional subject is a *self-transcending* subject, thus adhering, as Simmel teaches us, to the very essence of life.[68] This is not, however, in the sense of intentionally embarking on an ascetic path but rather in the sense of letting otherness come in, allowing its "intrusion."[69] Alterity can take on infinite faces and asks us to make the effort to recognize it—as it happens today with the other distant in space and the other distant in time—if we do not want to risk the apathetic or violent atrophy of a Self that votes itself and the world to death as it refuses to be contaminated with anything that is outside itself.

To be or, rather, to remain within the dynamics of the passions is to accept the challenge that comes from the other, letting ourselves be displaced from our sovereign position through the disturbing power of love and hate, envy and gratitude, shame and emulation, fear and compassion. This means welcoming the Freudian *unheimlich* [uncanny] and inhabiting the anxiety felt while awaiting the other's response. From this answer, the Self learns its own limits and strengths, failures and conquests, disappointments and hopes. "To be another, another, another," Canetti hypothesizes; "as another, you could see yourself again, too."[70] But that is not all. By adhering to the unpredictable flow of passions and responding to the other's "resistance," the subject exposes itself and the other to a metamorphosis and has the chance to understand, not through a solitary vertical momentum but through a dynamic and horizontal relationship that is generative of ever new forms of awareness, whether and how it wants to get involved to change its own life, whether and how it wants to manage the metamorphosis. Without this, no future is possible.

Notes

1. I share with Roberto Esposito, *Living Thought: The Origins and Actuality of Italian Philosophy* (Stanford, CA: Stanford University Press, 2012), the fundamental idea of a living thought, although, as is evident from the following reflections, I tend to explore different theoretical paths and to propose different perspectives.

2. Hannah Arendt, *The Human Condition* (Chicago: University of Chicago Press, 1998); Günther Anders, *Die Antiquiertheit des Menschen, I: Über die Seele im Zeitalter der zweiten industriellen Revolution* (Munich: Beck, 1956); Hans Jonas, *The Imperative of Responsibility: In Search of an Ethics for the Technological Age* (Chicago: University of Chicago Press, 1985).

3. Jonas, *The Imperative of Responsibility.*

4. Michel Foucault, "What Is Enlightenment?," in *The Foucault Reader*, ed. Paul Rabinow (New York: Pantheon Books, 1984), 46.

5. Max Horkheimer and Theodor W. Adorno, *Dialectic of Enlightenment: Philosophical Fragments*, ed. Gunzelin Schmid Noerr (Stanford, CA: Stanford University Press, 2007), xiv.

6. Herbert Melville, "*Bartleby*," in *The Piazza Tales* (New York: Dix & Edwards; London: Sampson Low, Son & Co, 1856).

7. Anders, *Die Antiquiertheit des Menschen, I.*

8. Axel Honneth, "*Pathologies of the Social*: The Past and Present of *Social* Philosophy," in *Handbook of Critical Theory*, ed. David M. Rasmussen (Oxford: Blackwell, 1996), 369–98.

9. I am alluding to the "emancipatory catastrophism" spoken of by Ulrich Beck, *The Metamorphosis of the World: How Climate Change Is Transforming Our Concept of the World* (Malden, MA: Polity Press, 2016).

10. Max Weber, *The Protestant Ethic and the Spirit of Capitalism with Other Writings on the Rise of the West*, trans. Stephen Kalberg (Oxford: Oxford University Press, 2009).

11. Massimo Cacciari and Paolo Prodi, *Occidente senza utopie* (Bologna: Il Mulino, 2016).

12. Dimitri D'Andrea, "Pensare la soggettività senza natura umana. Materialità e immagini del mondo in Max Weber," *Cosmopolis* 1, no. 13 (2016).

13. "The negative is then not only what should not be, but rather what cannot exist, what cannot be thought and lived, without contradiction"; see Rahel Jaeggi, *Critique of Forms of Life*, trans. Ciaran Cronin (Cambridge, MA: Belknap Press, 2018).

14. From Emmanuel Renault, *L'expérience de l'injustice* (Paris: La Découverte, 2004) to Amartya Sen, *The Idea of Justice* (London: Allen Lane, 2009).

15. Miguel Benasayag and Gérard Schmit, *Les passions tristes. Souffrance psychique et crise sociale* (Paris: La Découverte, 2003).

16. Martha Nussbaum, *Upheavals of Thought: The Intelligence of Emotions* (Cambridge, MA: Cambridge University Press, 2001).

17. Elena Pulcini, *Care of the World: Fear, Responsibility and Justice in the Global Age*, trans. Karen Whittle (Dordrecht: Springer, 2013).

18. Adam Smith, *The Theory of Moral Sentiments* (1759), vol. 1 of the *Glasgow Edition of the Works and Correspondence of Adam Smith* (Oxford: Clarendon Press, 1976).

19. See Zygmunt Bauman, *Liquid Modernity* (Cambridge: Polity Press, 2000).

20. See Fredric Jameson, *Postmodernism, or, the Cultural Logic of Late Capitalism* (London: Verso, 1991); *The Multiple Self*, ed. Jon Elster (Cambridge: Cambridge University Press, 1985); and Christopher Lasch, *The Culture of Narcissism* (New York/London: Norton, 1991).

21. Elena Pulcini, *The Individual without Passions*, trans. Karen Whittle (Lanham: Lexington Books, 2012).

22. "As can be said for every 'rational' asceticism, Puritan asceticism . . . worked to render the devout capable of calling forth and then acting upon their 'constant motives,' especially those motives that the believer, through the practice of asceticism itself, 'trained' against the 'emotions.' In this manner, and in *this* formal-psychological meaning of the term, Puritan asceticism socialized the believer to become a 'personality'"; Weber, *The Protestant Ethic*, 116.

23. Arendt, *The Human Condition.*

24. Anders, *Die Antiquiertheit des Menschen, I.*

25. Jean-François Lyotard, *The Postmodern Condition: A Report on Knowledge*, trans. Geoff Bennington and Brian Massumi (Minneapolis: University of Minnesota Press, 1984).

26. Herbert Marcuse, *Eros and Civilization: A Philosophical Inquiry into Freud* (London: Routledge, 1998), 159ff.

27. Bauman, *Liquid Modernity*.

28. Jameson, *Postmodernism*; Elster, *The Multiple Self*; and Michel Maffesoli, *The Time of the Tribes: The Decline of Individualism in Mass Society*, trans. Don Smith (London: Sage Publications, 1996).

29. Pulcini, *The Individual without Passions*, 125ff.

30. René Girard, *Deceit, Desire and the Novel: Self and Other in Literary Structure*, trans. Yvonne Freccero (Baltimore: Johns Hopkins University Press, 1965).

31. Lasch, *The Culture of Narcissism.*

32. Guy Debord, *Society of the Spectacle*, trans. Malcolm Imrie (London: Verso, 2009).

33. David Riesman, *The Lonely Crowd* (New Haven: Yale University Press, 1961).

34. Massimo Recalcati, *L'uomo senza inconscio* (Milan: Raffaello Cortina Editore, 2010).

35. Erving Goffman, *The Presentation of Self in Everyday Life* (London: Penguin, 1990).

36. Heinz Kohut, *The Analysis of the Self: A Systematic Approach to the Psychoanalytical Treatment of Narcissistic Personality Disorder* (London: Hogarth, 1971).

37. On indifference, disattention, and emotional void as characteristics of the contemporary Self, see the reflections by Zygmunt Bauman, starting with his *Postmodern Ethics* (Oxford: Blackwell Publishers, 1993). On indifference, see also

Adriano Zamperini, *L'indifferenza. Conformismo del sentire e dissenso emozionale* (Turin: Einaudi, 2007).

38. Jameson, *Postmodernism.*

39. See Richard Sennett, *The Corrosion of Character: The Personal Consequences of Work in the New Capitalism* (New York: Norton, 1998).

40. Lasch, *The Culture of Narcissism.*

41. Zygmunt Bauman, *In Search of Politics* (Cambridge: Polity Press, 1999), 157ff.

42. Zygmunt Bauman, *Globalization: The Human Consequences* (Cambridge: Polity Press, 1998).

43. On the concept of immunity, see Roberto Esposito, *Communitas: The Origin and Destiny of Community*, trans. Timothy Campbell (Stanford: Stanford University Press, 2010); and Roberto Esposito, *Immunitas: The Protection and Negation of Life*, trans. Zakiya Hanafi (Cambridge: Polity Press, 2011).

44. Arendt, *The Human Condition.*

45. All of Canetti's work is laced with the topic of metamorphosis. See, for example, Elias Canetti, *The Human Province*, trans. Joachim Neugroschel (New York: Seabury Press, 1978), 102: "How much I would like to listen to myself as a stranger, without recognizing myself, and only find out later that it was I"; see also Elias Canetti, *Crowds and Power*, trans. Carol Stewart (London: Phoenix, 2000); Leonard Mazzone, *Il principio possibilità. Masse, potere e metamorfosi nell'opera di Elias Canetti* (Turin: Rosenberg & Sellier, 2017).

46. Pulcini, *Care of the World*; for a brief but dense introduction to this important topic, see Alessandra Grompi, *V come Vulnerabilità* (Assisi: Cittadella Editore, 2017).

47. Emmanuel Levinas, *Otherwise Than Being or Beyond Essence*, trans. Alphonso Lingis (The Hague: Springer, 1991).

48. Judith Butler, *Giving an Account of Oneself* (New York: Fordham University Press, 2005).

49. "But this death, if it is a death, is only the death of a certain kind of subject, one that was never possible to begin with, the death of a fantasy of impossible mastery, and so a loss of what one never had. In other words, it is a necessary grief"; Butler, *Giving an Account*, 65.

50. Judith Butler, *Precarious Life: The Power of Mourning and Violence* (London: Verso, 2004), xiv.

51. Butler, *Giving an Account*, 100; see also *Precarious Life*, 43.

52. Maurice Blanchot, *The Unavowable Community*, trans. Pierre Joris (Barrytown: Station Hill Press, 1988).

53. On the differences between vulnerability, fragility, and precariousness, see Paul Valadier, "Apologie de la vulnerabilité," *Etudes* 2 (2011): 199–210.

54. Martin Heidegger, *The Question Concerning Technology and Other Essays*, trans. and introduction by William Lovitt (New York: Harper and Row, 1977).

55. George Herbert Mead, *Mind, Self, and Society*, ed. Charles W. Morris (Chicago: University of Chicago Press, 2015).

56. Jonas, *The Imperative of Responsibility*.

57. "One could assert that the state of indebtedness is introduced when he who receives, instead of rendering, gives in his turn"; see Jacques T. Godbout, "L'état d'endettement mutual," *Revue du MAUSS* 4, no. 210 (1994), own translation. Hence, it is a debt that we do not feel the need to pay off. Quite the opposite, we wish to remain in debt because it is proof of the value set by our constitutional dependence. The positive notion of "debt" crosses at several points, albeit in an indirect and sometimes unsystematic manner, authors like Levinas (*Otherwise Than Being*), Hannah Arendt (*The Human Condition*), and Paul Ricoeur ("Love and Justice," in *Radical Pluralism and Truth: David Tracy and the Hermeneutics of Religion*, ed. Werner Jeanrond and Jennifer Rike [New York: Crossroad, 1991], 182–202).

58. Nussbaum, *Upheavals of Thought*.

59. Jean-Luc Nancy, *Being Singular Plural*, trans. Robert Richardson and Anne O'Byrne (Stanford, CA: Stanford University Press, 2000).

60. Nussbaum, *Upheavals of Thought*.

61. Benedictus de Spinoza, *Ethics*, ed. and trans. G. H. R. Parkinson (Oxford: Oxford University Press, 2000).

62. Smith, *Theory of Moral Sentiments*.

63. Allusion to Ulrich Beck and Elisabeth Beck-Gernsheim, *The Normal Chaos of Love*, trans. Mark Ritter and Jane Wiebe (Cambridge: Polity Press; Cambridge, MA: Blackwell, 1995).

64. Daniel Goleman, *Emotional Intelligence* (New York: Bantam Books, 1995); Umberto Galimberti, "Gli analfabeti delle emozioni," http://www.feltrinellieditore.it/news/2002/10/08/umberto-galimberti-gli-analfabeti-delle emozioni-431/.

65. Nussbaum, *Upheavals of Thought*.

66. Adriana Cavarero, *Inclinations: A Critique of Rectitude*, trans. Amanda Minervini and Adam Sitze (Stanford: Stanford University Press, 2016). See also Guido Cusinato, *Periagogé. La singolarità e la cura del desiderio* (Verona: QuiEdit, 2017).

67. Thomas Hobbes, *De Cive*, ed. Howard Warrender (Oxford: Clarendon Press, 2002).

68. Georg Simmel, *The View of Life: Four Metaphysical Essays, with Journal Aphorisms*, trans. John A. Y. Andrews and Donald N. Levine (Chicago: University of Chicago Press, 2010).

69. Jean-Luc Nancy, "The Intruder," in *Corpus*, trans. Richard A. Rand (New York: Fordham University Press, 2008).

70. Elias Canetti, *The Secret Heart of the Clock: Notes, Aphorisms, Fragments 1973–1985*, trans. Joel Agee (London: Deutsch, 1991), 70.

Part Four

Everyday Life, Action, Transcendence

Nine

Everyday Life

For a Vision without Transcendences

Enrica Lisciani-Petrini

> There is no need to be a philosopher for one to be amazed by extraordinary things; but knowledge of philosophy is necessary to be dazzled by the most mundane aspects of everyday existence and of naked being in general.
>
> —Vladimir Jankélévitch

Introductory Remarks

In this chapter, among various considerations, I provide a sketch of what has been over the years the focus of my philosophical research, which has been influenced by such thinkers as Heidegger, Bergson, Jankélévitch, Simmel, Merleau-Ponty, and Deleuze. In dialogue with these authors, my work has crystallized in a theoretical perspective that constitutes both the outcome and a renewal of my research projects. The overall theoretical perspective that I wish to put forward aims at two connected goals: deconstructing a series of traditional parameters and opening up a transformed vision of things. To achieve these two aims, my theoretical hypothesis calls for *a radical interrogation of everyday life*. This question has become the core of my recent work, finding expression in a recent book titled *Vita quotidiana. Dall'esperienza artistica al pensiero in atto* [*Everyday Life: From Artistic Experience to Thought in Action*].[1] To delineate the cardinal points of the position that I fully develop in this book and that I outline more briefly in this chapter, I start with some preliminary considerations. As I begin from this general framework, the main focal points of the perspective that I intend to advance slowly emerge.

If there is an aspect of reality that culture in general, but also philosophy, has always confined to the realm of irrelevance, this is undoubtedly the sphere of everyday life. This is not to say that, ever since antiquity, art and culture have not dealt with the *hemerios*, that is, the everyday aspect of life. On the contrary, as is well known, Plato was interested in nothing else than human beings' destiny in the "cave" of everyday life. *Yet this is precisely the point*: this implied, for human beings, distancing themselves from everyday life through the *bios philosophos*, that is, through a philosophical mode of life that sought to tear human beings away from the sphere of merely material, opaque concreteness and direct them toward the luminous and disembodied world of ideas. Aristotle too spoke of life, but he distinguished only three forms of it, namely *bios apolaustikos* (life that finds its form in pleasure), *bios politikos* (life that is shaped through honor), and *bios theoretikos* (life that has the form of contemplation). All three are opposed to "naked life" (*zoe*), that is, to life in its everyday indeterminate (formless) flux. In short, in the Greek tradition, everyday life does not even have a name to designate it. This circumstance, which may appear bewildering or belonging to a forgotten era, is in reality not such at all. This becomes clear if one considers that the first use of the term *Alltäglichkeit*, "everyday life," occurs in a German dictionary only at the beginning of the nineteenth century—and this is not by chance, as we are about to see. This corresponds to what I have said so far.

The marginalization of the everyday is not the prerogative of philosophy alone. As mentioned above, in all cultural forms, and especially in art, in the course of the centuries, even when grasped in its ordinary temporal development, the dimension of everydayness is obscured and covered up with a very rich iconography made of life-forms that are sublimated, made heroic, and, in sum, idealized. They are built according to expert compositional arrangements characterized either by cold and solemn execution (one can think, for instance, of medieval art) or by a perfect harmonization of the single parts wrought within a framework that remains compact, no matter how full of movement and dynamism (one can think of art from the Renaissance to the Classical-Romantic age). In short, the fundamental intention of these works is to detach and tear the human gaze away from the lowly disorder of everyday life and lift it up toward a lofty world made of order and perfection. The implicit message is that *only* that higher world represents *true* reality. Indeed, it is sufficient to think of all those faces that, in the paintings from the past, are always turned upward, of those gazes that are lost in the distance of incommensurable heights. In sum, the strategy is to "dress up"—to use an effective Benjaminian expression—actual reality through an expert "*maquillage*" of auratic forms.[2]

Of course, one could object in a somewhat superficial manner by asking: Why speak of everyday life? Is this not the most obvious and ordinary thing? Is everyday life not always right here in front of us and so easily known as to be taken for granted? In reality, as Hegel says: "the familiar, just because it is familiar, is not cognitively understood."[3] There is nothing we think we know better and of which, instead, we know so little. Indeed, as Maurice Blanchot writes in one of the most incisive texts on this theme, "the everyday is the most difficult thing to discover" and grasp.[4] Why? Precisely because it is the dimension of the formless and the unqualifiable; it is "without qualities," as Robert Musil would say.[5] This dimension resists all forms instituted by knowledge because it comes before and finds itself beyond them all. It is true that such a dimension is nevertheless always inevitably "qualified" through such forms. *Yet, for this very reason*, it is transformed into its very opposite, namely, a life that pieces itself together within an actual form.

Still in Blanchot's terms, this is precisely what "scares," namely, the fact that everyday life "escapes" all attempts at delimitation within an established form; the fact that it is the "ungraspable" par excellence with regard to all forms of knowledge that pretend to fix it within the boundaries of a formal and epistemic framework. This, as is already clear, and as we will understand even better later, dismantles the truth claims and epistemological pretensions of those forms of knowledge. Here, then, lies the explanation for why the persisting attitudes toward everyday life have always taken one of two forms: either to go beyond everyday life to elevate oneself to the life of "spirit," thereby obscuring everyday existence or to assume everyday life yet in the attempt at "cleansing" its "un-qualifiable" and formless character, thereby sublimating it.

The theoretical perspective I wish to advance on the basis of some of the main philosophical reflections of the twentieth century is diametrically opposite to the one that has just been recalled and has been canonical up to the current times. The latter was concerned with creating an ideal world that stands above the "actual" world and is imposed as "the Truth." Hence comes *the necessity to engage precisely with everyday life*, to interrogate its lack of form and its disturbingly ungraspable character. There are two interrelated reasons for this necessity. First, when assuming a perspective that moves within the "lowly" aspects of a dimension where the constituted forms are continuously stripped of meaning, torn, and dispossessed of their conviction of *truthfully* coding reality, there is no place for that overarching gaze of "*survol*," as Merleau-Ponty calls it, which pretends to stand on an "elevation" from which one can see and capture things within an epistemic form. Second, and consequently, various notions and categories that have traditionally accompanied and conditioned us are made to disappear. Among such notions is, first of all, the idea of an individual and *personal* "subject" understood as the supreme master of its own knowledge, resisting all reductions to the level of the "anyone" and the "whoever," and constituting the perfect counter-aspect to everyday anonymity.

What opens up here is a broad and innovative process that not only leads to rethinking the "*subject*" in *impersonal* terms but also enables a reformulation of the entire view of things. This new vision is deeply transformed: first, because it recovers the material substrate of the real (for centuries marginalized in relation to the spiritual and ideal dimension), which is characterized by a *dynamism* that transforms (deforms and reforms) it continuously, and, second, because it lets emerge, from out of the real, a constitutive interrelationality of all entities. This interrelationality is certainly opaque and ambiguous, but also profoundly vital and dynamic.

It is important to emphasize that this discourse is not at all a sentimental "apology of small things." On the contrary, I intend to delineate a specifically philosophical position. First, I wish to reunite the two levels between which reality has always been split, namely the ideal-spiritual, transcendental plane and the actual-material, immanent one. My aim is to demonstrate their intrinsic connection. Second and consequently, I wish to reunite the forward-facing subject (in its univocal identity), which tradition has exclusively assigned to us and which certainly characterizes us, *and the impersonal, anonymous, and trans-individual dimension that always constitutes us*—as is clearly visible in everyday life—thereby uncovering the thick network of relations that exist beyond our identity and within which we are always caught.

The reversed worldview that ensues carries with it some important consequences with respect to the philosophical discourse and its methodology. In fact, it leads to a) a rethinking of philosophy no longer as a truth-disclosive, systematic (epistemic) procedure, but rather as a continuous referral of thought back to a formless substrate of reality, which incessantly gives rise to all the cognitive and representative forms that have been historically produced; b) a transformation of the very philosophical approach, which is no longer an "analytics" of reality and knowledge but a "creation of concepts," as Deleuze expressed it, aimed at possibly elaborating new categories capable of living up to the complexity of our current reality; c) a modification of the very methodology of philosophy, which now no longer proceeds through rigidly standardized systematizations and formalizations (which, today more than ever, are practiced and "fashionable" within certain analytic philosophy), but rather returns to having a "multidisciplinary" character; in this way, philosophy can unite (as it *already* did for Plato) philosophical speculation and the pleasure of reading, logical tension, and commitment to the "city," thus going back and forth between the languages of the concept and of art, of science and of politics.

This is a comprehensive reversal that, among other things, corresponds more adequately to the way in which thinking always emerges and takes shape: that is, precisely within the terrain of "actual," everyday life. Thinking should remain rooted in this terrain and remain exposed to it in order not to lose its energetic charge.

Metropolitan Life: Simmel

The turn of the gaze downward, toward everyday life began a long time ago—even though we still struggle to understand this move. As has always been the case, it was art that, with its rhabdom-like antennae, registered for the first time the "symptoms" of the change of vision that was slowly taking place starting with the second half of the nineteenth century.

In particular, it was with Baudelaire that, for the first time, everyday life in its chaotic, tentacular entanglement of anonymous existences, full of "horror [. . .] and inexpressible disorder,"[6] explicitly made its entry into history.[7] This occurred not only and not so much in *Les fleurs du mal*, where metropolitan, everyday "modern life" in its most brutal aspects was reproduced in a powerful and terrible portrait, *even though* one that remained confined within the perfectly balanced structure of a sonnet. Rather, it took place in the *Petits poèmes en prose*.[8] The prosaic nature of material life here truly ends up invading the poet's very writing and disrupts it. It is not by chance that these little poems were written "in prose." This prose is dissonant, errant, disconnected, and made of fragments that are hard to recompose—almost as if they were the debris of an unorderable everyday magma poured back into the poet's writing, bringing disorder to it. The subject matter is no longer the shimmering lives of heroes and/or heroines or the romantic adventures that painters loved to recreate with vaporous beauty as had been the case in art until a little earlier—one can think, to mention but one name, of Antoine Watteau. What appears now is only the frenetic network of city streets, "riling with greed and desperation"; only the "demonic courting" of continuous jolts against an everyday reality—made of withered old women, scraped walls and fusty furniture, and human faces without a name—through which the poet drags himself. This makes a real "mockery" out of any idea of salvation or any "ideal" vision of things.

From this moment on, art completely changes its register. Mythological and heroic scenes, divine and aristocratic figures, bucolic landscapes or muffled environments that were wrought through well-defined gestures and ethereal compositions are replaced with a "modern life" that resists any orderly idealization, slips away in all directions, is harsh and labyrinthine, even pointed and sharp in the perceptions it produces. The artists of the time felt compelled to reproduce this image of "modern life." A few examples are the literary works ushered in by Rilke and then by Musil, Döblin, Strindberg, and Brecht, to mention but a few; the paintings pioneered by the impressionists and Cézanne, and then by Grosz or Munch or Klee, also to name but a few here. And one should not forget the revolutionary novelties introduced in the field of photography by the "montages" of a certain Atget; the dissonances invented by Debussy and then incremented by Schoenberg, Berg, and Webern, to again mention only a few eminent artists. And finally, we must not overlook the extraordinary innovations created by the convulsed and syncopated rhythms of jazz. These are all expressions of that transformed way of looking at reality that became increasingly widespread and normal starting with the first half of the nineteenth century.

Why did such a radical change occur? What intervened, in everyday life, so as to profoundly modify human beings' rhythms and movements, spaces and temporalities, perceptions and thoughts?

As Georg Simmel explains superbly in some works that remain unsurpassed on this topic,[9] it is with the birth of metropoles, of "big cities," that is, with the transformation of the urban landscape into a mass, swarming with anonymous existences that meet and collide through quick and nervous contacts, that what is called "modern life" (as is the case in Baudelaire) or "everyday life" emerges. Here is therefore the explanation for why the first appearance of the term *Alltäglichkeit* is to be found in an early nineteenth-century dictionary. At that time, especially because of the changed socioeconomic circumstances brought about by rampant industrialization, individuals no longer recognized each other through stable identities and distinctly codified roles (the pharmacist, the blacksmith, the farmer, and so on). Masses of people went to fill the immense urban spaces of "the big cities," thereby creating the typical and depersonalized urban agglomerations that we know nowadays, where individuals are completely unknown to one another. This pushed to the forefront the indistinct magma of everyday life and ushered onto the stage of history, as its unique and true protagonist, the anonymous and impersonal crowd. With this, the classical hero, who was the author of extraordinary deeds, the character who was the main actor in so many adventures that were immortalized in symbolic images, got replaced with the common person, who remains nameless and even faceless and whose being is dispersed in the mundane and unnoticed business of everyday life.

From here originates that rapid, chaotic, and uninterrupted "succession of external and internal impressions" that is typical of metropolitan life. This is marked by a "continuous contact with an infinity of people," who not only unceasingly hit on the nerves of the inhabitants of the "big cities" (Grosz's works, like *Metropolis*, offer an unparalleled iconography of this) but also force the individual's "personality to adapt to forces that are external to it." This generates an unceasing "exchange of reciprocal influences" [*Wechselwirkung*] that one cannot escape. The result is "a form of extreme impersonality" through which "the individual is reduced to a *quantité négligeable*, to a small grain of sand confronted with an immense organization of things." From here derives that typical conformism of which fashion is the main embodiment and the most evident reverberation, as Simmel perceptively highlights.[10] This happens within a constant "interaction" between the individual and the collective so that everyone is caught in the influence of external factors. This has always been and still is the case today. One extremely effective representation of this, which conveys the idea vividly, is offered by a segment in the 2006 acclaimed film *The Devil Wears Prada*. It is the scene where Andy, the protagonist (Anne Hathaway), somewhat impertinently claims to have maintained her own freedom of judgment with regard to the bizarre trends promoted by the fashion industry (it is the scene where Andy becomes flustered trying to decide which leather belt goes with an indigo outfit). The perfidious Miranda (Meryl Streep) snaps back at Andy to say that her completely unremarkable light blue sweater, which she bought as an apparent statement against the dictates of fashion, is nothing but the residual product of the decision to make that color become world dominant for the purposes of a "*high fashion*" catwalk that took place a few years back. This was therefore a dictate that, imperceptibly, through obscure metropolitan networks, had succeeded in conditioning the indomitable yet unaware protagonist of the movie. In short, as Simmel highlighted already a century earlier, existence within metropoles "expands itself through concentric waves," and "the activities of all" become enmeshed in an organism that is so ramified that "a single man is not limited to the confines of his own body nor to those of the space that he immediately occupies through his activities. On the contrary, it extends to the sum of the effects of his actions which span out beyond him in time and space."

Naturally, right from the start, the negative side of all this did not escape Simmel's keen eye, namely "the predominance of what can be referred to as the objective spirit over the subjective spirit." That is to say, individuals are increasingly caught within objective dynamics that, on the one hand, reactively entail their locking themselves into an extreme form of individualism and, on the other, hand them over to an external, "reifying" force. *Money*, "the universal equivalent of all values," is the very symbol of this alienating process, a "frightful leveller" that drags the subject outside itself and reduces it to a mere cog, that is, a thing among things.[11]

It is no accident, therefore, that Simmel's most remarkable student, Lukács, focused his attention on this negative aspect and interpreted it, through a political Marxist prism, as the product of the bourgeois capitalist economy and the connected standardized "technical reproducibility" of all objects and actions.[12]

Nevertheless, this is but one negative side of the matter, which was definitely shaped and accentuated by the economic transformations and forces that intervened historically. The crucial point of the entire issue is perfectly identified by Simmel. For him, metropolitan life exposes the impersonal mechanisms that, no matter how invisible, have *always* tied individuals to the collective to which they belong, to the infinite network of "interactions" within which they are caught since birth. These impersonal mechanisms primarily intertwine precisely in everyday life—and therefore can be seen within it. From here originates Simmel's "micro-logical" attention (shared later by Benjamin) for the most banal and common objects and "fragments"; and this disrupts, among other things, the classical philosophical methodology and approach. But this also means—and here are the crucial points—that, now, with Simmel, first of all a dimension of everyday life that had hitherto remained marginalized or unremarked establishes itself within the realm of thought; and together with this—that is, precisely because of this, precisely because now the everyday life brings into the open the impersonal mechanisms that had not been noticed earlier—the very notion of "personal subject," which had been coined by Locke and Descartes and, for centuries up until then, had regulated the self-representation of each individual, fades away.

The overturn of the traditional framework is favored, in Simmel, also by his acquaintance with Bergson, that is, with the thinker who is among the first to focus his *philosophical* attention on *life* and its mechanisms. Following Bergson's footsteps, Simmel shines light precisely on this central, pivotal point, namely that, in all circumstances, we are always dealing with "life forms" (an expression he coined)—of which fashion, money, and so on constitute only some of the many epiphenomena—because it is life itself that cannot but "find shelter within these." At the same time, though, it is still life itself that, to maintain alive its own very "incessant flux," cannot refrain from engulfing them and incessantly producing new versions thereof. It is precisely this vital/mortal circuit that stands at the root of the "caducity" of fashion, which overturns all human forms and even the individuals, without human reason ever being able to master them. This movement makes our personal activity "spill outward" and "prevents that unity without which we would not be a personality in the absolute sense."[13]

The Fall of the "Modern" Subject: Freud and Heidegger

With Simmel, the intersection between the theme of life and the fall of the modern subject has already been given its principal outlines. The main thinker who, in philosophy, brings this intersection to precise conceptualization through the thematization of everyday "factical" life is Heidegger. This is done in the famous passages in *Being and Time* devoted to everyday life, but equally and even earlier in his writings from the 1920s focused, precisely, on "facticity" (*Faktizität*). The person who for the first time, starting with the end of the nineteenth century/beginning of the twentieth century, gives the final blow to the notion of a subject autonomously self-grounded on reason and consciousness is Freud. This, again, is done starting not from the analysis of extreme cases of insanity or evident abnormality, but from the study of the most everyday event possible, namely dreaming (the *Traumdeutung* is from 1900), and the most bizarre facts that happen to all of us on an everyday basis, namely gaffes, forgetfulness, and involuntary gestures, which are analyzed in the work that, significantly, is titled *Psychopathology of Everyday Life*.[14]

What is Freud's extraordinary and disruptive discovery? It is not only that each of us, each subject is in no way grounded on his/her own rationality and self-consciousness, but also that, in direct contrast, reason and consciousness are in themselves "ungrounded" by a kind of "black hole," an inner abyss that entirely escapes all attempts to bring it to the light of reason. This is the subconscious. As is demonstrated by everyday dreams, but also by gaffes and transient amnesias, the subconscious is "inhabited" by personalities that are different from the one we think we have. In fact, the latter constitutes the "mask"—the *persona*, following the ancient word *prosopon*—that we wear every day.[15] To give a mundane example of this, what happens when we involuntarily forget our house keys? We are probably perturbed by a thought *that derives from one or more people* so that (to mention only one of the possible explanations) our subconscious produces this forgetful action to stop us from coming back home, where we would stay to brood over that which torments us, for hours more. But then, *it is these other people* who have taken possession of our being and push us to exit the house hastily without our keys. It is precisely this bewildering discovery that Freud makes through the study of himself and his own forgetfulness. This leads him to speak of an unconscious "counter-volition," which he understands as interfering with himself. He goes so far as to liken his susceptibility to it to a "relation of slavery," so much so that he is compelled to conclude that "an unknown psychic power steals the availability [. . .] [of] my memory away from me."

This observation is powerful. The central node that we intend to bring into focus is clearly outlined by this example. In fact, what is brought to light is the *pre-personal* side (or, more accurately, the "*impersonal*" side, according to the lexicon that Freud himself will use in a later text, *Das Ich und das Es*) that ungrounds our "Self" and almost makes it go out of itself inserting it into other "Selves." We thereby discover that *normally*, and especially in everyday life, in its indistinct flow, we are "accompanied," as if we had a "double," by a living substrate that is *anonymous and undifferentiated*, in which we are always immersed, and which deconstructs the identity-profile that individualizes our subject-person. Thanks to this impersonal substrate, all of us continuously "interconnect" with one another. Not only does it drag us under the sway of unsurmountable automatisms (as is the case with our little everyday psychopathologies), but also, most importantly, it constitutes that widespread sphere of diffused thought that no one owns but that, precisely because of this, continuously forces us internally to harbor thoughts that belong to others. This is shown in the fact that, for example, when we are born, we enter a collective linguistic and ideological horizon, to which we belong rather than it belongs to us (it is not our own property). Thus, in the course of our lives, we always and incessantly think through a powerful network of thoughts that belong to everyone. Hence our very thinking—that is, that which is conventionally considered to be our most characteristic and individual ability, our most exclusive "property"—is in fact a "thing" that we have no reason to call our own "property."[16]

In sum, Freud sees clearly that between the personal and the impersonal there is a chiasmic circle that characterizes everyday life. And this completely calls into question the concept of subject-person that, from this moment on and throughout the entire course of the twentieth century, will undergo a radical dismantling.

As noted above, the first to conceptualize the decisive overcoming of the concept of subject-person is Heidegger. Indeed, there is something that should be clarified right away. It is with Heidegger that everyday life enters the philosophical reflection with the full force of its deconstructive reach into the personal subject. This already occurs with the first Freiburg lecture courses of 1919 to 1923.[17] In these lectures, Heidegger says explicitly that he wants his own investigation to take a "radical turn" precisely through an analysis of "factical life" (*das fatktische Leben*), that is, life as it is de facto and as we live it "every day" (*alltäglich*). Against the entire philosophical tradition that precedes him (from Plato up to Descartes and Kant), he establishes a central and decisive focal point, namely, that there is no external—whether transcendent or transcendental—reality that can be opposed to the "fundamental" and unique sphere that is "factual being." It is only within the latter that our "objective" encounters with things, animals, or others are determined, not to mention the institution of the "subjective" category of the "Self." What does this imply? It implies that, unlike what has traditionally been done, it is impossible to split factual existence and render it, through its subjugation, the external "object" of a sovereign "subject" that is each time understood as an "«I» [= «I think»], person, I-pole, centre of the act." On the contrary, facticity is that which resists any form of subjective and personal "power." Therefore, it is absolutely *impersonal.*

This is the initial impetus with which Heidegger's argument begins. Yet an entirely different theoretical endeavor unfolds within *Being and Time*. In fact, the first thing that stands out upon reading that text is that in Part I, where the existential definition of Dasein is developed, everyday existence is straightaway presented as the *only* horizon through which one can access the reality of Dasein because "factually [*faktisch*]," Dasein has *no other dimension than that of everyday life*. As is already the case in the Freiburg lectures, this approach immediately implies a clear distance from any idea of the "Self" or the "subject" or the "person" as a thinking, self-constituting ground of all contact with the world. There is no initial "subject" that establishes a relation with the world and posits the world or life as "objects" that are external to itself. First of all is the factual (or everyday) life that involves both. In fact, *only* through dealing—which is in the first place everyday dealing—with things and others, that is, only through its being "dispersed" outwardly in its *nonpersonal* exterior, can Dasein fold back onto itself and understand itself. This is as true of Dasein's relation with things as it is of its relation with others. For what concerns its relation with things, Dasein is, first and foremost, always already dealing, in a prethematic, that is, nonconceptualized way, with things, which are approached in terms of their "usability." This means that Dasein is "first and foremost, and on top of everything else, *no longer itself*," is not grasped and cannot grasp itself, precisely, as an autonomous and self-conscious subject that is separated from the world. This is what had emerged earlier in Freud's analysis—first and foremost, we live embedded within a flow of relations that precede and surpass us. This powerfully deconstructive and depersonalizing effect already emerges in the analysis of things, and it is even more evident in our relation to others. This relation bursts open the subjective shell of personal identity, revealing that it "is not there, nor has a subject without world ever existed," that is, "an isolated I." Each one of us is in an "originary" way and from the start dispersed—impersonally—in a being-with-others, in a "being-there-together," from which we do not even distinguish ourselves.

It is here, then, that "proper" and "improper," qualified "authentic" life and unqualifiable everyday life, personal life and impersonal life lose their opposite connotation and reveal themselves in a mirroring intertwining that turns one into the inverted image of the other. One could say, as Heidegger in fact does, that "the everyday" does not mean at all that Dasein loses its own personal being, identity, and individuality, that is, its "authenticity." On the contrary, these dimensions are so intertwined that the only form of authenticity, for Dasein, is its self-discovery as irremediably inauthentic, that is, as belonging to the everyday.

This is a radical outcome. The everyday envelops the entire dimension of Dasein, of the human being, and this very "authentic existence is not something that sets itself above everyday life in the latter's fallenness; existentially it [authentic existence] is only *a modified grasping of the latter*." Authentic existence—that is, the dimension of thought, of the sovereign subject that separates itself from reality to understand it and appropriate it, of the subject that pretends to give definitive forms to the world—is only a perspective, a glimpse of inauthentic life, a representation of the latter, and can never pretend to separate itself from it, giving us the illusion or the pretension of becoming authentic, fully defined, and well-rounded subjects. Factically (*faktisch*) we are, on the contrary, always within the magma or vortex of an impersonal flow that drags us away, along with the very forms through which we think we can order and close off the world and external reality, along with ourselves, to master it.

Of course, Heidegger's argument is not without oscillations. Right after the pages on "everyday life," Heidegger introduces the theme of "Care"; that is, the "call to consciousness" by way of which the subject must respond of its own actions to itself, which echoes Kant's transcendental framework. Then, in the "second section" of *Being and Time*, it is undoubtable that a "countermovement" is set in motion in the opposite direction, specifically with the introduction of the themes of "decision" and "being-toward-death." The "decision" is, in fact, a gesture that occurs in the context of the everyday, yet it only acquires a truly "decisive" character when it implies an anticipation of death—one really chooses only when one is totally free in the awareness of death. This produces transcendence with regard to our everyday dispersion. For now, instead of seeing itself caught within the fabric of everyday life, Dasein detaches itself from it and comes to see itself as "a totality," closed in between the beginning and the end of its own existence, reappropriating itself; and it can thereby reacquire its own "*Jemeinigkeit*" ("mine-ness"), that is, its proper sovereign will over things and therefore its "being-toward-authenticity." As Adorno will astutely observe, from this moment onward an "authenticity jargon" enters Heidegger's discourse. This follows a hieratic-heroic line that will soon lead Heidegger's thought to reach the poisonous conclusions we have presently come to know in full. In this way, the enigma of everyday life—which Heidegger analyzes for at least a decade with a hermeneutic subtlety that remains as of yet unsurpassed—can be said to have been resolved and dissolved through a personalist and heroic lexicon, which was typical of the very tradition toward which Heidegger was hostile and from which he intended to distance himself.

Nevertheless, two main points have been established. The first is the criticism of the notion of the modern subject, which was devised by Descartes and Locke, and over which Heidegger will unceasingly return (as one can see, for instance, in *The Age of the World Picture*).[18] The second follows from the first, and it amounts to a looping back of the subject onto and *within* the dynamics of the "given-ness of Being" and, therefore, human beings' belonging to a "facticity" they will never master by detaching themselves from it and making it become "the object" to be "governed" from a transcendent (or transcendental) position. At most, human beings can be its custodians and "shepherd[s]." Those initial pages of the 1927 work mark therefore the turning point—and a point of no return—for philosophy itself. And their effect is inescapable.

Toward a "New Ontology": Merleau-Ponty

Before proceeding, I quickly retrace what has emerged from our discussion thus far. The profound overturn in the general way of seeing things had been underway since the second half of the nineteenth century and, perhaps, even since the beginning of that century, if one considers the discovery of *bios* and biology. By the next century, these changes crystallized in three deeply transformed spheres: 1) The dissolution of the "modern subject" grounded on its own self-acting reason and its reinsertion into the complex and concrete dynamic of the real. 2) As a consequence, the dismantling of the traditional vision founded on a system of forms that were seen as universal and eternal (the Truth) and are now instead discovered to be simply *a* historical product of the human need to continuously give form to the chaotic reality that surrounds human beings and within which humans are immersed. 3) The rediscovery of the concrete terrain of the real, which is dynamic and hard to pin down, and from which there continuously rise forms that are historically produced by humans. This terrain is life in the pulsating, enigmatic, and labyrinthine facticity of the everyday. This is what we have called, indeed, everyday life.

Merleau-Ponty is the thinker who reformulates this fundamental conception in an original, intense, and fecund way. Despite never explicitly thematizing everyday life, his reasoning continually touches on this topic. This is also the case for phenomenology—to which Merleau-Ponty initially adhered, but on which he impressed a new twist—with its motto "back to the things themselves" and to their "genuine self-giving." It is not by accident that all the "places" or the innumerable examples that Merleau-Ponty employs—be they about the room in which the philosopher is sitting or the "red carpet" whose fluff is analyzed for paradigmatic purposes, and many other similar instances—always belong to the sphere of ordinary life. And it is precisely for this reason that Merleau-Ponty, despite never deviating from the plane of philosophical argumentation, continuously and transversally crosses the fields of art and politics, of science and psychoanalysis. In doing so, he deploys a methodology that is as fruitful as it is free from subservience to abstract frameworks that tend toward pure logicism or are closed within the self-referential nature that is typical of a certain philosophy. On the contrary, his methodology is situated precisely within the "impure" and opaque substrate of concrete life. Therefore, it is a methodology that is already, in itself, an effective expression of the "ambiguous" philosophy, as it has repeatedly been called, that Merleau-Ponty practiced.

As I have stated, right from the start this French philosopher impresses an original twist on Husserl's phenomenology. This twist already signals in the direction of that Husserlian "unthought" that will be explicitly addressed later on.[19] It is sufficient to open the first pages of *Phénoménologie de la perception* to understand straight away the problematic node that concerns Merleau-Ponty. He wishes immediately to clarify that beings, individuals, and meanings—that is, subjects and objects according to Descartes' formulation—should not be seen as closed entities within a sealed-off identity, in turn based on an ideal essence (a form) that is given from the start. On the contrary, identities are born "at the intersection" of various relational threads, that is, at the points of convergence of various dynamics that are themselves generated from the material fabric of life. This is why "every [being] is the mirror image of every other being." In other words, the whole of reality is a "reciprocal seeing/mirroring of one-self." And *this* is what establishes the meaning and identity of each thing. There is no identity outside this interrelationality.

Let us take as an example *this* table on which I am now writing. According to Merleau-Ponty, this table is not born in the ethereal realm of ideas, and its significance does not exist in an abstract conceptual world, as we have been mostly led to think. This table is the result of all the relational connections that surround it and make it be the table that it is: the room in which it is situated, the culture to which I belong that promotes writing essays, the era in which I live and because of which there is a computer on the table, and so on. If this table were situated in a dining room, its significance would change completely and it would become a dining table, supporting not books but plates, and so on. Conversely, if it were located in a sacred place, it would become the equivalent of an altar. Therefore, this table finds its entire meaning and significance here, in this room, in this network of relations within which it is caught and reflects itself, and without which it would not acquire its identity. No "table" can exist outside this system of relations. What applies to the existence of the table likewise applies to all other things and beings.

This means that, among all entities, there occurs "a kind of reciprocal mirroring" that is chiasmatic and insoluble. This is the same as the one that we experience in our own bodies when, for instance, our hands touch each other. As Merleau-Ponty writes in the essay *Signes*, which is dedicated to Husserl's "unthought," "when my right hand touches my left I sense it as 'a physical thing' [an object]; but in that very moment . . . an extraordinary event occurs: now my left hand, in turn, starts feeling the right [. . .] Therefore [. . .] my body accomplishes 'a kind of reflection' [. . .] the relation capsizes: the felt hand [object] is now the one which feels [subject] and I am forced to say that my body is a [. . .] 'subject/object.'" What does this famous example tell us? It highlights that what happens with our hands when they touch each other, when they simultaneously become subject/object for each other, happens precisely with all things, all beings of the world. Let us take our table again as an example: this table is not just "the object" against which I am leaning, *but* it is that *thanks to which* I am a person who here, now, has adopted a certain posture. No matter how paradoxical this may appear to our canonical view, the table "objectifies" and "identifies" me as the "writer" I am at this very moment. And this is true vice versa, as said earlier. Therefore, the table and I are, simultaneously, subject/object for each other. Far from being given, our identity is, on the contrary, the product of that continuous "reversibility" of one into the other. What is true for me and the table is true for anything, person or entity of this world.

In short, the I, the world, and all beings are like "the hands that touch each other," doubled into internal and external elements, like a page with two sides for which the front and the back are inseparable. And this is not all. The front and the back continuously pass into each other. This is why—and this is, as I said earlier, the central point of Merleau-Ponty's thought—beings cannot and do not exist as pregiven, stand-alone identities that, on top of this, are separated, as we are used to think. On the contrary, they are *the result* of a mirroring play of reciprocal reflections; so much so that, in the end, an identity is nothing other than "the virtual center" of all the infinite relations that surround it and thanks to which *only* it can be what it is. And it is only thanks to these relations that it *exists*.

Now it becomes clear why Merleau-Ponty could define as a "*new ontology*" this philosophical framework on which he principally worked during the last years of his life. It is a new vision according to which the entire texture of reality is an immense piece of "flesh" in which we are all caught and in which we all mirror one another.

Yet, and here is the decisive philosophical point, this immense relational and dynamic texture is not at all something that could be illuminated through the light of reason and known once and for all. On the contrary, it is that which is "un-reflected" and beyond all reflection, that from which all reflection emanates that is obscurely guided by it—as Husserl had already understood, but then he reabsorbed it into the noematic sphere of reflection and therefore it remained "unthought." Here we find again the thread we had encountered earlier and to which Merleau-Ponty's reflection offers a precise ontological explanation. For such an unreflected ontological texture, which is to be found obscurely at the base of all our gestures and even our entire individual existence, is nothing other than that "*impersonal*" sphere, as Merleau-Ponty explicitly says, that accompanies us every day. This impersonal sphere causes all of our experience, from its sensorial to its intellectual dimension, to be always caught within the flow of general existence, which is "anonymous" and which "flows through [us] *without [us] being its author*." Therefore, our entire life is steeped in a "*pre-personal*" and "*trans-individual*"[20] dimension whose cradle is precisely everyday life with its labyrinthine intrigues.[21]

The ontological interpretation elaborated by Merleau-Ponty on the theme of the impersonal has implications that are of the highest significance for the political sphere.

On the political level, to say that the entirety of reality is an immense flow of relations means that the world is a movement of shared identities; that is, it is produced by continual reciprocal intersections. This is such that every identity is "im-plicated—in the literal sense that it is folded back—into itself and its other," that is, what is "foreign." The latter is therefore no longer properly the "foreign." It is rather the "other of" [*di-verso*] something: the *verso*, "*the other side or the rear*" with regard to which each one of our identities is the *reverse*. As such, the latter has always been "embedded" within our identity, so as to invalidate any affirmation of it that is closed in and on itself. For example, my being Italian is constituted—and constitutes me—precisely because I am not Moroccan, Nigerian, Chinese, French, and so on. For this very reason, though, my being Italian remains intrinsically "*implicated*" *in and by* these "others" who, "turning back" onto me as the *reverse* of my *recto*, as the "flipped side" of my frontal being, make me identical with my identity: the being that I am, namely an Italian.

This perspective is clearly entirely different from all identitarian, "appropriating" thought as well as from all communitarian positions in the sense of an "organic community" that creates identification and closure. It is also completely different from all perspectives based on the separation of the individuals understood as "autonomous subjects" that are sovereign self-masters, whether they are singular personal individuals or singular institutional individualities such as nation-states, according to the typically modern political perspective (put forward by thinkers ranging from Hobbes and Locke to Kant). This perspective is, today, more relevant than ever if we want to think about politics beyond the sovereignist divides that have dangerously come back to haunt the world stage. Conversely, as Merleau-Ponty teaches us, to go back to understanding ourselves as entities that are immersed in a reality that we are not able to grasp but only, at most, manage within partial and sectorial realms; to lower our gaze from the "lofty" position of "*survol*" from which, for centuries, human beings have believed that they could dominate the world; to reimmerse ourselves into that dimension that is life in its everyday and ungraspable transformations; to understand that we are *literally made* of all the relations that surround us, and therefore of the animal, vegetable, mineral, and inorganic ones as well—these are the only gestures that, today, can perhaps save humanity.

This is the lesson that is to be found within a philosophy of the everyday. This is the "message" in the bottle that has reached us from the flows of everyday life.

Conclusive Remarks

Before closing the discussion, I make some final remarks in relation to the argument that I have developed so far through some of the major thinkers of our time.

As has been evidenced, the path that we have embarked on has the theme of everyday life as its main thread, as though this were a musical motif; we could even say, the theme of life *tout court*. If, over the centuries, there has been a thought that has constantly intersected this sphere, protruding itself into it, and rooting itself in the earthly, disorderly, corporeal, and sanguine *humus* [soil], instead of lifting it up solely toward transcendent and metaphysical heights; if there has been a thought that has honed in on especially the civil and political life of the individuals, this thought is Italian thought. It has spanned the entire period from Dante, despite the solemn vision that seems to drive him, running through the whole of Humanism, passing through Vico, then going on to Leopardi, and ending with twentieth-century Italian philosophers.[22] On this last topic, it is worth recalling that it was Bergson, that is, one of the thinkers who have been best able to do philosophical work on the theme of life, who inspired (as was already the case with Simmel) some of the Italian thinkers of the early twentieth century, not to mention more recent ones. Moreover, one Italian artistic movement, Futurism, sought precisely to express Bergson's "vital energy."

This is why the framework that has been developed above can be fruitfully taken up and reinterpreted also through the lens of the theoretical and cultural development of "Italian thought." This is what I have attempted to do in the most recent phase of my work.[23] The characteristically impure[24] connotation of Italian thought in comparison with the detached procedures of the more systematic philosophies of other countries; its transversal movement between the spheres of art (in all its configurations) and politics, over and above philosophy; its rooting within the "factual" substrate, to say it in Machiavelli's terms, of the concrete dynamics of history—all this makes Italian philosophy apt to contribute to a general change in the view of things along the lines outlined above. It is also from this capacity for renewal that the recent discovery and success of what has become known as "Italian thought" arises. Such a success was born beyond the national boundaries—it has come "from outside."[25] "Italian thought" is represented today by some philosophers who share, directly or indirectly, knowingly or unknowingly, that cultural origin. The present chapter, written by an Italian thinker, intends to intercept this broader intellectual movement, offer a contribution to it, and meanwhile open a possible additional line of inquiry onto which my current philosophical path is moving.

Notes

1. Enrica Lisciani-Petrini, *Vita quotidiana. Dall'esperienza artistica al pensiero in atto* (Turin: Bollati Boringhieri, 2015).

2. This is how Benjamin expressed himself when speaking of photography and E. Atget, who, by portraying the most ordinary and poor aspects of the everyday reality of Paris, "undressed" reality as it had been represented up until then by "pictorial" and "auratic" photography. See Walter Benjamin, "Das Kunstwerk im Zeitalter seiner technischen Reproduzierbarkeit," in *Schriften*, vol. I (Frankfurt a. M.: Suhrkamp, 1955).

3. Georg Wilhelm Friedrich Hegel, *Phenomenology of Spirit*, trans. A. V. Miller (Oxford: Oxford University Press, 1977), 18.

4. For this and the following citation, see Maurice Blanchot, *L'entretien infini* (Paris Gallimard, 1969), 360–71.

5. The obvious reference is to Robert Musil, *Der Mann ohne Eigenschaften*, in *Gesammelte Werke*, ed. Adolf Frisé (Reinbeck bei Hamburg: Rowohlt, 1978).

6. See Rainer Maria Rilke, *Die Aufzeichnungen des Malte Laurids Brigge* (Leipzig: Insel, 1910); as is well known, this work in prose is dedicated to Parisian metropolitan life and is openly inspired by Baudelaire.

7. I highlight this explicitly because, in reality, this argument does not lend itself to any historicist interpretation. In fact, on closer inspection, it is possible to trace various other cases of artists who have grasped the restless and chaotic aspect of everyday existence within dominant culture, well before the nineteenth century. It is sufficient to mention one name: Caravaggio. Unfortunately, developing this argument here would take me beyond the scope of this chapter. It deserves, however, a separate elaboration elsewhere.

8. See, also for the references that follow, Charles Baudelaire, *Les fleurs du mal*, in *Œuvres complètes* (Paris: La Pléyade, 1975); *Petits poèmes en prose*, ibid. See also *Le peintre de la vie moderne*, ibid.

9. Specifically see Georg Simmel, "Die Großstädte und das Geistesleben" (1903), in *Brücke und Tür* (Stuttgart: Koeler Verlag, 1957), 227–42. The following citations are taken from this text.

10. The reference is to Georg Simmel, "Die Mode" (1919), in *Philosophische Kultur* (Leipzig: Klinkhardt, 1911).

11. It is important to remember that Simmel has dedicated to this theme a famous essay: *Philosophie des Geldes* (Leipzig: Duncker & Humblot, 1900).

12. On this point, following in the footsteps of Lukács, see also Henri Lefebvre, *Critique de la vie quotidienne*, 3 vols. (Paris: Grasset et L'Arche, 1947–1961).

13. Georg Simmel, *Philosophische Kultur. Gesammelte Essays* (Leipzig: Klinkhardt, 1919).

14. Sigmund Freud, *Zur Psychopathologie des Alltagslebens* (1901), in *Gesammelte Schriften*, vol. IV (Leipzig/Wien/Zürich: Internationaler Psychoanalitischer Verlag, 1981). The following citations are taken from this book.

15. The term "person" derives from the Greek word *prosopon*, which designated the mask donned by the actor on a theatrical stage.

16. This point has been abundantly analyzed by Roberto Esposito, *Due. La macchina della teologia politica e il posto del pensiero* (Turin: Einaudi, 2013).

17. The works to bear in mind are Martin Heidegger, *Phänomenologische Interpretationen zu Aristoteles. Einführung in die phänomenologische Forschung* (1919),

in *Gesamtausgabe*, vol. LXIII, 1988; *Sein und Zeit* (Halle: Niemeyer, 1927). The citations that follow are taken from these texts.

18. Martin Heidegger, "The Age of the World Picture," in *The Question Concerning Technology and Other Essays*, trans. W. Lovitt (New York: Harper & Row, 1977), 115–36.

19. This is a reference to the work dedicated to Husserl, "Le philosophe et son ombre," in Maurice Merleau-Ponty, *Signes* (Paris: Gallimard, 1960), 201–228. Merleau-Ponty's other works, from which the following citations are taken, are *La phénoménologie de la perception* (Paris: Gallimard, 1945); *Le visible et l'invisible* (posthumous and edited by C. Lefort) (Paris: Gallimard, 1964).

20. It is worth noting that Merleau-Ponty's second major and most famous student after Lefort was Gilbert Simondon, who indeed theorized the "trans-individual."

21. The author who was best able to express this—that is, the fact that we are the product of a labyrinthine network of relations, which extends in time and onto a "screen" onto which, ultimately, "our image" (our identity) is projected—is without doubt Marguerite Yourcenar, who penned a splendid trilogy that was, by no accident, called *Le labyrinthe du monde* (Paris: Gallimard, 1974–1984).

22. This genealogy of contemporary Italian thought has been, recently, carefully reconstructed by Roberto Esposito, *Pensiero vivente. Origine e attualità della filosofia italiana* (Turin: Einaudi, 2010). It has then been taken up again and rearticulated with reference to the beginning of the nineteenth century (and to authors such as Rensi and Tilgher) in Roberto Esposito, *Da fuori. Una filosofia per l'Europa* (Turin: Einaudi, 2016).

23. See Enrica Lisciani-Petrini and Giusi Strummiello, eds., *Effetto Italian Thought* (Macerata: Quodlibet, 2017), and especially my postface, "Un pensiero dell'attualità."

24. This is how Remo Bodei defined Italian Thought in *Il noi diviso. Ethos e idee dell'Italia repubblicana* (Turin: Einaudi, 1998). See also Remo Bodei, "Una filosofia della ragione impura: il pensiero italiano," in Lisciani-Petrini and Strummiello, *Effetto Italian Thought*, 55–70.

25. See above note 22.

Ten

The Symbol in Action

Maria Cristina Bartolomei

Understanding the Symbol Starting from Symbolic Action

The central aim of this chapter is to propose, as the title suggests, an interpretation of the symbol starting from symbolic action rather than from how "the symbol"—understood as something that is already established and known—acts. The intention is to examine the theoretical (and practical) benefits of looking at the symbol from a less customary perspective, that is, not from its consideration in terms of the cognitive dimension but rather from the perspective of action with a view to grasping specifically what is manifested in and by symbolic action.

A proposal of this kind is, of course, not an absolute novelty. The present perspective is situated within the broader context of the contemporary consciousness, which recognizes the symbol's deep connection with what it means to be human. This idea and connection are succinctly articulated in Ernst Cassirer's well-known definition of the human being as *animal symbolicum* [symbolic animal].[1]

In this regard, an even more significant point of reference can be found in Paul Ricoeur's hermeneutics when it moves "from text to action"[2] as *topos* [place] for the exercise and verification of hermeneutics. The move to action does not imply abandoning and, even less, denying the significance of all references to text and discourse; nor is it, in turn, an arbitrary choice. Rather, it is a choice that is necessary for and demanded by an integral philosophical anthropology. Ricoeur, in fact, connects his theory of action with a theory of history by integrating a consideration of imagination in discourse and action.[3] In a passage on the text as paradigm, the pivotal point of Ricoeur's discourse is the connection between *explaining* and *understanding*, which are understood not in a dichotomous or alternative sense but rather as dialectically correlative.[4] Conceived in this manner, the connection represents, on the one hand, the architrave under which Ricoeur situates his trilogy of theories of text, action, and history; on the other hand, the connection arises precisely from the tie between these three *foci* of Ricoeur's theory. In each of these theoretical areas, in fact, similar *aporias* arise that prompt Ricoeur "to question the methodological dualism of explanation and understanding and to substitute a subtle dialectic for this clear-cut alternative."[5]

In particular, regarding action, Ricoeur says that "if explanation belongs to the domain of system theory and understanding to that of motivation (of intentional and motivated human action), we perceive that these two elements—the course of things and human action—are intertwined in the notion of *intervention* in the course of things."[6] This notion of intervention, he notes, refers to an idea of cause different from Hume's causality insofar as it is synonymous with an agent's initiative. Yet it is not opposed to, but rather includes, the idea of cause as motive "since intervention in the course of things implies that we are following the articulation of natural systems,"[7] yet with an *intention* to make something *else* happen.

What is most interesting here is the analogy that Ricoeur recognizes between the theory of the text and the theories of action (considered to be a "quasi text"[8]) and history. In the theory of action, the ideas of cause, motive, intention, and effect are all involved; in the theory of history, the connection between narrative and action comes to light. The notion of the text, in particular, "is a good *paradigm* for human action and . . . action is a good *referent* for an entire category of texts."[9] Action leaves in fact a trace that can then be interpreted by future readers in new contexts; and for many texts, the referent is action itself.[10]

All this offers an interpretive key that is particularly suitable for opening the access to another form of action in which the intervention in the course of things is of a very peculiar nature. That is the *symbolic action*, which is indeed the primary case in which text, action, history, intention, cause, and meaning are mutually implicated.

To grasp the connection between symbol and action and, better yet, between action and symbol, we must turn to Schleiermacher and to the theory of Christian action he develops in his work *Die christliche Sitte*.[11] This, in turn, illuminates the action that is altogether peculiar to Christianity, namely, the sacrament. Even the latter, as symbol, philosophically "gives rise to thought." When we adequately reconsider this sacramental and liturgical dimension, we can find in it a particular inspiration that Christianity offers to culture and philosophical thought.

Foundations for Understanding the Symbol

An adequate consideration of symbolic action presupposes a general conception of the symbol that we must now make explicit. Analogously to what Aristotle affirms with regard to the concept of being, the symbol can be spoken of "in many ways."[12] But it is also understood in many senses, with great semantic variations—from, on the one end of the arc, considering it as merely synonymous with a purely conventional sign to, on the other end, emphasizing its "natural" link (by analogy or similarity) with what is symbolized, rendering it close to an icon. Meanwhile, on the linguistic level, the symbol is made to be close to an allegory or a metaphor.[13]

The space for the reflection on the nature of the symbol is opened up and individuated by two coordinates of reference for the perspectives under consideration. On the abscissa, there is, on the one hand, a conception of the symbol as something that "comes to us," that "offers itself" as a threshold [*soglia*] of access to the beyond and, on the other hand, a conception of the symbol as the product of the mind, of the symbolizing consciousness, and of the imagination. On the ordinate, we can distinguish an interpretation "from above" and one "from below." The interpretation "from above" sees the symbol as a manifestation of transcendence; in giving itself, the symbol manifests the inclination of the human consciousness to go beyond itself, toward the Originary. The interpretation "from below" highlights the fact that symbols originate from and reflect a specific cultural and linguistic context that is historically determined, and they develop and evolve over time.

The conception of symbolic action proposed in this chapter aligns with a line of understanding of the symbol that goes from Kant to Ricoeur, passing by way of Cassirer.[14] Its first landmark is to be found in Kant's *Critique of Judgment*, where the symbol is understood as an articulation of a kind of intuitive representation, different from the representation that belongs to the schema.[15] Whereas the latter is direct and demonstrative, the former is indirect and analogical. According to Ricoeur, the symbol can be defined as "*any structure of signification in which a direct, primary, literal meaning designates, in addition, another meaning which is indirect, secondary and figurative and which can be apprehended only through the first.*"[16] The relation that enables the connection between the two meanings can only be analogical: the "nature" of the symbol is linked to that of the reality it designates. Precisely for this reason, one can say that the symbol "gives rise to thought."[17] That is, the symbol offers something to be thought but also "prompts thinking," makes one restless, stimulates.

The symbol is an occasion for exercising thinking in a rigorous sense. This is due, above all, to its intrinsic referential dynamic. The symbol is, in fact, an entryway from an experiential meaning to a meaning beyond itself, reachable by analogy and never directly. In connection with this, the symbol gives rise to thought because of its relation of circularity but also of dialectic with respect to the concept. It would be completely misleading to oppose the one to the other.[18] With complete separation, both would perish. The concept does not exhaust the polysemy of the symbol. Yet apart from the concept, the symbol cannot understand itself. In turn, the concept is open to the symbol. In fact, philosophical thought employs symbolic and metaphorical language to lean toward the unthought.[19]

Within the symbol, a similar circular and dialectical relation concerns the connections between word and thing; between "precision [*puntualità*]" of the symbol's meaning and stratification of meanings;[20] between the singularity of the symbol and the dynamics of synergy and symphony of many symbols and symbolic behaviors (such as happens in every "liturgy," whether secular or religious); and between timelessness and the historicity of the cultural roots. In this light, what becomes clear is a problematic, paradoxical structure of the symbol, namely, its being the point of tension and synthesis between maximum of concreteness and maximum of transcendence.

The lethal threat affecting the symbol is its reification, its transformation into a "thing," and, thereby, its absolutization, its being released from the conditions of its giving and of its being interpreted, of its being capable of communicating the meaning to which it refers.

Among the conditions needed for the "symbol" to exist, the presence of an intention is essential. The symbol—whether concrete, iconic, linguistic, or gestural—is such because what is present at its origin and maintaining its existence is an intention to communicate meaning, an intention that becomes decodable within a shared horizon of meaning. The same symbolic element may take on different meanings in different cultural contexts. The triangle, for example, is a geometric shape. It can become a symbol when an intention supplies it with symbolic meaning, which is by definition polysemic. Hegel notes that a triangle can be a symbol for the Trinity within a Christian church, painting, or sculpture but not outside such a context; it could not be decoded as such by someone who has no notion of the Christian perspective.[21]

Thinking the symbol, thinking from the way the symbol gives itself should not be confused with a vaguely "symbolic thought." In order not only to be registered and noted, but also to be truly brought to thought, the symbol must be thought conceptually within a tension of perspectives: the symbol that comes to us, that "is there" *or* the symbol as product of the mental faculty, of the intention of the one who creates it, of the attribution of meaning within a specific linguistic-cultural constellation. On the one hand, there is the theophanic symbol and, on the other, there is the symbol as function of the consciousness that, through the symbol, leans toward the Originary.

The path we have followed so far considers the symbol (and its linguistic side, the metaphor) under the theoretical aspect, that is, in the sense of the interpretation, production, and conceptualization of the symbol. In this perspective, symbolic behaviors seem to be an "application" of symbols that exist prior to them. The prevalent modality of consideration of the symbol assigns it to the noetic realm, albeit with different modulations, from the gnoseological/truth-related to the aesthetic, and there also is no shortage of modalities that focus on the ethical, political, and social dimensions of the symbol.[22]

Thinking the Symbol Starting from Its Action

The symbol not only reflects or "speaks" though; it also acts. Indeed, the symbol "speaks" by acting. By acting, through a specific modality of action, it also fulfils a communicative and affective function. Practices, which are symbolic behaviors, are the cradle and humus of the symbol and of symbols; they are the starting place from which symbols become active, on a noetic and practical level. Thinking the symbol adequately requires that we consider symbolic practices and behaviors.

Here, the origin of the *symbolon* has much to teach us. Originally, the *symbolon* was a clay tablet (which bore an inscription or image) attesting an alliance into which two parties had entered or, more modestly, an agreement or contract they had reached. The tablet was broken in half so that, even at a great spatial or temporal distance, when meeting again, the owners of the two halves could recognize each other as parties to the pact and reactualize it. Here, the key idea seems to be that of an originary unity that must be found again and reconstituted. But where, how, and when is the *symbolon* a symbol? It is such neither at the beginning nor at the end, which is its goal but also its termination. The symbol is in the in-between; it is there that its power unfolds. The end of the action of the symbol is not the reconstitution of the originary unity; it is much more, and different. In-between is the arrival and the *recognition* of something new. The *symbolon* is driven, it is important to note, by a "principle of hope."[23]

Returning to the originary scene, then, the symbol already gives rise to thought. What is, specifically, the symbol? The whole tablet at the origin? Or the reconstitution of its parts by the two parties who hold them? Are each of the two halves symbols? Perhaps, to answer the question, we must modify its formulation by correcting the "what." The tablet is a symbol for the *intention* to break it and later reassemble it. The clay that is made whole again is a symbol for the *recognition* that the two parties exchange. The two halves, while they are separated, are symbols inasmuch as each one *points to* the other, carrying the memory of a past event (the breaking) and anticipating a future event (the bringing together) within human experience, which is an experience of distance, separation, and lack of knowledge. In the in-between, between the initial and the final moment—that is where the symbol is most truly symbol. It is a symbol specifically *there*, where it is essentially a pointer to an absence that, however, is not simply a "lack," because it is evoked by the symbol itself. Rather than being a "thing," the symbol is above all the experience that "the not" [*il non*] is.[24]

Representational Action

The matter is not simply that the symbol speaks by acting. Rather, acting itself can have a symbolic nature. This requires that we consider the different ways in which acting occurs, because certainly not every action has symbolic relevance.

The "fact" of human action has been a constant object of investigation in the history of thought, from ancient philosophers to the medieval to the modern. Because of challenges from sociology and other humanities and social sciences, the debate about a philosophy of action has been especially broad and lively in the contemporary period. In particular, within analytic philosophy and in dialogue and dialectic with it, a theory of action—initially in connection with the theory of language—has developed in various stages and turns. The dimensions of free will, the antecedents of action, intention, motivation, the correlative interplay between finality and causality, rationality, freedom, decision, and impulse have all played a role in this development. It would be impossible to offer an adequate account of all of this here.[25]

Schleiermacher obviously precedes all these subsequent elaborations and inquiries. His thought, however, offers an interesting and original element and perspective that serve not as alternative but as complement to the subsequent reflection, opening the way to a deeper articulation.

In his examination of the different modes of acting, Schleiermacher articulates the fundamental distinction (which, it must be noted from the start, cannot be understood as an opposition) between effective action (*wirksames Handeln*) and representational action (*darstellendes Handeln*).[26] Having made this distinction, Schleiermacher focuses on representational action, placing it within a context that gives it ontological value: "Every representation is nothing other than the stable realization of the human essence itself."[27]

The specific context within which Schleiermacher articulates this concept is his treatment of Christian life and, specifically, Christian worship. The articulation falls within the broader picture of Schleiermacher's philosophical thought, which sees human beings, in their finiteness and self-consciousness, as being in an originary relation with the world and the divine Infinite, a relation of both freedom and dependence.[28] By virtue of their cognitive function, human beings welcome the world within themselves; by virtue of their organizational function, they shape the world according to reason until nature becomes a symbol of reason.

This is linked to the fundamental distinction between *wirksames Handeln* and *darstellendes Handeln*, effective action and representational action. The first is analogous to the organizational function; the second, to the cognitive one.

Schleiermacher notes that there are actions by which we do not intend to achieve anything. This is the case for all forms of representations, art, and play.[29] These actions do not have the purpose of producing or accomplishing changes; they are expressions of one's inwardness that have no efficaciousness or external end or purpose.[30] The interiority of the human being is expressed in a representation of the self so as to achieve communication with others.[31]

This distinction is established and applied for heuristic purposes in order to understand what happens in the act of worship. Within the Christian perspective, worship presents in fact a paradox. Worship is clearly an action performed by the community. At the same time, though, worship is also the site and time of an action of God, whom the community and each of its members stand open to receive. It is both activity and passivity. How can these two aspects be held together? Schleiermacher offers an overall understanding of worship as feast or festival (*Fest*), in which spontaneity and receptivity intertwine. This is made possible by identifying the type of action that characterizes worship in the strict sense.[32]

The action that is performed in worship is a purely representational action. Indeed, worship is the general "type" of representational action.[33] In the act of worship, Christians do not "work"; rather, says Schleiermacher, they "represent" themselves as instruments of God's action. They represent passivity and openness to divine action so that, in the representational action of Christians, it is Jesus Christ himself who "acts" through them. The human (representational) action of Christians is the experience of the working of the Holy Spirit. What we observe here is, therefore, a symbolic action in a strong sense: it is an action that refers to some other who otherwise is not directly accessible, an action that "makes present" some other as an active agent, and that in so acting reveals the other. In this perspective, the sacraments that are celebrated in Christian worship are not punctual and extrinsic acts; rather, they are the result of an overall symbolic action that is, at the same time, revelatory. This leads to delineate a symbolic behavior as the place within which individual symbols are situated and to circumscribe an action that has cognitive and revelatory meaning. This link between action and knowledge is not so obvious within the philosophical tradition, but it is well rooted in the biblical and Christian traditions.[34]

That which Schleiermacher brings to focus as "typical" representational action (that is, Christian worship) illuminates the relevance of human representational action in general. That is, it highlights the way in which symbolic behaviors act and reveal and how symbols arise from such behaviors, how the symbolic can be grasped in its entirety only in its being practiced.

Throughout his work, Schleiermacher theorizes and practices a constant going back and forth between philosophy and theology, keeping them quite distinct and autonomous, yet refusing to consider them as exclusive or as mutually negating.[35] Instead, he activates continuous synergies between the two.[36] The theological horizon of the specific essay in which Schleiermacher deepens the distinction between the two types of action includes a very broad exercise of philosophizing.[37] Starting with a theological question and pre-comprehension, the philosophical arguing is led to an encounter with a practice of faith (the Christian liturgy) and, by reflecting on that practice, the philosophical arguing turns into theological arguing, which produces a better understanding of that very practice and its implications.

On this ground, there emerges the multiple philosophical relevance of Schleiermacher's elaboration: in itself, that is, insofar as it contributes to enriching the reflection on the symbolic and, beyond this, in that it offers a perspective of inquiry that is also applicable—with due differences—to the consideration of other forms of action and practice. Looking through this lens at the polymorphous forms of human representational action within the contexts of politics, society, art, gender studies, and personal interactions enables a better grasp of their depth and implications.

More directly, moreover, Schleiermacher's theme of representational action has recently been the object of renewed interest and has been retrieved in many forms and areas of knowledge such as religion, aesthetics, and pedagogy, even finding points of contact with recent research on ritualism and theater.[38]

Among contemporary philosophies of action, Schleiermacher's perspective can, for example, be brought close to the implications of the idea of novelty and the "epiphanic" dimension linked to action in Hannah Arendt's conception.[39] By distinguishing among labor, work, and action, Arendt highlights how action is the manifestation and actualization of the human condition.[40] Inherent in the human condition is the ability to initiate, to set in motion, and thus to create the conditions so that something truly new may happen.[41] In acting that—inasmuch as it is always relational to others, political—is intertwined with discourse, an uncontrollable "revelation" of the person takes place.[42] Especially interesting is the way in which, in an entirely secular sense and key, there emerges here the connection between the dimensions of action and of revelation.

An Exercise in Philosophizing: The Center and Its Extending Rays

The coring into Schleiermacher's thought offers a valid example of the possible fecundity of overcoming the vision, present in much contemporary philosophy, of philosophy and theology as two forms of knowledge (to the extent that one is even willing to concede that theology be knowledge at all) that are entirely opposed to each other, destined to mutual elision. After philosophy's laudable, difficult, and painful attainment, in modern times, of its independence and autonomy from all theological authority, it had seemed as if these two fields could only either ignore or battle each other.

This antagonistic perspective, though, which has been particularly present within the Italian cultural context, has undergone a change in recent decades. Engagement with the theological tradition has become interesting again and is pursued by believing and nonbelieving philosophers alike, regardless of their personally religious and confessional creeds.

This is not to say that the relation between the two fields now can be characterized as one of good neighborhood. Neither philosophy nor theology would tolerate a similar kind of minimization and disregard of their respective differential profiles.[43] What rather should be underscored is the dialectical relation between the two—not two disciplines that are extraneous to each other, but two movements of thought that animate human discourse, that cannot be added to each other, but that can be integrated in their dialectical relation to each other. In fact, over the course of their multicentury journey, they have historically developed into what they are through differentiation from within a constitutive relation, both sharing the same concern for "the ultimate questions."[44] Conflicts between them, even to the point of mutual disavowal,[45] have been stages in a process of disengaging from an undifferentiated and confusing unity or from relations of submission of one to the other.[46] Having achieved mutual autonomy, they went through a period of reciprocal disregard as a way to prevent further attempts at mutual swallowing up. Now, though, the two fields can take a renewed interest in each other. This increasing proximity risks being understood and practiced as a softening of their irreducibility, thereby prefiguring new forms of fusion. At its best, however, the proximity takes place in the reciprocal recognition and appreciation of the mutual differences so that each may find (and may wish to find), in the other, an *ezer kenegdo* (Genesis 2:18): a "helpmate at one's front," that is, the sort of help that comes from the one who engages and resists us, with whom we confront and measure ourselves, in a relation that is not trivially peaceful but rich and fruitful.

The dialogue between philosophy and theology is also one of the paths and fundamental aspects of the philosophical exercise of the author of this reflection. Specifically, the study of the historical relation between philosophy and Christianity and the theoretical meta-reflections of the philosophy of religion have represented two of her primary areas of investigation.

This philosophical exercise finds its origin and center in the fundamental philosophical gesture of radical and critical questioning, in its conditions, and in the dialectical progression of its search for truth.[47] It is precisely in virtue of this gesture of questioning that philosophy cannot avoid interacting with other exercises of thought that are grasped phenomenologically and recognized as relevant.[48] This certainly includes philosophy's theological alter ego. But also, while always maintaining a clear distinction of ends and methods, philosophy cannot avoid asking itself about "who" [*chi*] poses the philosophical question in the concreteness of one's own existence, one's intellectual and psychological life, one's individual dimension and political actualization, and therefore also in the dimension of one's own gender. In the same way that philosophy cannot help but ask itself regarding "who" and "what" is revealed in the philosophical discourse, likewise it cannot avoid inquiring into "who" and "what" may be obscured and concealed by this very same discourse.

Lines of research such as the ones just mentioned may appear at first to be divergent and unrelated. On the contrary, they are rather brought together, on the one hand, by their focusing on a deep excavation of the philosophical questioning and, on the other hand and simultaneously, by their exploring the wide range of research paths that such a philosophical questioning connects and opens up.

A Brief Excursus on the Question of the "Who" in Philosophy

The question concerning the "who" may seem and, depending on how it is posed, may indeed entail a slide [*scadimento*] into the kind of psychologism denounced by Husserl, with a confusing, lethal mix-up between "my circumstance," as Ortega y Gasset would say—that is, "the empirical self," as Kant would have it—and the exercise of *nous*, that is, the production of thought and the universality of reason. Were such a question to become *the* central question of philosophical thinking, then it would indeed become a suffocating reduction [*restringimento*].

Yet the question about the "who" is the impertinent question that pertinently opens up all critiques of ideology. In all cases and especially when the matter is that of the relation between woman or the feminine [*femminile*] and philosophy, it is the removal of what has been repressed. It is a question that neither weakens nor, even less, endangers the radicality of the philosophical question. On the contrary, it does it justice.[49]

The dimension of argumentative rigorousness of the philosophical discourse is, in fact, always intertwined with its semantic dimension, with its identifying realms of experience and reality that need to be brought to concept and thought. As Jürgen Habermas says, there are always interests, whether they are conscious or unconscious, which move toward this form of knowledge; therefore, one should always engage in their critical identification, unveiling, and control. In this sense, even the question regarding the "who" is not only legitimate but also necessary.

In turn, this question benefits from its contextualization within a perspective of inquiry focused on the symbolic dimension. On the one hand, the symbolic dimension in fact unravels and "loosens up" the attention on the "who," thereby preserving it from being a biunivocal reference to individualized and isolated subjectivities. On the other hand, the passage through symbolic constellations and, primarily, the review and exploration of symbolic *behaviors*, of the "symbol in action," provide access to kinds of "who" that are stratified and intertwined, thereby enriching the field of experience and the very notion of the "who."

Contextualizing the contemporary consideration of gender within the horizon of the symbolic is also a fitting occasion for a critical rethinking of the concept of gender and, vice versa, a felicitous provocation for a philosophical reflection that engages the symbolic dimension.[50] On this path, one may also arrive to claim that the question of the gender of the subject is, in fact, a philosophical question, as it is not given at the biological or purely factual level but, rather, it is constituted at the level of symbolization, where the intertwining of individuality, intersubjectivity, structuring, and interpretative and cultural horizons comes to pass.[51]

Philosophy and Symbol: Dialectic and Conversation[52]

Given the conceptual and logical-argumentative interweaving of the philosophical discourse, the reflection on the symbol is, in the first place, truly a confrontation with the other-than-oneself considered also as opposite and stranger, and it indeed carries to fruition the fecundity of the encounter with alterity. At a subsequent stage, however, it becomes clear that this "other," even though it remains other, is implied in the very origin of philosophizing, that it nourishes and accompanies its unfolding both by offering ever new matters "to be thought" and by precipitating (in the chemical sense of salt precipitation) in the metaphors employed by discourse. At the same time, the dimension of the symbolic in turn acknowledges its need for the conceptual in order to be able to express meanings, even though it maintains an unexhausted reserve of potential meaning.

Exploring the symbol turns out to enable the integration of interests in theology, religion, biblical hermeneutics as well as psychoanalysis, politics, and gender studies. Through the reflection on the symbol, such areas of research appear not as subsequent stages along a journey, but as connected paths extending outward from a central point.

In turn, the symbolic feature that essentially qualifies theological discourse and religious language, the divisive and controversial question of the role of the symbolic in one's mental life as brought to light by psychoanalytical inquiries, and the critical reconsideration of the culturally and socially relevant symbolisms emerging from the areas of both political theory and gender studies—all this leads to deepening, in a properly philosophical key, the question of the symbolic dimension. This deepening sheds new light on the areas of thought that are investigated; it also centers the appeal, which such areas address to philosophy, to be "brought to thought" and focuses the contributions that come from them.

In the space available here, it obviously is not possible to carry out an exhaustive consideration of this whole range of themes, which nevertheless are mentioned, yet only in passing. The present reflection instead has focused on illustrating through an example the philosophical interest of a specific theological elaboration as a concrete exemplification of the meaning and power of the symbol in action. Through such an example, it has aimed to show that an increased understanding of the symbolic in its acting and the confrontation with the other-than-oneself can indeed be fecund for the philosophical discourse.

Notes

1. According to Cassirer, in the human animal, in addition to the receptive system and the reactive system, there is a symbolic system, which transforms our entire existential situation so that we live not in a merely physical universe, but in a symbolic universe. The definition of the human being as *animal rationale* retains—especially in the face of all irrationalistic theories—its value, because human activity is mainly characterized by rationality. However, reason does not explain all the richness and variety of the forms of cultural life, which are symbolic. Therefore, "instead of defining man as an *animal rationale*, we should define him as an *animal symbolicum*"; see Ernst Cassirer, *An Essay on Man: An Introduction to a Philosophy of Human Culture* (New Haven: Yale University Press, 1944), 26.

2. Paul Ricoeur, *From Text to Action: Essays in Hermeneutics, II*, trans. Kathleen Blamey and John B. Thompson (Evanston, IL: Northwestern University Press, 1991).

3. See Ricoeur's essays "Explanation and Understanding," 125–43, and "The Model of the Text: Meaningful Action Considered as a Text," 144–67, both contained in Ricoeur, *From Text to Action*.

4. Ricoeur, "Explanation and Understanding," 125–27. Ricoeur writes, "By dialectic, I mean the consideration that, rather than constituting mutually exclusive poles, explanation and understanding would be considered as relative moments in a complex process that could be termed interpretation"; see Ricoeur, "Explanation and Understanding," 126.

5. Ricoeur, "Explanation and Understanding," 126.

6. Ricoeur, "Explanation and Understanding," 136–37.

7. Ricoeur, "Explanation and Understanding," 137.

8. See Ricoeur, "Explanation and Understanding," 137–38.

9. Ricoeur, "Explanation and Understanding," 137.

10. See Ricoeur, "Explanation and Understanding," 137–38.

11. Friedrich Daniel Ernst Schleiermacher, *Die christliche Sitte nach den Grundsätzen der evangelischen Kirche im Zusammenhang dargestellt*, ed. Wolfgang Erich Müller (Waltrop: Spenner, 1999).

12. See Aristotle, *Metaphysics*, IV, 2, 1003a33: "*to on pollachos legetai*," being can be said in many ways.

13. See Maria Cristina Bartolomei, "Il simbolo si dice in molti modi: Saggio introduttivo," in *L'interrogazione del simbolo*, ed. Maria Cristina Bartolomei (Milan: Mimesis, 2014), 11–24.

14. More accurately, it goes from Ricœur to Kant, because the contemporary reconsideration of the nature of the symbol, in Ricœur as well as in other thinkers, finds in Kant a basis for a new approach.

15. "All the intuitions [*Anschauungen*] that are placed under *a priori* concepts are either schemata or symbols: the former contain direct presentations, the latter indirect presentations of the concept. The former do it in a demonstrative way, the latter by the aid of an analogy"; see Immanuel Kant, *Critique of Judgment*, trans. James Creed Meredith (Oxford: Oxford University Press, 2007), 179.

16. Paul Ricoeur, "Existence and Hermeneutics," in Ricoeur, *The Conflict of Interpretations: Essays in Hermeneutics*, trans. Kathleen McLaughlin (Evanston, IL: Northwestern University Press, 1974), 12–13 (italicized in the original).

17. See Paul Ricoeur, "Le symbole donne à penser," *Esprit* 27 (1959): 60–76.

18. Cassirer notes that the concept of "the unity of the rule" implies that the conceptual structure represents an ideal point of reference for the very construction of our perceptive and intuitive world. See Ernst Cassirer, "Zur Theorie des Begriffs," in Cassirer, *Philosophie der symbolischen Formen*, vol. 3 (Hamburg: Meiner, 2002), 323–61.

19. Adorno emphasizes that, because philosophy possesses its object only insofar as it surpasses it, if in philosophy "no more words were used that would say more than what it has to say here and now, at this particular point, philosophical thought would then be completely impossible"; Theodor W. Adorno, *Philosophische Terminologie*, vol. I (Frankfurt: Suhrkamp, 1973–74), 68.

20. See Elio Franzini, *I simboli e l'invisibile: Figure e forme del pensiero simbolico* (Milan: Il Saggiatore, 2008).

21. See Georg Wilhelm Friedrich Hegel, *Vorlesungen über die Ästhetik*, in *Werke*, vol. 13 (Frankfurt: Suhrkamp, 1970), 346–48.

22. For example, on the ethical dimension, see Giampaolo Azzoni, "La duplice trascendenza del simbolo," in *Symbolon/diabolon: Simboli, religioni, diritti nell'Europa multiculturale*, ed. E. Dieni, A. Ferrari, and V. Pacillo (Bologna: Il Mulino, 2005), 27–36; and on the political and social dimensions, see *La legittimazione simbolica*, ed. Roberto Cipriani (Brescia: Morcelliana, 1986).

23. In the Blochian sense of human consciousness, which, by virtue of the principle of hope that animates it, has the capacity to anticipate, to imagine what does not yet exist, thus making historical development possible. See Ernst Bloch, *The Principle of Hope*, 3 vols. (Cambridge, MA: MIT Press, 1995).

24. "By the expression 'experience of the symbol' is meant *an original openness (and possibility) of man and his logos inclined in the direction of a being 'not'* "; Giuseppe Zarone, in Fausto Pellecchia and Giuseppe Razzino, "Le ragioni del simbolo: Un colloquio tra filosofi e teologi," *Filosofia e teologia* 5, no. 3 (1991): 354.

25. Two key references suffice: Paul Ricœur, *La sémantique de l'action. Première partie: Le discours de l'action* (Paris: Èditions du Centre National de la Recherche Scientifique, 1977) and Franco Chiereghin, *Possibilità e limiti dell'agire umano* (Genoa: Marietti, 1990).

26. See Schleiermacher, "Das darstellende Handeln," in *Die christliche Sitte*, vol. 2, Second Part, 502–706.

27. "Alles Darstellen nichts anderes ist, als die beständige Realisation des menschlichen Wesens selbst"; Schleiermacher, *Die christliche Sitte*, 517.

28. See F. D. E. Schleiermacher, *Der christliche Glaube nach den Grundsätzen der evangelischen Kirche im Zusammenhang dargestellt*, ed. M. Redeker (Berlin: De Gruyter, 1960), 26.

29. See Schleiermacher, *Die christliche Sitte*, 37.

30. See Schleiermacher, *Die christliche Sitte*, 48.

31. See Schleiermacher, *Die christliche Sitte*, *Beilage* A, § 69, 24.

32. Schleiermacher does not isolate worship from life, the representative action from the effective action that must arise from it. He does not forget that, in the broad sense (according to Paul's "Letter to the Romans," chapter 12), the "spiritual" worship offered to God is one's entire life and action in the world, without which, he says, worship becomes superstition. But this aspect is not relevant to the matter of the present chapter.

33. See Schleiermacher, *Die christliche Sitte*, *Beilage* A, § 53, 17.

34. It is not by chance that we find the influence of these traditions on Ricœur, who, as we have seen, establishes links between the three theories of text, action, and history.

35. As regards philosophical and theological morality, see Schleiermacher, *Die christliche Sitte*, 24–28.

36. It is interesting to note, for example, that Schleiermacher claims that any theory of worship must always rely on aesthetics; see Schleiermacher, "Die praktische Theologie nach den Grundsäzen der evangelischen Kirche im Zusammenhange Dargestellt," in Schleiermacher, *Sämmtliche Werke*, ed. J. Frerichs (Berlin: de Gruyter, 1983), 1, 13, 798.

37. Throughout his years teaching in Berlin (1807–1834), Schleiermacher regularly offered courses in both philosophy and theology, although he published none of the treatises of these philosophical courses (dialectics, ethics, aesthetics, psychology, pedagogy and politics, history of philosophy) during his lifetime. Certainly, his dialectical, hermeneutic, and aesthetic perspectives are intertwined in the Schleiermacherian approach to representational action. But it is in particular in terms of Schleiermacher as scholar, translator, and interpreter of Plato that his consideration of the symbolic comes most into play. See F. D. E. Schleiermacher, "Einleitung," in Schleiermacher, *Platons Werke* (Berlin: Akademie Verlag, 1985);

Wilhelm Dilthey, "Il Platone di Schleiermacher," appendix to *Introduzione a Platone*, ed. G. Sansonetti (Brescia: Morcelliana, 1994).

38. See Ulrich Bogun, *Darstellendes und wirksames Handeln bei Schleiermacher* (Tübingen: Francke, 1998); Martina Kumlehn, *Symbolisierendes Handeln. Schleiermachers Theorie religiöser Kommunikation und ihre Bedeutung für die gegenwärtige Religionspädagogik* (Gütersloh: Chr. Kaiser/Gütersloher Verlagshaus, 1999); Inken Mädler, "Schleiermachers Gottesdiensttheorie im Schnittpunkt von Kunst und Religion," in *Christentum—Staat—Kultur*, ed. A. Arndt, U. Barth, and W. Gräb (Berlin: de Gruyter, 2008), 147–64; Victor Turner, *The Ritual Process: Structure and Anti-Structure* (Chicago: Aldine, 1969); Victor Turner, *From Ritual to Theatre: The Human Seriousness of Play* (New York: PAJ Publications, 1982); Victor Turner, *The Anthropology of Performance* (New York: PAJ Publications, 1986); and David Plüss, *Gottesdienst als Textinszenierung* (Zürich: Theologie Verlag, 2007).

39. See Hannah Arendt, *The Human Condition* (Chicago: University of Chicago Press, 1958).

40. "Philosophically speaking, acting is the human response to the condition of being born"; see Hannah Arendt, *On Violence* (Orlando: Harcourt, 1970), 82.

41. "The fact that man is capable of action means that the unexpected can be expected from him, that he is able to accomplish what is infinitely unlikely"; see Arendt, *The Human Condition*, 178.

42. "This revelatory quality of speech comes to the fore where people are *with* others. [. . .] Although nobody knows whom he reveals when he discloses himself in deed or word, yet he must be willing to risk the disclosure"; see Arendt, *The Human Condition*, 180.

43. Notable is the solution proposed by Paul Tillich. Rejecting the idea of the possibility of a "Christian philosophy," he argues that neither conflict nor synthesis is possible between (Christian) philosophy and theology. Both philosophy and theology ask the question of being, but from different perspectives, referring to different sources, and with different contents, because the philosopher's concern is cosmological while the theologian's is soteriological. However, alongside this divergence, there is also a convergence of the two viewpoints in the concrete persons of the philosopher and the theologian, which nevertheless does not necessarily result in a common ground between the two disciplines. See Paul Tillich, *Systematic Theology* (Chicago: University of Chicago Press, 1951), 21–32. For systematic theology, Tillich advocates the "method of correlation." Analyzing the human situation in light of the various forms of creative self-interpretation of the human being, in the various cultural areas (philosophy, narrative, psychology, sociology, poetry, dramaturgy), Tillich then shows that the content of the Christian faith is a response to the questions that arise from existence (see Tillich, *Systematic Theology*, 67–73). Through correlation, a modality of dialogue and synergy between theology and philosophy is re-created. However, the view that theology would find the answers to the questions that are articulated in philosophy has obviously raised doubts and criticisms from a philosophical point of view.

44. "Philosophy and theology are both characterized by an *ultimate concern*, that is, by being focused on the 'ultimate interests'"; see Tillich, *Systematic Theology*, 11–18. See also Paul Tillich, *Dynamics of Faith* (New York: Harper & Row, 1958), 1–12. And such ultimate concerns can only be expressed through symbolic language; see Tillich, *Dynamics of Faith*, 41–54.

45. See Helmut Gollwitzer and Wilhelm Weischedel, *Denken und Glauben: Ein Streitgespräch* (Stuttgart: Kohlhammer, 1965).

46. Referring to the conflict between the philosophical faculty and the theological faculty, Kant takes up the medieval image of philosophy as *ancilla theologiae*, observing, however, that it is unclear whether philosophy carries the lady's dress from behind or precedes her with a torch in hand; see Immanuel Kant, *The Conflict of Faculties*, trans. and with an introduction by Mary J. Gregor (New York: Abaris Books, 1979), 45.

47. "I define philosophy . . . as the movement of the spirit whose specific and proper intention is truth, without it being able to presuppose having this truth as something ready and definitive, contained in one of its particular propositions or in any other immediate form"; see Adorno, *Philosophische Terminologie*, vol. I, 88: "*So würde ich . . . Philosophie definieren als die Bewegung des Geistes, deren eigene Intention Wahrheit ist, ohne daß sie wähnte, nun in einem ihrer einzelnen Sätze oder in irgendeiner Gestalt der Unmittelbarkeit diese Wahrheit als ein bereits Fertiges zu haben.*"

48. According to Badiou's sharp analysis, which sees in the sciences, in poetry, in political thought, and in psychoanalysis "generic procedures" of truth, philosophy is "the act of Truth with respect to truths," which de-absolutizes them and declares them to be compossibile in the circulation of sense. See Alain Badiou, *Manifesto for Philosophy*, trans. Norman Madarasz (Albany: State University of New York Press, 1999), 142.

49. See Maria Cristina Bartolomei, "Alètheia? Tra Lete ed Eunoè: il soggetto e l'origine," in *La filosofia come vocazione: "Seconda Navigazione," Annuario Filosofico 1997* (Milan: Mondadori, 1997), 99–115.

50. In many respects, one can observe a reciprocal, albeit not unsurmountable repugnance between gender thinking and symbolic horizon insofar as gender thinking would imply precisely the liquidation of the symbolic dimension [*simbolicità*].

51. See Maria Cristina Bartolomei, "Simbolicità e prospettiva di genere," in *La dimensione simbolica* (Naples: ESI, 2009), 247–80.

52. "Conversation" is here to be understood not merely in the usual sense of a verbal exchange but rather in the etymological sense of the Latin verb *conversari*, that is *cum*, with, together, and *versari*, that is, dwelling, being in contact, keeping company, sharing a space in order to understand one another in an interchange in which one handles matters together.

Coda

Eleven

Mimetic Inclinations

A Dialogue with Adriana Cavarero

Adriana Cavarero and Nidesh Lawtoo

Introduction

A prominent figure within feminist thought and the thought of sexual difference, Adriana Cavarero is undoubtedly one of the most renowned Italian philosophers on the international scene.[1] Across political and classical philosophy, poststructuralism and gender studies, and even in dialogue with literary studies and art history, Cavarero's thought transgresses disciplinary boundaries to focus on immanent ethical and political problems rather than on delimited historical periods or fixed theoretical paradigms. Often in the company of Hannah Arendt and in critical dialogue with a patriarchal philosophical tradition that lists Plato among its initiators, Cavarero has written influential essays on the theme of human vulnerability, on the role of narrative and the formation of subjectivity, on terrorism, on violence against the helpless. She has developed a relational ontology that is more attentive to birth than death, and to the relationship with the other instead of an autonomous and egocentric subject. Among her published works, translated in various languages, are *Nonostante Platone* (1990), *Corpo in figure* (1995), *Tu che mi guardi, tu che mi racconti* (1997), *A più voci* (2003), *Orrorismo* (2007), and, more recently, *Inclinazioni: Critica della rettitudine* (2013).[2]

The following interview took place in Verona, where Cavarero taught for several years. We began with one of her more recent books, *Inclinations*, and proceeded to a dialogue about a concept that, unlike "voice," "story," "stately bodies," or disfiguring "horrorism," does not appear often or explicitly in her writings, yet an attentive reading will find that it underlines relational ontology throughout her work. This interview seeks to bring to the surface the concept of *mimēsis*, which lies at the intersection between philosophy and literature, two of Cavarero's main interests that are often in opposition within the patriarchal tradition but that Cavarero's thought helps bring into relation. A protean concept, usually translated as "imitation" or "representation," mimesis is at the center of many recent developments within continental philosophy, literary theory, but also the social and experimental sciences that, from different perspectives, are attentive to relational mimetic phenomena (such as identification, sympathy, affective contagion) that bind and, perhaps, incline the self toward the other. Whether mimesis so understood is in fact implicated in Cavarero's relational thought is what this dialogue-interview seeks to uncover.

Ancient Shadows

Nidesh Lawtoo: Let's begin with *Inclinations* in order to talk about mimesis, subjectivity, and politics. Given that the concept of mimesis goes back to Plato, the subject of one of your earliest books, following the thread of mimesis will perhaps allow us to weave in a figure in movement that characterizes an aspect of your thought that is little discussed but informs it implicitly and in a fundamental way nonetheless.

Adriana Cavarero: Gladly. Why don't we start with one of your definitions of *mimēsis* as a reference, to frame our talk, before we enter Plato's labyrinth?

NL: Sure. As you know, the Greek concept of *mimēsis* is difficult to define because it wriggles and escapes, as the god Proteus does, just to recall a Homeric image. In literary studies, for instance, mimesis continues to be thought of in terms of the Aristotelian model of representation of reality and is therefore reduced to realism. This definition is perhaps due more to Eric Auerbach's most important book, *Mimesis*, with the subtitle *The Representation of Reality in Western Literature*,[3] than to Aristotle, according to which *mimēsis* is not a representation of reality but of an action (*muthos*), constructed in an organic and unitary way, having a beginning, a middle, and an end. In any event, this realistic conception of mimesis is often mentioned. Less acknowledged is a fact of which Aristotle reminds us at the beginning of *Poetics*. That is, that at its origins, mimesis had something to do with corporeal ritualistic practices such as dance and music, which, through rhythm and melody, induce mimetic movements that would generate what Aristotle calls a "mimesis of character, of emotions, and of actions." This second, more archaic definition, according to which *mimēsis* induces the subject to imitate, often unconsciously, the other, and which defines us as mimetic beings (the most mimetic ones!), is the definition that interests me the most. Thus, mimesis can be understood not only as realism or, if we think of Plato, as a copy or a deteriorated shadow of the ideal reality. Rather, mimesis can be considered as a mimetic behavior that is embodied, immanent, contagious, and relational; through it, the I imitates the other, is exposed to the other, maybe is even possessed by the other, so much so that the I becomes a copy, a shadow, or a phantom of the I.

It seems to me that defined in this double sense, understood both as a degraded shadow of an ideal vertical world and as an affective force that has the power to charm and bend the subject, mimesis seems to play a double-sided role in *Inclinations*. Whereas you are critical of the former definition, and of the vertical ontology that underlines it, it seems you might be interested in the second notion because of its power of inclination. Starting with your critique of Plato, which you discuss in an intriguing chapter of *Inclinations* titled "Plato, *Erectus Sed*," could you articulate the relation that, in your assessment, exists between, on the one hand, mimesis and the Platonic vertical ontological device, which you oppose, and, on the other hand, the inclined subject that you propose?

AC: When I read the mimetic parts of Plato's myth of the cave, I read them in the Platonic spirit, which implies a negative attitude toward mimesis, and we need to keep this in mind. According to Plato, mimesis is not something that brings us close to knowledge or truth but something that distances us from truth, a distance of a few degrees: the shadows are the furthest degree. In the myth of the cave, reaching verticality would create the greatest distance from mimesis. Thus, within the Platonic framework, where mimesis has a much greater degree of distance from knowledge, whereas knowledge of the good is in fact the summit, the vertical point, what you suggest works wonderfully. This is to say that the Platonic mimesis is closer to inclination in the sense that there is, for sure, an attraction to or a fascination with shadows in the prisoners that are sitting in the cave. Therefore, we have mimesis along with fascination, which are always together in Plato, because mimesis is art, and art succeeds because it deceives and charms. Verticality is instead entirely on another side, because you reach it by leaving this magnetic field of attraction/fascination. This is what I would like to say to frame the myth of the cave.

NL: There is therefore an anti-Platonic tendency in your thought that brings you, *against* Plato, to celebrate what mimesis entails: narration, artistic representations, immanent and affective corporeal relationships. Would you agree that mimesis, similarly to *eros*, has the power to bend the I toward the other, to move the I's center of gravity, and possess it?

AC: Yes, but we need to clarify. I celebrate what Plato condemns, but not so much mimesis as he understands it. I celebrate a type of inclined subjectivity that is not self-created, that cannot be by itself, that needs the other and the inclination of the other in order to be. This is typical, for instance, of maternal inclination, a figure I employ because it is the most well-known and transparent icon. I have recently argued in an essay that in Plato I see the archeology of the foundation of the subject. Obviously, it is inappropriate to apply a term such as "subject" to Plato. The subject is a modern concept, and I am generally against taking the categories of modernity and attaching them to the Western macro-narrative from Homer to our day. Undoubtedly, however, in the myth of the cave, there is already an intimation of the subject, which is the philosopher, who stands up, changes direction, ascends, and then contemplates the sun and stands vertically in the direction of the Good. It is a self-sufficient subject, or, to say the least, its story is the narration of a story of self-sufficiency. In my view, this is the greatest fallacy of the entire Western metaphysics: the idea of the ego, self-created and self-sufficient.

On the contrary, in my theoretical perspective, subjectivity is entirely constituted by others. Therefore, there is a relationship with others that is not something added onto the self-sufficient subject: there is no self-sufficient and autonomous subject to start with. This is the scheme of the social contract: they are all rational, autonomous, and self-sufficient individuals who make a pact to give themselves a government. It is clearly an abstract narrative full of metaphysical fallacies. In my view instead, the subject is originally and irremediably constituted by relationships; we start from relationships, instead of starting from the I. This is why I do not know if what you mean by "*mimēsis*" can fit with my perspective since, in my view, there is no fusion with or substitution of the other. To put it in a more drastic way: the relationship with the other is not a relation tending to a fusion—in such a way that I become other, I otherize myself. In polemic with a certain postmodern usage of the theme of alterity, I want to underline that these embodied and relational subjectivities are distinct and unique among them. I am clearly referencing here what Hannah Arendt calls "uniqueness." In Arendtian terms: there is uniqueness in plurality;

therefore, there is no fusion or confusion or overlapping. I think this is the point you and I need discussing.

Modern Phantoms

NL: Yes, I agree. This is what I wanted to come to. Perhaps in mimesis as I understand it, there is both a risk of fusion and the possibility of maintaining uniqueness, depending on the context. Let me explain. On the one hand, it is true that, from my position about mimesis, there emerges a diagnostic interest in the form of affective contagion that risks, if not completely fusing or confusing, at least radically diminishing or diluting the ontological difference between the self and the other. I do not become completely other in the sense of Rimbaud's "*Je est un autre*"; but in some relational or collective contexts—watching a movie in a room that evokes Plato's cave, for instance—I can become unconsciously receptive, open, and vulnerable to what the other feels. There is a form of sympathy, of *sym-pathos*, constitutive of mimetic relations that interest me, that is contagious, that transgresses the principle of individuation and ties the I, in the good and in the bad, to the other.

On the other hand, I find some modern philosophical and literary authors who, though anti-Platonic, are inspired by Plato as you are, and who insist on oxymoronic concepts that seem to point to a double back-and-forth movement in this form of mimetic contagion. Let's take, for instance, the Nietzschean concept of the "*pathos* of distance" (*Pathos der Distanz*). This concept is often reduced to the position of distance that Nietzsche takes with respect to the mimetic subjects he condemns (slaves, women, masses, or, as he calls them often, the herd) in order to celebrate instead the sovereign and autonomous individual (the master). Yet he calls this relationship a "*pathos*," an affective concept that is at the heart of sympathy and that, if considered more closely, seems to indicate a vulnerability that makes him, Nietzsche, extremely receptive to the mimetic affects he himself condemns. In his thought, as in the thought of other philosophical or literary authors, I find a double back-and-forth movement, which is central to my conception of mimesis as a double-edged concept: on the one hand, one that relates affectively the I to others, risking to generate simulacra or "phantoms of the ego," as Nietzsche says; on the other hand, this allows the I, although permeable to the pathos of the other, to maintain a critical distance that preserves the difference and a degree of individuality, even though this individual is not indivisible but is constituted by the mimetic relationship with the other.

In this, I find an isomorphism, or at least a resonance with your thought, which is, to say the least, twofold. On the one hand, you insist on uniqueness, which you share with Arendt and which brings you to underline the unity of the figure. You show this aspect brilliantly, for instance, in *Relating Narratives*, in your comment on the tale by Karen Blixen and the figure of the stork that is traced on the sand as a unitary figure of the I. On the other hand, the affective dimension of mimesis reveals a relational conception of the subject, which is open, permeable, and vulnerable to the other. Could you talk a little more about this tension between the unity of the figure and its ontological openness to the other, which is characteristic of inclination?

AC: I would not speak of a double movement, because the figure of uniqueness, as I understand it, is structurally open and vulnerable. Just like the self-sufficient and sovereign subject of the tradition, the Cartesian subject, is closed, ideally invulnerable, "hard as a nut," as Virginia Woolf writes,[4] so is the unique subject vulnerable. As Arendt says too, uniqueness is ontologically founded on birth, in our first appearing, and it is actualized and expressed with the "second birth" that is action. Action is the total exposure of the self, of *who* you are, to others, while you are totally exposed and bent toward the outside (*estroflesso*): you appear, you show yourself. In this total exposure, there is structural openness and vulnerability. Naturally, we can view this exposure in exhibitionist and Narcissistic terms, which is something well known in modernity. Arendt herself, after all, recognizes that there could be a certain emphasis on such exposure; she says that the Homeric heroes, for instance, reveal themselves in an emphatic manner. But in a non-heroic situation, this exposure is also, in the first place, an exposure to the wound. It marks a constitutive vulnerability, a condition of dependence, which, as I have tried to argue in *Inclinations* along with Levinas, does not lead necessarily toward an ethics of reciprocity; rather, it forces us to rethink ethics in terms of unbalance and asymmetry.

Moreover, I would not confuse unity with uniqueness, because the concept of unity suggests something that is always singularly compact. Certainly, the stork that the protagonist of Karen Blixen's tale draws with his steps is a unitary figure; but it is so symptomatically, not because he wanted to draw it; rather, because at the end and without his intention, it "results" from the footsteps he has left on the wet ground. In my reading of Blixen, the stork, the unity of a figure that makes sense still remains an ideal goal. In other words, that our life has a unitary meaning is an object of our desire, not a given. No one has a life with a definitive meaning that is complete and closed in a wonderful unity. We can only wish to have such a life. However, if it is true that the desire of the narratable self is to aspire to the completion of unity, it remains clear in my argument that "uniqueness" is not at all synonymous with closure. On the contrary, in terms of the Arendtian speculation, which I like to resume and elaborate, it is synonymous with openness and vulnerability in the literal sense, that is, openness to the wound.

NL: This desire for a figural unity, even only as an ideal, is perhaps less present in the Nietzschean tradition on which I rely. However, the vulnerability and the openness constitutive of the I, at birth, by way of the other, is something that we share, it seems to me. My problem is that if the I is structurally open to the other, vulnerable to forms of affective contagion, predisposed to a mimesis that is often unconscious and involuntary, the risk of dissolution, of fusion, and of loss of the I remains big. We shall come back to this. For the time being, could you clarify the role that, in your view, the other plays in such a delineation of a figure of the I that is open, yet not unitary?

Mimesis and Narration

AC: This is another fundamental point that I have learned from Arendt: the narration of the self by itself, the autobiography *in primis*, is a falsification. As you know, this is, after all, a commonplace in literary studies as well. A good number of literary critics who comment on Augustine's or Rousseau's *Confessions*, for instance, underline that the self narrating itself is substantially a *fiction*. Arendt provides some very interesting philosophical explanations of this autobiographical falsification to which, even according to the postmodern critique, we are drawn. She says that uniqueness, which she calls the "who," that is, the subject of the question "who are you?" (an altogether different question from "what are you?"), being totally exposed to the other, comes from the other, in that it is only the other who has a vision of this "who." The only way to see myself would be by looking into the mirror; but in doing so, we would be right in the field of the most ostentatious Narcissism. Arendt says that no one knows *who* he or she is while acting. We can reflect on what we have done, on how we have acted, and we can narrate our actions to ourselves. In doing so, we tend to falsification because no autobiographical narrator has properly seen himself or herself. Following Arendt, it is worth taking the question of vision seriously. The others are also those who see you, you expose yourself to their organ of sight. Where the self is looking at itself, where there is a mirror, there is in fact a danger of mimesis. But *who* you are, Arendt insists, the narratable uniqueness that your story tells, is structurally entrusted to others.

As a matter of fact, "who is Homer?" Arendt asks. He is the first narrator and the first historian of Greece who tells the story (the history) of Greece, the war of Troy, but also the personal stories of singular and exposed lives: Achilles, Hector, Ulysses, Andromache, Penelope. In narrating these life stories, we can say, he saves them from ruins, in the sense that, as the Greeks and Homer knew well, every life is unique and singular, is a temporary and precarious existence—mortal. The Greeks are obsessed with the theme of death—human beings are called "mortals" (*hoi brotoi*). The narration, which tells a life story, saves life from the ruin of death, that is to say, from oblivion; but it does not save it in the Empyrean or in some place beyond. It saves it for posterity, in the world of human beings, in the fully human sphere of the world. We know the figure of Ulysses, we know his story because Homer has told us this story. It is saved in our entirely worldly dimension. There is no metaphysical salvation in the sense of the self. According to Arendt, the sense of every unrepeatable and singular existence, a unique existence, is historically immanent to the world in which it has appeared by exposing itself to others.

NL: In listening to you and in seeing how you trace your relation to figures such as Plato, Arendt, but also literary authors such as Homer and Blixen, I see a way of philosophizing that seems different from the predominant, patriarchal tradition in at least two ways: on the one hand, in your relation to literature; on the other, in your relation to the models that come before you. These are two themes that touch upon mimesis, often in a combined fashion. In thinking about the relationship between Plato and Homer, for instance, we have a relationship of rivalry, which is the rivalry both of Plato against Homer and of philosophy against literature. This rivalry continues all the way up to our time. Let's start with your relation to the philosophical models in order to arrive to literature.

In your relation to the philosophical figures that come before you, you distinguish yourself from the paradigm of mimetic rivalry that, within the patriarchal tradition from Plato to René Girard, often leads to violence and death. One of the many virtues of your approach is that you underline birth, affective relations, and life. Arendt plays an essential role in your thought, among other reasons, precisely because she celebrates birth. You even talk about imitating the "Arendtian model," but you do not do this on the basis of the mimetic rivalry model. There is, nonetheless, a form of confrontation or mimetic agonism that opens a new way of reconnecting to the models that come before us in a creative or productive way, bringing their thought elsewhere. How would you define your relation with the philosophical models from which you draw?

AC: I consciously imitate Arendt's method because I find it very effective. Her method consists in bringing some intuitions, some ideas to their extreme consequences, that is to say, to force, radicalize, and bring a thesis to its extreme. In doing so, obviously one may incur in speculative and interpretive errors. But who does not incur in this type of error, after all? Arendt, however, succeeds in constructing strong theoretical structures, which then become frameworks that are useful to move further, go beyond, and redraw what seems known, if not perfectly known. As a matter of fact, I imitate this method very often. For instance, in *Inclinations*, I recover the significant figure of the mother with child, which is a very famous icon within the European Christian tradition, and, by forcing its stereotypical representation, I push it to its extreme consequences and redraw its meaning. My strategy is fruitful, I hope. I am convinced that by bringing intuitions and images to their extreme consequences, it is possible to attain the result, which I find decisive, of making stereotypes speak differently. Our language is rich in stereotypes, obviously. Those about the masculine and the feminine, for example, are the most well known, and I have been working on them for some time. But there are also the various stereotypical representations of different ethnic, religious, and moral identities; or the formulas that pretend to synthesize the ideas of East and West, and even of good and evil, of just and unjust, and so on. Through the operation of bringing on and forcing the images, these stereotypes, so to speak, are torn apart and enable us to see possible meanings that are often different from or even opposite to those that the stereotype suggests.

Many years ago, in *In Spite of Plato*, I called this method the "technique of theft."[5] I think that it can still be called so. In my first years of study, when I was young, I happened to encounter Plato's texts. If one begins with Plato, it is difficult to leave him behind, because he is an author still on the threshold of philosophy; it is philosophy in its making, the philosophizing process itself, which constructs itself as a discipline and reckons with its own foundation. Plato is full of ways of reasonings, images, or, as Derrida would say, figural explanations and intuitions that still have an undecidable side. This explains why I look at Plato as an author who, first and before others, has left us images, traces, and pieces of constructions from which we can take and steal, tear off the context, and rearrange, think of, or imagine differently. I think that this is a fecund speculative method, and I always encourage young scholars in philosophy and literature, whether they are men or women, to adopt it.

NL: You adopt the "technique of theft" with respect to the patriarchal tradition . . .

AC: I steal from Arendt as well (she laughs) . . .

NL: Yes, but you are often very explicit in your debt toward her.

AC: Yes, it is true. The dangerous part of mimesis is repetition and, therefore, sterility. If mimesis is done with literary stealing, I think that it becomes more productive and maintains something living in it that does not become congealed. Then there are big treasures, large deposits. Certainly, Plato is a large deposit, and surely Homer is too. But in my view—as you know, because you do the same thing—literature is the largest deposit par excellence. If we, who do philosophy, limit ourselves to the philosophical macro-narrative, we leave out the biggest treasures, which are the literary ones.

Imitation and Gender Relations

NL: Would you say that this method of stealing, which reconnects with literature and therefore with a mimetic tradition, belongs properly to the feminine symbolic order in opposition to the "ideal" philosophical order, often based on the rivalry of a patriarchal mold?

AC: I don't know if it is feminine. Let's say that it is feminine if we think of the figure of women gatherers. Or of women embroiderers as great creators of patchworks. That is to say, to be able to take pieces, snatch them, save them, rearrange them, and reweave a different canvas. It is an operation that does not waste the treasure, the literary or figural deposits, but combines them in a different way, and therefore can needle them into an embroidery. It is not by chance that the figure I was inspired by, in my early book *In Spite of Plato*, was Penelope, the weaver, the one who does and undoes. This means that the weaver does not waste but utilizes threads that have already been used for a previous fabric. This does not mean that there are no new threads; naturally, the time and the story, the experience bring in new threads. It means, however, that in order to say new things we can tap into great deposits, we can draw from Homer and from the literature of all times. For example, you and I love to tap into Conrad—it is a deposit that one cannot avoid tapping into, as a matter of fact! Conrad's imagination is wonderful! Why not take advantage of this imaginary, which also takes place at such an important historical moment, namely, a time of transition to imperialism, of great technical, social, and political transformations? You yourself take advantage of the great literary deposits . . . therefore you understand what I am trying to say.

NL: Yes, I try to do that, and I find dazzling intuitions about mimesis, about which "my" authors know a lot. I also share your passion for the affirmative—Nietzsche would say "gay"—spirit of your method, a method that could also be called genealogical in the sense that it is turned toward figures of the past: not just for its own sake, but in order to reweave threads or in order to recover figures or concepts of the past, such as that of mimesis in fact, and reweave them in a productive way in view of addressing ethical and political problems of the present and the future. There is a strength turned not toward death, but toward birth—another great Nietzschean theme—in this gesture of yours that leads me to the next question.

You snatch, recover, and reweave the concept of birth, taking it from Arendt; at the same time, you radicalize it by putting the accent on the figure of the mother, in a way that goes beyond Arendt's thought in order to anchor the category of natality in the life of the body of the mother and of the infant. Very often, when you speak of philosophers of the patriarchal tradition, as in the case of Kant for example, you remind us that we have to deal not just with abstract minds, but also with embodied persons, who have lives, habits, and some experience—or lack of experience. What role does the experience of birth play in your radicalization of this concept?

AC: As I have argued in *Inclinations*, I accuse Arendt—and I think I am right in this—of having been able to give value to the category of birth by placing it at the foundation of her political thought without, however, considering, not even as a theme, that necessary figure, always present at birth, that is the mother—and actually, not even the infant is considered. Arendt speaks of a "newborn," one who has just been born, who is already congealed in this stage of novelty, beginning, namely someone who always remains a newborn and does not grow. It is clear, obviously, that the newborn will grow, will become an adult, will act, and will experiment that which Arendt calls his or her second birth; but what happens in the meantime, we don't really know in Arendt's terms. Therefore, there is a blindness in Arendt in the way she discusses birth as a relational scene between mother and infant, an infant that is a vulnerable creature, exposed both to wound and care and that needs caring in order to grow and become an "actor." Allow me to insist on the realism, even material realism, of the scene of birth, where there are at least two persons, namely: the mother and the newborn. What is important to me here is to illustrate the foundation of ontology as a scene that is already constitutionally relational. In other words, the meaning of birth is not given as a pure apparition of a newborn; it is given, rather, as a relationship of the newborn with the mother and vice versa. It is not enough to make of birth a concept: we must conceptualize birth as a credible scene, concrete, avoiding turning it into an abstract category of philosophy.

The experience of maternity is, naturally, the experience of a relationship strictly connected to the body, an experience of tactility, also of vocal and affective correspondences with the infant who, in all evidence, is not the Arendtian newborn, congealed in his or her paradigmatic function of a "new beginning," but rather a creature who extends his or her existence in a long period of infancy, which is a long period of absolute fragility and vulnerability. Therefore, the experience of maternity is an experience of subjectivity, the maternal subjectivity, which, besides being in herself vulnerable like all subjectivities, is structurally put into relationship with the absolute—and exemplarily helpless—vulnerability of the infant. It seems to me that, in fact, this is a very interesting model for rethinking ontology and, with it, ethics and politics. I add, but this seems obvious to me, that I speak of the mother, and I have in mind an ordinary representation of this figure: namely, a woman who has a child and then raises such a child. But, aside from giving birth, the maternal figure can obviously be substituted by anyone else who takes upon himself or herself the care of the absolutely helpless because otherwise, as Hobbes says, if no one looks after him or her, the infant dies. And let's not forget that, for Hobbes, the power of life and death is sovereign power. There is something frightful in the originary relationship with the absolute helpless who enters the scene through the experience of maternity. Arendt does not take this into consideration, but, in my view, it is a decisive aspect of the operation of grounding ontology in the human condition of natality.

NL: I find this aspect of a constitutive relationship that you radicalize in Arendt also central to the problem of an affective and unconscious mimesis that, from birth on, ties the subject to the model, *in primis*, of the maternal one or the parents and then to teachers, friends, but also television and movie models, and, increasingly, even virtual models. I agree with you that the mimetic relationship with the other precedes the constitution of subjectivity, or better said, it is the mimetic relationship that, after the first birth, enables subjectivity to emerge in what Plato already calls a second birth. A starting point for me is to think how this mimetic relationship, which is also a relationship of inclination, comes paradoxically from philosophers who are often, and rightly so, considered patriarchal, phallocentric, and frankly misogynous thinkers, such as Nietzsche or, in a different way, figures such as D. H. Lawrence or George Bataille. Nevertheless, between the lines of their sexism, they describe, often not without admiration, the relationship of nonverbal communication between mother and newborn with great sensibility. They even anticipate recent developments in child psychology that seem to support your thesis concerning a constitutive relational ontology. It has been discovered, as a matter of fact, that newborns respond in a mimetic and reflexive manner to the facial expressions of the parents, the mother first of all, much earlier than was previously thought. The predominant model in developmental psychology came from figures, such as Piaget, who put imitation at a late stage in the development of the infant. Instead, these mimetic reflexes that, for the good or the bad, open subjectivity to the other, happen very early—the records show they happen at around forty-two minutes from birth.

These experiments show that mimesis, not as mirror of reality but as unconscious mimetic behavior, is perhaps at the origin of human subjectivity. They show, based on empirical evidence, that we are a species that, as already Aristotle said, is the most mimetic of all and that, for lack of originality, I call *homo mimeticus*. As I understand it, *homo mimeticus* is also opposed to the traditional figure of *homo erectus* because it reminds us that, from birth on, we are inclined to mimesis and mimesis inclines us, with our body but also with our psyche, toward the other and vice versa. On this point, I think our interests intertwine around what we could call, if you agree, "mimetic inclinations" that—through bodily affective experiences such as facial expressions, touch, voice—from birth on, place relationship as originary. What do you think about these developments?

AC: It seems to me that mimesis as you describe it now says, in more concrete terms, what I was saying in philosophical terms. That is to say, in your own words, mimesis shapes the vulnerable subjectivity. The vulnerable subjectivity is so exposed to the other that it just imitates the other in gestures, voices, sounds, and facial expressions, and, therefore, it is a subjectivity totally formed by the other. I think that, in this, we are very close. I think that my fear to adhere unconditionally to your position comes from the risk of fusion. In other words, in the very concrete and affirmative discourse of the formation of subjectivity, in the constitutive relationship that forms subjectivity, I follow you perfectly. My fear is that, in what comes after that, there is a postmodern drift, falling therefore into a formula according to which "every self is never a self, but always already the other." Here it is—I do not share this formula or the language that it evokes. First of all, because I do not share the idea of the subject as the starting point to which that formula is opposed in a decisive way, that is to say, the ghostly idea of a self totally autonomous and sovereign. We are never autonomous, even less at birth, because we are expelled by another body and exposed to the world. In short, there is never an isolated self without the other, and the other is constitutive for the formation of the self.

In my view, being able to recognize the constitutive bond of such a self—namely, the relational function in the ontological condition of subjectivity—as well as to recognize, to put it in your own terms, that mimesis shapes and continues to reshape this subjectivity in time, is important in order not to fall into the verticalizing abstractions of the philosophy of the sovereign and autonomous subject. I am therefore very suspicious toward all postmodern suggestions that risk modifying the relational substance of the self, making the self an alteration of the self-in-the-other. It seems to me that this is an aesthetic game that does not captivate me when it comes to political philosophy. As a political philosopher, as a matter of fact, one of the central categories is, for me, that of responsibility. I need an anchoring subject that does not fuse with the other than oneself; that is, I need a subject that is determined, that is able to receive the interrogation and respond. You understand that now I am not referencing Hannah Arendt but Emmanuel Levinas, who is another of my inexhaustible treasures, one of my deposits!

Masses and Plurality

NL: What you say makes me think also of the ethical implications of this mimetic openness for the dominant models of the contemporary political scene. My preoccupation concerning the dissolution of the self is not so much aesthetic but, as you say as well, ethical and political. In particular, it concerns the problem of the relation between mimesis, which, in my opinion, often works in an unconscious and involuntary way, and the masses, a relation that accentuates the permeability of the self and makes it very vulnerable to leaders and their ideological suggestions. If we think of Plato's old distinction, that mimesis can function both as therapy and as poison, we could say that, on the one hand, the mimetic inclination leads to a living openness if the models are good but also, on the other hand, to a potentially pathological one if the models are harmful, as seen in the relation between populist leaders and the masses in the age of Twitter.

AC: This is the dangerous, demagogic, and populist mimesis, a theme about which we understand each other well! It may be because I am a Platonist, but I fear this version of mimesis deeply, also because I have studied the phenomenon of totalitarianism. I fear mimesis, contagion, attraction, and the dissolution of subjectivity. This too means, for me, to shake off one's responsibility: all guilty, no one guilty.

NL: Yes, we share this sentiment of consciousness of the power of the masses that dissolves, influences, and conditions the individual often in a pathological and unconscious way. When I say unconscious, I do not mean this on the basis of a repressive Oedipal hypothesis but on the basis of those mimetic involuntary reflexes that are visible in infancy but also in adult masses, and that I collect under the category of "mimetic unconscious." At the same time, you propose the notion of a "plurality" that does not identify with mimetic masses. By way of conclusion, could you reflect on this relation between masses and plurality in connection with the projects you are working on now, and perhaps even tell us about them?

AC: At the moment, I am reflecting exactly on the difference, if not opposition, between plurality and masses. Masses are a form of collectivity in which subjectivity dissolves and, through a mimetic process, becomes only one enormous and amorphous subject that is called, in fact, masses. Plurality—a category that I take from Arendt—is the exact opposite. It is the paradoxical plurality of unique beings, namely, in Arendt's terms, the human condition par excellence. Not only does individuality not dissolve in the plurality; on the contrary, it is exalted in the sense that uniqueness and plurality go together. If we are unique, it means that our collective form is the plural form; if our collective form is plural, then it means that we are unique. In Arendtian terms, uniqueness and plurality are just two categories that implicate one another reciprocally. In this sense, they are the opposite of the masses.

Moving from this distinction, at present, I am reflecting on the sonorous and acoustic aspect that is manifested in the difference between masses and plurality. We are dealing with two phonospheres, two soundscapes about which literature—our famous literary treasure!—provides us with punctual descriptions. For example, the typical example of the voice of the masses is the singing of the national anthem, but we could also mention, to make this more modern, the singing of hymns at soccer or football stadiums. On the voice of the masses, I have found some very interesting things in the novels by Émile Zola but also in Elias Canetti and, obviously, in the writings of Georges Mosse. The voice of plurality is instead a more difficult theme, but I have found interesting analyses in autobiographical texts by Canetti himself and by Roland Barthes. What interests me is that vocal plurality as well as vocal masses have also to do with the word, and not just with pure sound or a roar. Since in plurality everyone is unique, the ideal voice of plurality, as Roland Barthes says, suggests that every one of these unique subjects has a different speech, or that there is a plurality among many different dialogues, between me and you, between two others, and so forth, maybe simultaneously. From the acoustic position of the one who listens, the result would then be a kind of cacophony. I, on the contrary, try to argue that it is instead a *pluriphony*, in the sense that the vocal plurality emits its own particular noise or buzzing, in which it is possible to perceive the uniqueness of the voices that constitute it; it is a particular noise, a kind of distinctive phonosphere that is profoundly different from the voice of the masses, which sounds tendentially in unison, both in form as in roar, as well as in the national anthem. Canetti says that the voice of the masses is like the voice of the sea: a repetitive rumble and a roar, a wave, something that is sweeping.

I fear that the recent surge in populism, both in Europe and in the United Stated, is a return of the masses. For sure, it is for the most part a dispersed mass, connected through the new media and social media; and this too, as you know well, is a problem of mimesis! As you yourself have written, it is symptomatic of the contagious mimesis of the masses, above all in the totalitarian form, as well as in a sonorous mimesis. In my opinion, the sonorous dimension conveys this contagion very well, this *reductio ad unum*; namely, it makes it very effective and easily perceptible. Crucially, in the case of plurality, the mimetic element understood as contagious is not there; however—and this is the concept I make allusion to when I speak of pluriphony—it seems that the unique voices tune in at a specific level of sonority.

NL: It seems that in this dialogue, on the one side, tied to mimesis and, on the other, in opposition to it, we find an original journey that draws a figure of your thought as it moves. We started with your early works on Plato, passing through your relationship with Arendt, your passion for literature, and we have come to your most recent projects. Images change, but you continue to weave and reweave the threads that are constitutive of mimetic phantoms that project a shadow on the present and on a plurality that, we can only hope, opens the I to the future.

A *word of thanks*—Nidesh Lawtoo wishes to thank Adriana Cavarero for accepting to weave a mimetic thread that we "picked up" informally at Grand Central Station in New York in June 2017, we rethreaded more calmly at the Università di Verona, in April 2018, and allows us to continue to dialogue.

(Translated by Elvira Roncalli)

Notes

1. This project has received funding from the European Research Council (ERC) under the European Union's Horizon 2020 research and innovation program (grant agreement No. 716181: HOM).

2. See Adriana Cavarero, *In Spite of Plato: A Feminist Rewriting of Ancient Philosophy* (New York: Routledge, 1995); *Relating Narratives: Storytelling and Selfhood* (New York: Routledge, 2000); *Stately Bodies: Literary, Philosophy, and the Question of Gender* (Ann Arbor: University of Michigan Press, 2002); *For More Than One Voice* (Stanford: Stanford University Press, 2005); *Horrorism: Naming Contemporary Violence* (New York: Columbia University Press, 2008); *Inclinations: A Critique of Rectitude* (Stanford: Stanford University Press, 2016).

3. Eric Auerbach, *Mimesis: The Representation of Reality in Western Literature*, trans. Willard R. Trask (Princeton, NJ: Princeton University Press, 2013).

4. See Virginia Woolf, *A Room of One's Own* (London: Hogarth Press, 1929), chapter 6.

5. Cavarero, *In Spite of Plato*, 5.

Contributors

Maria Cristina Bartolomei completed a postgraduate specialization in philosophy after graduating in philosophy from the University of Padua. In addition, she holds a license in theology from the Pontificio Ateneo Anselmianum in Rome. Until retiring in 2016, she was associate professor of moral philosophy at the State University of Milan, where she taught moral philosophy and philosophy of religion. She is part of the editorial board of many philosophical journals and book series and of the executive committees of various philosophical and theological associations. She has been one of the main promoters of the Centro Interuniversitario di Studi sul Simbolico (CISS). At the center of her research projects are the relations, on the one hand, between hermeneutics and dialectics and, on the other, between philosophy and theology, studied both historically and theoretically; both relations are thematized particularly by focusing on the symbolic dimension of thinking and on the relation between symbol and concept. Among her publications are *Tomismo e principio di non contraddizione* (1973); *Ellenizzazione del cristianesimo* (1984); *Intersezioni tra scrittura e interpretazione: la Bibbia* (1990); *Psicoanalisi e teologia. Ermeneutiche a confronto* (1992); *La dimensione simbolica. Percorsi e saggi* (2009); and *Filosofia della religione* (2015). She has also edited or coedited various volumes, among which are *Il male in questione* (2009); *La filosofia e il Grande Codice* (2012); and *L'interrogazione del simbolo* (2014).

Laura Bazzicalupo is professor of political philosophy at the University of Salerno, collaborates with numerous journals, and directs *Soft Power*, an interdisciplinary journal published in English and Spanish and centered on issues of neoliberal governmentality, international exclusion processes, and forms of hierarchization from postcolonial to gender discrimination. She has worked on the political dimension of the symbolic and art in Mitteleuropean literature (Mann, Musil, Broch, and Burchkardt) and has written monographs on passions (*Superbia. La passione dell'essere*, 2008; translated into Spanish and Hungarian) and on singularities that embody a not merely formal freedom (*Eroi della libertà. Storie di rivolta contro il potere*, 2012). The focus of her research is the attention to the concreteness of the living within politics, from the crisis of representation (*Hannah Arendt: La storia per la politica*, 1995) and mimesis to the opening to *aisthesis* in the current biopolitical turn (*Biopolitica. Una mappa concettuale*, 2010; translated into Spanish and Portuguese) where the body and power are central (see her essays on Deleuze) but also exposed to the control and management of desires (see her essays on Lacan). In particular, she highlights the economic ratio of governmental practices extended today to the whole living (*Il governo delle vite. Biopolitica ed economia*, 2006). The ambivalence of biopolitics, the risks it represents for representative democracy in crisis (*Politica. Rappresentazioni e tecniche di governo*, 2013), but also the empowerment of subjectivities that can promote a radically participatory democracy are the center of her current scholarly work (see her various essays in the journal *Filosofia politica*).

Silvia Benso is professor of philosophy at the Rochester Institute of Technology, Rochester, New York. Among her areas of interest are ancient philosophy, contemporary European philosophy, the history of philosophy, ethics, and aesthetics. She is the author of *Thinking After Auschwitz: Philosophical Ethics and Jewish Theodicy* (1992, in Italian), *The Face of Things: A Different Side of Ethics* (2000), and *Viva Voce: Conversations with Italian Philosophers* (2017); and the coauthor of the volume *Environmental Thinking: Between Philosophy and Ecology* (2000, in Italian). She has also coedited various volumes such as *Contemporary Italian Philosophy: Between Ethics, Politics and Religion* (2007); *Levinas and the Ancients* (2008); *Between Nihilism and Politics: The Hermeneutics of Gianni Vattimo* (2010); *Thinking the Inexhaustible: Art, Interpretation, and Freedom in the Philosophy of Luigi Pareyson* (2018); and *Open Borders: Encounters between Italian Philosophy and Continental Thought* (2021). During the past decade, she has devoted herself to the promotion of Italian philosophy; she is the general coeditor for the SUNY Press series on Contemporary Italian Philosophy and the codirector of SIP, the Society for Italian Philosophy.

Maria Luisa Boccia is president of the Fondazione CRS-Archivio Pietro Ingrao. She has taught political philosophy at the University of Siena and has been senator for the Italian Republic during its fifteenth legislature. A representative of both theoretical and political feminism, she is the founder of various feminist journals such as *Rosa* in 1974; *Memoria. Rivista di storia delle donne* and *Orsaminore* in the 1980s; and *Reti. Pratiche e saperi* *di donne*, which she directed from 1987 to 1993. Her topics of research and writing include feminist political thought, theories of subjectivity with specific relation to the body and the concept of freedom, forms and instruments of democracy and citizenship, and reproductive technologies. Her authors of reference are Carla Lonzi, Hannah Arendt, Simone Weil, Karl Marx, Immanuel Kant, Michel Foucault, Jacques Derrida, and Judith Butler. Among her publications are *L'io in rivolta. Vissuto e pensiero di Carla Lonzi* (1990); *L'eclissi della madre. Fecondazione artificiale. Tecniche, fantasie, norme* (with Grazia Zuffa, 1998); *La differenza politica. Donne e cittadinanza* (2002); "Il problema della pace e le vie della guerra," in *Guerra e pace*, ed. Giuseppe Prestipino (2004); "Faire autrement de la politique. Théorie et pratique dans le féminisme italien," in *Les femmes dans l'espace pubblique*, ed. Christiane Veauvy (2004); *Con Carla Lonzi. La mia vita è la mia opera* (2014); and *Le parole e i corpi. Scritti femministi* (2018).

Laura Boella is professor of moral philosophy and environmental ethics in the Department of Philosophy of the State University of Milan. She has worked on twentieth-century women thinkers, especially Hannah Arendt, Simone Weil, María Zambrano, and Edith Stein. Her volume *Il coraggio dell'etica. Per una nuova immaginazione morale* (2012) develops themes and problems in contemporary ethics. Her book *Le imperdonabili. Milena Jesenská, Etty Hillesum, Marina Cvetaeva, Ingeborg Bachmann, Cristina Campo* (2013) introduces some extraordinary authors' contributions that are essential for an understanding of our current times. Her research focuses on themes of intersubjective relations, empathy, and sympathy; she also advances a critical confrontation between current research in the neurosciences and the phenomenological perspective. She is the editor of the Italian revised edition of Max Scheler, *Essenza e forme della simpatia* (2010). Among her publications are *Sentire l'altro. Conoscere e praticare l'empatia* (2006); *Neuroetica. La morale prima della morale* (2008); *Empatie. L'esperienza empatica nella società del conflitto* (2018); and *Hannah Arendt. Un umanesimo difficile* (2020).

Adriana Cavarero is an Italian philosopher and honorary professor at the University of Verona. She has been visiting professor at Warwick University, at the Universities of California at Berkeley and at Santa Barbara, and at New York University. Her writings focus on ancient and contemporary philosophy, political thought, feminist theory, Hannah Arendt, theories of narration and vocality, and on a wide range of issues in the arts and literature. Among her books translated into English are *In Spite of Plato: A Feminist Rewriting of Ancient Philosophy* (1995); *Stately Bodies: Literature, Philosophy and the Question of Gender* (2002); *Relating Narratives: Storytelling and Selfhood* (2000); *For More Than One Voice: Toward a Philosophy of*

Vocal Expression (2005); *Horrorism: Naming Contemporary Violence* (2009); *Inclinations: A Critique of Rectitude* (2016); and *Surgin Democracy: Notes on Hannah Arendt's Political Thought* (2021).

Simona Forti is professor of political philosophy at the University of Eastern Piedmont and in the graduate program of philosophy at the University of Turin. She also teaches regularly in the philosophy department at the New School in New York City and has been visiting professor at Columbia University in 2017 and Fulbright visiting professor at Northwestern University in 2014. She graduated with a degree in philosophy from the University of Bologna and received her PhD in the history of political thought from the University of Turin. She is widely known in Italy and abroad for her work on Hannah Arendt's thought, especially Arendt's notion of totalitarianism, and for her more recent work on biopolitics, Nazi biopolitics of souls and democratic biopolitics of bodies, and the contemporary reshaping of the notion of evil. Among her various publications in English are the volume *The New Demons: Rethinking Evil and Power Today* (2015) and the book chapters "Hegel, Marx and Arendt," in *Hannah Arendt: Critical Assessments of Leading Political Philosophers*, ed. G. Williams (2006); "Spectres of Totality," in *The Ashgate Research Companion to the Politics of Democratization in Europe*, ed. K. Palonen, T. Pulkkinen, and J. M. Rosales (2008); "Parrhesia between East and West: Foucault and Dissidence," in *The Government of Life: Foucault, Biopolitics and Neoliberalism*, ed. V. Lemm and M. Vatter (2014); and "The Soul as Site of Dissidence," in *Thinking After Europe: Jan Patočka and Politics*, ed. F. Tava and D. Meacham (2015). She is also the author of *Il totalitarismo* (multiple reprints, the most recent in 2016); *La filosofia di fronte all'estremo* (2004); and *Hannah Arendt tra filosofia e politica* (2006).

Nidesh Lawtoo is assistant professor of philosophy and English at the KU Leuven as well as principal investigator for a five-year European Research Council (ERC)–funded project titled *Homo Mimeticus: Theory and Criticism*. His work is located at the intersection of literary theory, continental philosophy, and political theory, with a special focus on theories of mimesis, contagion, and identification. He is the editor of *Conrad's* Heart of Darkness *and Contemporary Thought* (2012) and the author of *The Phantom of the Ego: Modernism and the Mimetic Unconscious* (2013) and *Conrad's Shadow: Catastrophe, Mimesis, Theory* (2016; this work received the 2018 Adam Gillon Award). His latest book, titled *(New) Fascism: Contagion, Community, Myth* (2019), focuses on the case of Trump to diagnose the power of mimetic actors to turn the political into a fiction.

Enrica Lisciani-Petrini teaches theoretical philosophy at the University of Salerno. She is part of the editorial boards of various philosophical journals and book series and the director of the Italian Thought Network. Her research engages nineteenth- and twentieth-century philosophical thought, especially Heidegger, Bergson, Jankélévitch, Merleau-Ponty, and Deleuze. Her work unfolds along two primary themes, namely the intertwining and problematic relation of philosophy with politics and the human sciences in general on the one hand, and the relevance and role of artistic expressions within the twentieth-century philosophical horizon on the other. More specifically, she focuses on issues of the body, identity, subjectivity, and personhood, which she analyzes from a deconstructive perspective geared toward unfolding a different conceptual framework centered on notions of life, subjectivation, and impersonality rethought in the sense of a philosophy of the everydayness also in light of contemporary Italian thought. Among her publications are *Tierra en blanco. Música y pensamiento a inicios del siglo XX* (1999); *Il suono incrinato. Musica e filosofia nel primo Novecento* (2001); *La passione del mondo. Saggio su Merleau-Ponty* (2002); *Risonanze. Ascolto Corpo Mondo* (2007); *Charis. Saggio su Jankélévitch* (2012, translated into French as *Charis. Essai sur Jankélévitch*, 2013); and *Vita quotidiana. Dall'esperienza artistica al pensiero in atto* (2015). She is the Italian translator and the editor of various works by Vladimir Jankélévitch, such as *La musica e l'ineffabile* (1996); *La morte* (2009); *Il non-so-che e il quasi-niente* (2010); *Da qualche parte nell'incompiuto* (2012); *Debussy e il mistero* (2012); *Il puro e l'impuro* (2014); and *L'avventura, la noia e la serietà* (2018).

Lea Melandri has been the founder, with psychoanalyst Elvio Fachinelli, of the journal *L'erba voglio*, one of the most independent and significant voices of political-cultural dissent and anti-authoritarian critique of society in the 1970s. During the same period, she became actively involved with the women's movement. From 1987 to 1997, she directed the journal *Lapis. Percorsi della riflessione femminile*, which has recently also become available online. Currently, she gives lectures and courses at the Milan *Associazione per una Libera Università delle Donne* (Association for Women's Free University), which she has promoted since 1987 and of which she is the current president. Among her publications are *L'infamia originaria* (1977, 1997, 2018); *Lo strabismo della memoria* (1991, reprinted in 2019); *La mappa del cuore* (1992); *Una visceralità indicibile. La pratica dell'inconscio nel movimento delle donne degli anni settanta* (2000); *Le passioni del corpo. La vicenda dei sessi tra origine e storia* (2001); *Come nasce il sogno d'amore* (2002); *Preistorie. Di cronaca e d'altro* (2004); *La perdita* (with Rossana Rossanda e Manuela Fraire,

2008); *Amore e violenza. Il fattore molesto della civiltà* (2011, translated into English as *Love and Violence: The Vexatious Factors of Civilization*, 2019); and *Alfabeto d'origine* (2017). She is an honorary citizen of Carloforte (on San Pietro Island, in Sardinia) and received the "Ambrogino d'oro" from the city of Milan in 2012 in recognition of her role as feminist thinker.

Luisa Muraro studied philosophy at the Catholic University of Milan, where she began an academic career soon to be interrupted because of the 1968 events. Shortly afterward she became involved with the feminist movement. She has remained loyal to the initial trend of feminism later called "thought of difference," which inspired most of her subsequent work. From 1976 to 2006, she taught philosophy at the University of Verona, where in 1983 she cofounded the women's philosophical community Diotima. She is a founding member of the *Libreria delle Donne* (Women's Library), created in 1975 in Milan, for which she coedits the journal *Via Dogana*. She has advanced the most original ideas of Italian feminism at various international conferences in Chicago (1997), Santiago del Cile (1998), and Sana'a (Yemen, 1999). She has taught as part of the master's program in *Estudios de la libertad femenina* at the University of Barcelona. Her works comprise more than a thousand titles including books and contributions to conferences, journals, periodicals, and online publications. Some of her writings that have been recently published in English are the essay part of the volume *Another Mother*, edited by Cesare Casarino and Andrea Righi (2018), and the book *The Symbolic Order of the Mother* (2018), which is the most significant and well-known work in her vast political-philosophical production.

Elena Pulcini earned her PhD at the Université de Paris III Sorbonne Nouvelle and is now professor of social philosophy in the Department of Social and Political Science at the University of Florence. Her central interests are the topics of passions within the theory of modernity and modern individualism, the ethics of care, the theory of the gift, and the theory of the female subject. Her current research focuses on the transformations of the subject and the social bond in the global age and on the possible emotional foundation of an ethics for the future, proposing a philosophy of care for the global age. She has published numerous essays in national and international journals and edited volumes. Among her more recent books (since 2000) are *Il potere di unire. Femminile, desiderio, cura* (2003); *The Individual without Passions. Modern Individualism and the Loss of the Social Bond* (2012); *Care of the World. Fear, Responsibility and Justice in the Global Age* (2012; the Italian edition of this volume received the 2009

First Prize in Philosophy "Viaggio a Siracusa"); *Envie. Essai sur une passion triste* (2013); and *Specchio specchio delle mie brame. Bellezza e invidia* (2017). She is also the coauthor of *Responsabilità, uguaglianza, sostenibilità* (with S. Veca and E. Giovannini, 2017); *Felicità italiane. Un campionario filosofico* (with D. D'Andrea and others, 2016); and *Emotions and care* (with Sophie Bourgault, 2018); and the coeditor of the volumes *Filosofie della globalizzazione* (2001) and *Umano post-umano. Potere, sapere, etica nell'età globale* (2004).

Caterina Resta is professor of theoretical philosophy at the University of Messina, where she teaches philosophical hermeneutics and twentieth-century philosophy. She focuses on contemporary continental philosophy and, in particular, on the topics of the deconstruction of the subject, the relation between identity and otherness, the notion of the human, the question of technics and nihilism, and geophilosophy (globalization, the Mediterranean, and Europe). Among her books are *Il luogo e le vie. Geografie del pensiero in Martin Heidegger* (1996); *L'evento dell'altro. Etica e politica in Jacques Derrida* (2003); *L'Estraneo. Ostilità e ospitalità nel pensiero del Novecento* (2008); *Stato mondiale o* Nomos *della terra. Carl Schmitt tra universo e pluriverso* (2009); *Geofilosofia del Mediterraneo* (2012); *Nichilismo Tecnica Mondializzazione. Saggi su Schmitt, Jünger, Heidegger e Derrida* (2013); and *La passione dell'impossibile. Saggi su Jacques Derrida* (2016).

Elvira Roncalli is associate professor of philosophy at Carroll College, Helena, Montana. She studied philosophy at the State University of Milan and received her PhD from the Université Catholique de Louvain-La-Neuve, in Belgium, with a dissertation titled "Life of the Mind and Love of the World: The Crucial Role of Judging in Arendt's Thinking." Her interests include the philosophy of Hannah Arendt, twentieth-century European thought, Italian philosophy, social and political philosophy, and feminist and gender theory.

Index

www.ingramcontent.com/pod-product-compliance
Lightning Source LLC
LaVergne TN
LVHW040157080826
844660LV00001B/12

* 9 7 8 1 4 3 8 4 8 4 9 1 4 *